Voices of the Fleet Air Arm

– BRIAN SKINNER –

An environmentally friendly book printed and bound in England by
www.printondemand-worldwide.com

This book is made entirely of chain-of-custody materials

www.fast-print.net/store.php

Voices of the Fleet Air Arm
Copyright © Brian Skinner 2011

ISBN 978-178035-209-1

First published 2011 by
FASTPRINT PUBLISHING
Peterborough, England.

Contents

Editor's Preface

For some time now I have been recollecting with former friends and colleagues about the things we got up to in Borneo between 1962 and 1966. Although there are articles on the web and now some books are beginning to appear, there seems to be no authentic 'hands-on' stories written by those who were there in what was actually a considerable campaign over nearly four years, involving very large numbers of ships, aircraft and men from British and Commonwealth armed services and many of their supporting units.

Many of us have referred to Borneo as a 'forgotten war' and, although this may be an exaggeration, I feel that it is fair to say that there is little written coverage as to what we actually did in those days and the conditions in which we worked.

This book therefore sets out to present the untold and largely unknown story of the vital contribution of the Royal Navy helicopter squadrons to the highly successful containment of the Brunei Rebellion and the subsequent Indonesian Confrontation campaigns by presenting the personal stories of the helicopter pilots, observers, aircrewmen and maintainers of the Fleet Air Arm and other supporting units during this conflict. This Preface sets the scene as to how we came to be making our way to Borneo in the first instance.

Following experiences of the Suez Crisis in 1956, it was realised that troops in general, and the Royal Marines in particular, needed to be made available anywhere in the world where force projection was needed. At Suez, troops were transported ashore from World War 2 landing-craft or squeezed into other warships without suitable amphibious capabilities. In addition though, and for the first time, some troops were successfully landed in the Whirlwind helicopters of 845 Squadron. This led to the decision to convert HMS *Bulwark* from a fixed-wing Aircraft Carrier to a Commando Ship, and she recomissioned as such in 1960 with Whirlwind Mk 7 helicopters. This role proved a success and the government of the day decided to convert a second Carrier to this role, and HMS *Albion* was duly taken in hand and recomissioned in the new role on 1st August 1962. The political support for these role changes was thought to be largely driven with the aim of replacing expensive shore bases around the globe with cheaper and more mobile floating bases, particularly East of Suez.

For *Bulwark's* deployment East of Suez in the Commando Role from 1960 to 1962, she was equipped with the Whirlwind Mk 7s of 848 Squadron. This petrol-fuelled, 14 radial-cylinder, rotary-engine helicopter proved versatile but was constrained to lifting only a few troops ashore at a time or an underslung Citroen 2CV vehicle, a light WOMBAT anti-tank weapon, or a net of stores. Nevertheless, with these dedicated Commando Role helicopters it was proved possible to project troops, weapons, ammunition and stores ashore and to recover them more quickly than had been achieved at Suez in 1956.

Albion's conversion to a helicopter-carrying Commando Ship required a number of extra helicopter pilots to be acquired and trained quickly. Furthermore, the Whirlwind Mk 7 was to be replaced in the Commando role by the new Wessex Mk 1, which could carry a greater number of troops and lift heavier loads. To achieve this, during 1960 and 1961 the Admiralty invited already sea-trained junior officers who were not yet scheduled for other specialist training to volunteer for helicopter training. I was serving in HMS *Chichester* at the time and duly volunteered and was accepted.

I joined the Fleet Air Arm for survival training at Seafield Park in April 1961 and then basic fixed-wing flying for four months at RAF Linton-on-Ouse with 97 Helicopter Specialist Pilot (HSP) course, flying the Chipmunk, in May 1961. This was followed by six months with "contracted-out" training with British United Airways (BUA) at Redhill Aerodrome, with the Hiller 12C and Whirlwind Mk 1 helicopters. The BUA manager at Redhill was the famous Alan

Bristow, and most of the instructors were ex-Service pilots. At the end of this phase we received our pilots' wings, awarded by Rear Admiral Percy Gick (Flag Officer Flying Training). Then we went down to 706 Squadron at Culdrose for a six-week Wessex HAS Mk 1 Conversion. Finally, we crossed the airfield to join 845 Naval Air Commando Squadron, which formed officially on 10th April 1962 with twelve Wessex "Helicopter Utility" or HU Mk 1 aircraft. This aircraft was basically the Westland Wessex "Helicopter Anti-submarine" or HAS Mk 1 aircraft already in service and equipped with a single Napier Gazelle gas-turbine engine. Instead of dunking sonar for anti-submarine detection work, the Wessex HU Mk 1 had seats for 14 troops and a substantial underslung cargo hook.

So, we had arrived in our newly-formed front-line squadron after a scrambled training course. We were somewhat inexperienced at flying, to say the least (I had an overall grand total of 222 flying hours). 845 had an experienced pilot Commanding Officer (Alan Hensher), who had done his Wessex helicopter conversion in 706 with us, an experienced ex-848 pilot in *Bulwark* (Geoff Andrews) as Senior Pilot (SP), an experienced ex-fixed- wing third pilot (Digby Lickfold) and a second tour helicopter pilot from 848 in *Bulwark* (David Creamer). All the rest of us were first-tour pilots, and our ex 97 HSP team was followed by 98 HSP 3 months later. Against this, we did have varying degrees of General Service experience behind us and so were familiar with keeping watch on the bridge, Divisional Officer work, boat handling, ocean navigation and star sights, but flying was new to us and we hadn't yet attempted to land on a ship!

On 8th May 1962, 846 Naval Air Commando Squadron, our sister squadron destined for *Albion*, formed with eight Whirlwind Mk 7s. They fared no better experience-wise than us in 845. Their CO (David Burke) and SP (Peter Williams) were experienced fixed-wing pilots but the rest were first tour pilots, mostly formed from HSP 99.

For our pre-embarkation work up at Culdrose, with our Wessex 1s we trained hard at Royal Marine troop movements and load lifting of their Land Rovers and the Artillery's 105 mm howitzers by day and night. Four pilots were sent off to Paris to master the SS 11 air-to-ground wire-guided missile. Besides the SS 11s, the Wessex could also be fitted with fixed, forward-firing machine-guns and pods of seven 2-inch anti-tank rockets. We achieved deck-landing qualifications with *Albion* on 6th September 1962.

The work-up culminated with an Operational Readiness Inspection on the 27th and 28th September 1962 by FOFT (Rear Admiral Percy Gick), who chose to fly in the left-hand cockpit seat of my aircraft for the final troop lift. This proved interesting because halfway through this part of the inspection my radio headphones failed, but we continued the exercise with the Admiral shouting to me verbally the instructions he heard on the radio; quite interesting on the final phase which was close-formation flying from Predannick aerodrome back to Culdrose.

We finally embarked in *Albion* on 2nd November 1962 for a 'routine' deployment to East of Suez to relieve *Bulwark*. On the way through the Mediterranean we carried out an amphibious exercise in the Libyan desert before traversing the Suez Canal and arriving at Aden on 20th November 1962, where we found *Bulwark* eagerly awaiting us. Then it was off to Kenya for another 4-day amphibious exercise before setting off for Singapore. Off Gan on 9th December, the call came to steam to Singapore 'with all despatch' in order to embark further Royal Marines and stores before proceeding to Borneo, where a rebellion had broken out. After 6 days at 27 knots we arrived at Singapore and, after a hurried loading programme, we sailed again and landed our first troops in Borneo on 14th December 1962.

Foreword

By Major General Julian Thompson Royal Marines

Denis Healey, Secretary of State for Defence during the last two years of Confrontation, commenting in his memoirs on this highly successful campaign, said it was a 'textbook demonstration of how to use economy of force, under political guidance for political ends'. The passage of time has not produced any evidence to refute this assertion. What is also clear is that the campaign was a textbook demonstration of how to use helicopters. Indeed without helicopters Denis Healey would not have been able to write what he did, because the British would have lost the campaign; indeed they would have been foolish even to embark on it in the first place.

The terrain along the 900-mile-long border between East Malaysia (Sabah and Sarawak) and Indonesian Kalimantan, along with all of the island of Borneo, is some of the most inhospitable in the world. Except for patches of cultivation and extensive mangrove swamps, the island consists of huge mountain ranges, deep valleys, and rolling plateaus covered with dense, tropical rain forest, interspersed by large and frequently fast-flowing rivers. These sometimes provide a means of movement by boat, but just as often the rivers are an obstacle to movement. Even if their course is more or less in the desired direction of travel, rapids and falls, except near the sea, can make all but the shortest boat journey a considerable undertaking. In the mid-1960s there were few roads outside the towns and larger villages, and almost all were on the coast. A few logging tracks penetrated a little way inland in areas where timber was being felled. In the steamy heat, trudging up and slithering down the sometimes near- vertical hillsides, often through thick secondary growth, heavily-laden Royal Marines and soldiers could take several hours to cover even a mile. On one occasion it took a Gurkha patrol three days to walk 5,000 yards; a helicopter traversed the same distance in three minutes.

Confrontation, following the Brunei revolt, was divided into three phases. From April 1963 to February 1964, the Indonesians pursued a combination of subversion and guerrilla warfare. The next phase involved the Indonesian Army, employing deep penetration raids to set up guerrilla bases, and shallow incursions to intimidate the local population. Indonesian regular soldiers accompanied the raiding parties. From time-to-time these raiding sub-units not only stood their ground, but occasionally counter-attacked. The Indonesian units on the border at this time probably numbered no more than 2,500, one third of them regulars. In January 1965 the Indonesians increased the pressure, and committed regular army units to cross-border attacks on British bases in Borneo. Accordingly the Indonesian strength in border areas increased to possibly as high as 30,000.

The Marines and soldiers were based in a series of jungle forts at intervals along the border and usually a few miles back. These were not intended to form a stop line to incursions, but acted as a base from which troops patrolled and sortied to harry the Indonesian incursion parties. Despite excellent work by British and Gurkha troops, by the end of 1963 the Indonesians still held the initiative and crossed the border when and where they pleased. In 1964, as mentioned earlier, the Indonesians changed tactics and the campaign intensified with attacks on British bases, sometimes by up to two companies at a time. In response, starting in August 1964, British and Gurkha troops mounted a series of successful operations into Indonesian territory to attack their bases; these, codenamed 'Claret', remained classified Top Secret for years afterwards.

The Indonesians in Borneo were far better equipped, and more aggressive and dangerous than the Communist Terrorists whom many of the older hands had encountered in Malaya a few years previously. Some Gurkha officers, who had fought the Japanese in Burma, rated the Javanese, the best Indonesian troops, on a par with the Japanese. When engaged, the Indonesians fought back and company-sized battles were not uncommon. They were not guerrillas but well-equipped soldiers operating from behind their own frontier, and well supported by mortars and artillery, provided they were within range. They established bases, usually near the border with Borneo, from which they sortied to raid the British and Gurkha, and later Malaysian, bases. The Indonesians had one weakness - they lacked air superiority and could not therefore use helicopters to lift troops across the border, whereas the British used helicopters extensively in the follow-up of Indonesian parties after incursions and raids.

The majority of British jungle bases were supplied by helicopter, a few, usually the bigger ones, by air drop from Beverley or Argosy aircraft, or Twin Pioneers landing on short strips. Everything came by air: sandbags, rations including live chickens in crates, ammunition, spares, radio batteries, medical supplies, replacement jungle boots and clothing, mail, newspapers, reinforcements – everything. Similarly almost everything came out that way, including casualties. Troops were inserted into the jungle, and extracted, by helicopter. Descending into a tight landing-spot surrounded by tall trees, with a heavy load of troops in the underpowered Wessex was hazardous, even more so in the Whirlwind with its lamentable engine. Lifting out of such a spot could be even more 'heart-stopping'. On occasions it was necessary to rope down. An extraction by helicopter sometimes necessitated cutting sufficient space for it to descend. To make this possible explosives, hand-saws, and even buzz-saws were lowered through the 100-200-foot jungle canopy from a helicopter hovering overhead. Added hazards to flying were the violent tropical storms that transpired without warning, low cloud concealing the mountain tops, and morning mist in the river valleys. Most of the flying was in hot and high conditions on the absolute limits. There are numerous accounts in this book of the hazards of flying helicopters in this demanding environment.

Far and away the majority of helicopter sorties during Confrontation were flown by the Fleet Air Arm, which was involved from the first days of the Brunei revolt in December 1962 right up to the end of Confrontation in mid-1966. The Fleet Air Arm had a reputation for being a 'can do' organisation in a way that the RAF seemed, and still seems, unable to match. The Fleet Air Arm helicopter aircrews would take on tasks that the RAF turned down on grounds of safety or because they were contrary to the 'rule book'. To be fair, this was largely the fault of the chairborne senior RAF officers who wrote and enforced the 'rule book', rather than the aircrew themselves. At the time the RAF regarded flying an airborne 'truck' in support of ground troops as very much a third-rate job, far behind piloting a fast jet, or even a transport aircraft (a perception that lingers to this day). As third-class citizens, very few 'chopper' pilots achieve high rank in the RAF; and in the 1960s, none. Any helicopter pilot stepping outside the 'box' risked being leaned on heavily by an unsympathetic 'jet jockey' senior air staff officer, or air commander, who certainly was not going to have his career prospects jeopardised by supporting anyone who infringed the regulations, however good the operational reason for doing so. Having pioneered the support of ground troops in the Malayan emergency in the 1950s, taken part in the first ever helicopter-borne amphibious assault in history, at Port Said in 1956, and developed the helicopter carrier concept in the early 1960s, the Fleet Air Arm had a very different mind-set; and it showed. Few, if any, calls for support from soldiers and Royal Marines in Borneo went unanswered by the Fleet Air Arm.

The key to success in Borneo was the helicopter; and the Fleet Air Arm turned it.

Political Background to the Borneo Confrontation Campaign

The full record of events leading up to the formation of the Federation of Malaysia in September 1963 is complex and beyond the scope of this book. However a brief summary of the key political activities between 1961 and 1963 will help to set the scene for the four-year military campaign that ensued to counter Indonesia's armed intervention in Borneo in opposition to Malaysia, and for the personal memories recounted herein.

The concept of combining the Federation of Malaya, Singapore, Sarawak, Brunei and British North Borneo (later renamed as 'Sabah') into a new federation of 'Malaysia' was initially suggested by the Prime Minister of the Federation of Malaya, Tunku Abdul Rahman, in 1961. He saw the threat of Chinese Communist activities, especially from Singapore, as a threat to stability in the area and that a larger, combined state with a larger number of non-Chinese ethnicities would balance out this threat.

The Prime Minister of Singapore, Lee Kwan Yew, and the Sultan of Brunei both supported the proposal (although both had opposing pro-Communist factions in their countries). The British Government appointed a commission, chaired by Lord Cobbold, to study the preferences of the people of the British Borneo territories and Singapore. A referendum was held in Singapore and about 70% voted in support of the merger proposal.

There were, however, problems in Brunei. The Sultan had to deal with objections to Malaysia from a number of areas: internal political dissent, the question of payments for Brunei oil royalties and the future status of the Sultan. These problems could not be solved at the time and Brunei withdrew from the Malaysian proposal.

Furthermore, an anti-colonialist liberation military wing (with pro-Indonesian sympathies) had emerged in Brunei and started an armed rebellion on 8th December 1962. This was opposed and contained by British Army troops, including Gurkhas and Royal Marines and, by 17th December, the rebellion was largely over, with some 40 rebels dead and 3,400 captured.

Accordingly, the British Government agreed to Sabah and Sarawak joining Malaya and Singapore to form the Federation of Malaysia. They also set up the Lansdowne Commission to draft a constitution for Malaysia. Brunei was to remain an independent Commonwealth member and as such, would continue to be defended by Britain.

A draft constitution for Malaysia was drawn up and planned to take effect from 31st August 1963.

However, Indonesia and the Philippines opposed the idea of Malaysia as a neo-colonialist plot by the British. President Sukarno of Indonesia was backed by a strong Communist party opposed to the idea of Malaysia and the Philippines objected to Sabah joining a Malayan-led federation.

A United Nations team of 8 members was formed to determine whether Sabah and Sarawak really wanted to join Malaysia, and they did indeed confirm that the majority of the people in Sabah and Sarawak were content to so join. This further investigation delayed the planned introduction and Malaysia was formally established on 16th September 1963.

Indonesia was increasingly involved in political and military opposition to Malaysia until mid-1966.

Following the replacement of Indonesian President Sukarno by Suharto in 1966, Indonesian aggression to Malaysia gradually declined and Malaysia was eventually recognised by them.

Prologue

By Captain Alan Hensher MBE Royal Navy

This account, previously published in the *Fleet Air Arm Officers' Association Journal* and the *Naval Review*, tells of the part played by the Commando Ship HMS *Albion* and her helicopters in the Borneo campaign 1962-1964. It tells at the same time of the Royal Navy's role in Borneo and, altogether, gives a summary of a facet of Fleet Air Arm history which has previously not had the attention it deserved. The report was written by the late Rear Admiral Colin Madden who, as Captain Madden, was in command of *Albion* at the time and myself, Alan Hensher, in command of 845 Naval Air Squadron embarked in *Albion*. This account is presented as an introduction to the whole Borneo campaign.

HMS *Albion* was relieved by HMS *Bulwark* in April 1964 and *Albion* reappeared in 1966 to take over once again for the last few months of Borneo Confrontation until November 1966.

Fig. 1 HMS *Albion* - The Commando Carrier which became the 'Old Grey Ghost of the Borneo Coast'

The Royal Navy's role in the Borneo Confrontation Campaign involved many ships, aircraft and personnel over a four-year period.

Coastal Minesweepers acting as offshore patrol vessels, Frigates, Destroyers, Cruisers, Aircraft Carriers and the Commando ships, *Albion* and *Bulwark*, all played their part. In the latter stages these forces were supplemented by units from the Royal Malaysian Navy, the Royal Australian Navy and the Royal New Zealand Navy.

The rugged nature of the terrain in Borneo and the primitive lines of communication by road meant that movements by air, inland waterways and coastal sea passage were vital to the success of the operation. In each of these the Royal Navy made a significant contribution, deploying and resupplying troops, undertaking anti-coastal infiltration patrols, maintaining control of the harbour at Brunei, and providing essential radio communications.

The original Borneo Defence plan 'ALE' did not include naval participation. Nonetheless, right from the outset, thousands of troops (from 40 and 42 Commandos Royal Marines, *The Queen's Own*

Highlanders, 1/2 Ghurkha Rifles, the First Battalion *Greenjackets,* and *The Queen's Royal Irish Hussars*) were lifted by the cruiser HMS *Tiger,* the destroyer HMS *Cavalier,* HM frigates *Alert, Blackpool* and *Woodbridge Haven,* the coastal minesweepers *Fiskerton, Chawton, Wilkeston* and *Woolaston* to a wide area of Sarawak and Brunei. Ashore, Naval Party ALF, of one officer and eleven technical ratings, maintained key radio and other services in Brunei. Not to be forgotten was the vital logistic support from the Royal Fleet Auxiliary ships *Gold Ranger, Wave Sovereign* and *Fort Charlotte* in providing Replenishment at Sea (RAS) and other essential supplies to the HM Ships deployed off Borneo, as well as those front-line units ashore.

But it was the arrival of *Albion* on 14th December, 1962 with her two Squadrons of Commando Helicopters (twelve Wessex from 845 Squadron and eight Whirlwinds from 846 Squadron), landing-craft and embarked Royal Marine Command Brigade HQ and 40 Commando that was to prove such a decisive factor in bringing stability to the region and containing the immediate insurgency threat. This initial report deals with *Albion's* activities and some of the important techniques and procedures that emerged from the Commando ship and her Squadrons operating in an unusually hostile environment.

Narrative of Events

Albion, the newly-commissioned Commando ship, bound for the Far East Station, had just fuelled from an RFA due south of Ceylon. At the traditional crossing-the-line ceremony the Captain, Colin Madden, was about to be ducked in tribute to King Neptune when the Chief Yeoman of Signals interrupted proceedings with an extremely urgent message from the Admiralty: 'To *Albion* - FLASH - Proceed at full power to Borneo. Acknowledge.' The ship immediately increased speed to full power and she sped across the Indian Ocean faster than she had ever gone before. Further signals from the Commander-in-Chief Far East Station followed later: 'Situation Brunei still obscure but clear that rebels more numerous than supposed. *Albion* is diverted to Labuan and will arrive about 14th December, 1962. *Albion* to call at Singapore to load personnel and vehicles, land the Royal Artillery battery and replenish.'

Albion secured alongside Singapore Dockyard early pm, 13th December and in five hours embarked the Commando Brigade HQ, extra stocks and equipment, refuelled and immediately sailed for Borneo. A Wessex helicopter sortie to Kuching was launched 100 miles ahead of the ship and established from the Royal Marines already ashore that the capital was secure. An hour or so later at 1930 on Friday 14th December, just five days after receiving the first signal, *Albion* anchored off Kuching at the western end of Sarawak and disembarked 40 Commando and HQ 3rd Commando Brigade. The following day she anchored off Seria in Brunei, where 846 Squadron was disembarked with authorisation for the Land Commanders on the spot to use the helicopters as required, without having to refer to the ship. The Commandos and Squadrons were sent in to establish airfields, after which the ground crews followed. These Forward Operating Bases (FOBs) were set up as a well-practised procedure for Naval Commando Helicopter Squadrons for long periods at a time. The ground forces now had helicopter support close at hand.

Fig 2. Jungle Landing: Wessex 1 coming into land after a Borneo sortie

During *Albion's* periods in Brunei and Borneo the ship and all her hands worked tirelessly, with the helicopters and landing craft operating in concert to fly and ferry the troops with all their kit and equipment deep into the jungle. This support enabled the troops to move significant distances in only a matter of hours, which would otherwise have taken days on foot in such rough terrain. *Albion* was ready with all spares and equipment, food and any other help required. A good illustration was the deployment and support of 'A' Company 40 Commando Royal Marines in the Danau area by Wessex helicopters of 845 Squadron operating from the ship. Known as 'Pug Force' after its aggressive Commander, Major 'Pug' Davies, they were an important early military presence.

Christmas and the New Year were spent steaming up and down the coast of Brunei at 'assault stations', always ready for the 'next lift'. Casualties and prisoners were embarked and the landing-craft went in to support as required. The concept of a mobile airfield was understood immediately by the command ashore.

During the 26 days following her arrival off Borneo, *Albion's* helicopters flew 1,200 sorties in direct support of 'A' Company 40 Commando at Danau and elsewhere. Because of her frequent appearances off the coast, generally coming in at first light, *Albion* quickly became known as 'The Old Grey Ghost of the Borneo Coast!'

On the morning of Tuesday 8th January, *Albion* weighed anchor and left Borneo for Singapore and a short self-maintenance period which gave both her engines and the Ship's Company a welcome short period of respite. A few days before the ship's departure, six Wessex helicopters of 845 Squadron were disembarked to the airfield on Labuan Island and set up a FOB. Facilities and accommodation were limited and most of the Squadron lived in tents, in the same way that 846 Squadron did at Brunei. There were now six Wessex and eight Whirlwind helicopters operating ashore.

In Singapore, as soon as the last nut and bolt were in place, *Albion* resumed her trooping role. The 1st/2nd Ghurkha Rifles and the *Kings Own Yorkshire Light Infantry* (KOYLI) were embarked and the ship sailed for Borneo. She then returned to Singapore with relieved army units including The Queen's Own Highlanders, where they disembarked before proceeding for a short break in Hong Kong. However, by mid-March, *Albion* had returned once more to Borneo. The opportunity was taken to use her flight deck in the practice role of an extra landing strip that was much appreciated by the Army Austers and Beavers and by the RAF Pioneers. They all became regular visitors, having discovered the quality of the food on board and the ship's hot showers!

From the middle of December 1962 until January 1963, *Albion*, with her Royal Marines and helicopters, gave the support so urgently needed to stabilise the military situation. The immediate threat from Indonesian guerrillas and local rebels was contained. The longer-term problem of infiltration from across the border with Indonesian Borneo Kalimantan was still to be faced.

In January and February, excessive rains made survival in the remote kampongs extremely difficult. Normally reached by river and the occasional road, these were now impassable. Fortunately, the Wessex helicopters operating from Labuan were able to provide relief by flying in rice and other food to the beleaguered villages in weather which left a gap, often, of less than 50 feet between the dense, low cloud cover and the 200 foot-high tree canopy. This relief work was an important factor in winning over the hearts and minds of the local Ibans and Dyaks. They, in turn, gave invaluable help to our FOBs and the hospitality for detached helicopter aircrew and maintainers in the Long Houses became legendary. However, their habit of smoking while helping to refuel the aircraft was somewhat worrying.

Sibu, the major town in the third division of Sarawak, was a major trading-post where there was a FOB (at the small airfield just outside the town) and the River Rajang made an unmistakable navigation guide and also allowed small ships and coastal craft to unload and load at the dock.

Fig 3. Sibu on the River Rajang

Operating conditions for helicopters were hostile. High temperatures and humidity, rugged terrain with dense tree coverage of 200 feet or more, mountains up to 6,000 feet, violent and sudden rain storms, virtually no navigation aids and no reliable maps (aircrew had to insert their own contour lines!), all made for a very demanding environment in which to conduct help operations. As a result, the Squadron Commanders decided at an early stage to fly helicopters in pairs whenever operationally practical. If one went down in the jungle there was then at least a known position that single aircraft in difficulty might not be able to transmit or be received. A circular slide-rule produced by Lt David Creamer gave the pilot at a glance the available payload, in troops or pounds, based on fuel state/temperature. The 'Creamer Computer' was an invaluable aid.

The Indonesian confrontation had spread into Sabah and Sarawak, adding to everyone's work, and *Albion's* half of 845 Squadron together with some Whirlwinds of 846 were flown into Kuching, whilst the remaining Wessex of 845 disembarked to Sibu.

FOBs became an enduring feature of the campaign. Those at Sibu, Nanga Gaat, Labuan and Kuching enabled the helicopters to react swiftly to a rapidly-changing military situation. And we should not overlook the skill and adaptability of the Fleet Air Arm Maintainers who, maintaining aircraft in 'workshops' which were open to the elements, achieved remarkable levels of aircraft serviceability against all the odds. Engine changes and other complex technical tasks once regarded as impracticable in the field became common practice.

The initiative by 845 Squadron to provide volunteer aircrewmen for the larger Wessex helicopters resulted some years later in the establishment of a new branch of Commando aircrewmen. At the time, volunteers were recruited from the Squadron Maintenance ratings who fulfilled this important function, allowing a proper link between the pilot and the troops being lifted, and the safe handling of internal and external payloads. CAF Kentsbeer played a crucial role in encouraging the young maintenance ratings to volunteer as aircrewmen. The ship's Supply Officer, in a stroke of admirable initiative, devised a way of paying these irregular aircrew by invoking a little-used clause in the Naval Pay Regulations. This permitted additional pay for onerous or dirty work and the like. So the volunteer aircrewmen were rewarded with a kind of flying pay that was probably more irregular than the recipients.

Command and control arrangements of naval helicopters operating ashore presented no problems. Although very little in the way of joint operating procedures existed, the RN's approach, generated by years of working with the Royal Marines was, and still is, one of professional pragmatism with good lines of communication between ship and shore, and with local operational control delegated to the senior ground force commander. Much of this was informal, but it succeeded because there was a willingness by the personalities involved to make it work. The RAF's position on command and control was more formal.

September 1963 was spent plying between Singapore and Borneo, but this was cut short by the decision to move a number of RAF Whirlwind and Belvedere helicopters from the UK to Singapore to relieve *Albion's* aircraft. The ship was to pick these up at Tobruk, where they could be flown on board. Before setting sail on this 32-day, 11,000-mile round voyage, all the ship's helicopter personnel and stores had to be disembarked and dispersed between Singapore and Borneo, only to be re-embarked on her return, a long and tedious task.

Albion sailed again on 8th December to Borneo with the 1st King's Own Yorkshire Light Infantry (KOYLI) on board, together with some of the RAF Belvederes and other helicopters that had been brought from Tobruk bound for Labuan. This time, once the troops had disembarked, the Whirlwinds of 846 Squadron, having been relieved by the RAF's 225 Squadron, were re-embarked with some of the Wessex, and the Greenjackets. The soldiers were dropped in Singapore and the ship then had a very rough passage to Hong Kong so that some of the helicopters could be overhauled at Kai Tak aerodrome. There was welcome short local leave for those who could be spared from the ship and squadrons.

The Christmas period passed all too quickly, as *Albion* was called away four days early because tension had once again increased in the Sabah region. 846 Squadron was required urgently and, on 13th January, they were landed at Tawau, once more living in tents. *Albion* was back in her support role and 3 days later 845 Squadron was landed at Sibu in Sarawak.

Within two weeks of having landed her Squadrons in Borneo, world events once again shaped the course of *Albion's* Commission. In Zanzibar the government was overthrown, followed by African troop mutinies in Tanganyika, Uganda and Kenya. British help was requested and *Albion's* assistance was now required in East Africa.

Fig 4. Naval Air Power – Seven Wessex deployed at Belaga during Confrontation

Once again in her Commando role, and having left her other Squadrons to carry on with their important task in Borneo, *Albion* collected helicopters and troops *en route* from other ships. Fortunately, before arriving on station, the unrest in the former East African colonies had eased and *Albion* was able to return the helicopters she had borrowed from HMS *Victorious*. On 18th March 1964 she left for Aden, where she was to be relieved by *Bulwark*.

After two days transferring personnel, stores and equipment, including her four landing-craft, *Albion* sailed for the UK, arriving in Portsmouth on 15th April 1964 - one and a half years after she had left these shores. During that time the ship had steamed 85,000 miles and carried 12,000 troops; her helicopters had made more than 10,000 operational sorties.

The contribution to this campaign of the Commando ship *Albion* and, later, *Bulwark*, followed by *Albion* once again, was an important early lesson in the military significance of well-directed joint operations, underpinned by good communications, pragmatic delegation of tactical command, and reliable logistic support. Not only were the Commando helicopters an essential component in the military process of denial and containment through the rapid deployment of disproportionately smaller forces, but the ship provided essential support services and the vital launch platform for Commando and army units, including Special Forces, to be lifted to wherever needed ashore. The supply line from Singapore by RAF air was effective but limited, especially at the outset. Heavier equipment, including replacement helicopters, was carried by *Albion*. The workshops on board were able to provide instant engineering support ashore, and the ship's extensive communication nets were a key asset throughout.

On 15th April, 1964, the Commanding Officer of 846 Squadron was presented with the Boyd Trophy for their outstanding contribution to naval aviation during 1963. 'In atrocious conditions of tropical rains, high temperatures and in spite of almost complete lack of normal servicing facilities, the Squadron flew over 2000 operational sorties over dense primary jungle'. An outstanding achievement, which was equally applicable to 845 Squadron, who duly received the Boyd Trophy the following year.

It is interesting to reflect that the experience level of the pilots who flew in these demanding conditions was quite limited. For example, in 845 Squadron 14 of the 18 pilots arrived in Borneo with around 300 hours total flying, and much the same applied to 846 Squadron. Great credit is due to them for their telling contribution to the success of this campaign.

Part 1

The Brunei Rebellion December 1962 to March 1963

Thoughts of a Helicopter Squadron Commander.

By Lieutenant Commander Alan Hensher Royal Navy – C.O. 845 Squadron (Wessex 1)

The onset of the Confrontation Campaign was quite rapid. The political background of the introduction of 'Malaysia', the Indonesian opposition to this and, in particular, the geography of the area of conflict, were largely unknown to us. But as the prospect of being committed to operational deployment became inevitable, an air of excitement grew in the Squadron.

For me, the excitement was tempered with real concern at the low level of flying experience of the majority of my pilots. Of the 18 pilots 14 had less than 300 hours total flying. When, a little later, the true and hostile nature of the terrain in Borneo became clear, I began to think how best to accommodate some easing of pressure on pilots with fulfilling the varied operational tasks involved in:

- lifting troops and heavy equipment,

- 200ft-plus high trees in dense areas of jungle,

- violent and sudden changes of weather with low cloud base and very limited visibility, combined with primitive maps and no navigational aids,

All of which would pose a daunting flying environment to any pilot.

My policy was first, where possible, to avoid demanding too much from the less experienced pilots until they had gained a level of in-country experience: not always a practical option. Second, at first until more experience was gained, I required aircraft to fly in pairs even if the task could be done with one. This way, if a helicopter was forced down there was a buddy aircraft to assist and ensure the location was known. It also generated confidence in the pilots' minds. Oddly enough, the RAF later criticised this practice as wasteful of resources. I remain confident of the efficacy of the procedure. It must be said that the young pilots managed these considerable difficulties remarkably well and I was soon able to drop the pairs requirement.

The principal factor that influenced my approach to the relationship with the several Army units we supported was to replicate our established practice with the Royal Marines of giving operational control of tasking to the Ground Commander. I can claim that the rapport we developed with the Army at every level was a major foundation of a successful campaign.

As the Squadron was deployed ashore operating from Forward Operating Bases (FOB) for almost the entire period, I was able and very content to act independently of the parent ship command. Technical and logistic support from *Albion* was excellent. However, there was little or no guidance forthcoming except for a frequently-voiced desire to get the helicopters back on board. In retrospect I suspect that the command in *Albion* was not attuned to the unique character of this campaign and found it difficult to accept that the squadrons needed to operate mainly ashore from FOBs. This led to a misconceived view that the ship was misemployed by not being in constant and direct close support of the squadrons. The logistic support and ferrying of heavy equipment and helicopters to and from Singapore was felt to be less than fulfilling the ship's potential. In fact, it demonstrated the great value of the ship's versatility in performing so many vital tasks.

Fig 5. 845 Squadron Aircrew and Air Engineer Officers December 1962

I was immensely proud of the way that everyone in my Squadron performed, often in very demanding conditions. Apart from the aircrew, the maintenance people were superb under the leadership of a very young Air Engineer Officer and the highly-skilled Aircraft Artificers. They achieved many things in a primitive environment, including engine changes that were said not to be possible: a true example of Fleet Air Arm commitment to succeed.

Main Helicopter Bases in Sarawak and Brunei

The main Bases developed and used by the Naval Air Commando Squadrons during Confrontation are shown on this sketch map. Note that the spelling of some names have changed slightly.

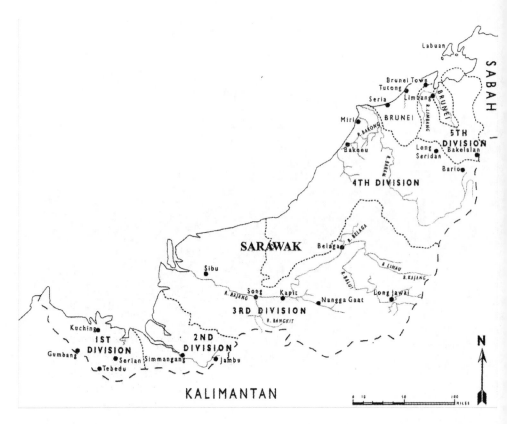

Fig 6. Sketch Map of Sarawak and Brunei

HMS *Albion* and the Brunei Rebellion December 1962 and January 1963

By Lieutenant David Storrie RM (845 Squadron Pilot Wessex 1)

In late 1962, 40 Commando Royal Marines transferred from HM Ships *Bulwark* to *Albion* in Aden Harbour. *Albion* then conducted an amphibious exercise in Kenya prior to turning eastwards towards Singapore, the Commando looking forward to reunion with families and friends and the Ship's Company, including 845 and 846 Squadrons, anticipating their first 'Far East Run Ashore'!

However, events in Brunei and eastern Sarawak on the island of Borneo during the first week of December 1962 caused the Ship to increase engine revolutions and make haste for the Singapore Naval Base to re-ammunition and re-supply overnight on 12-13 December, prior to setting sail for action.

To counter the rebel activities of the guerrilla 'army' of the 'North Kalimantan National Army' (TNKU), 42 Commando RM, 1st Royal Greenjackets, the 1/2nd KEO Gurkha Rifles and The Queen's Own Highlanders had deployed to Brunei and Sarawak, taking advantage of the unsecured airfields at Brunei and Seria. Brigadier Glennie commanded this Force, and the quick deployment of the Gurkhas and Highlanders to secure important points in Brunei Town and the oil towns of Miri and Seria, plus the gallant action by 'L' Company 42 Commando in capturing Limbang and releasing the hostages taken by the TNKU, meant that an incursion by Indonesian forces, poised on the Brunei border, was forestalled.

On *Albion's* arrival off the Sarawak coast on the 14th December 40 Commando, commanded by Lieutenant Colonel David Hunter MC, was landed by the helicopters of 845 and 846 Squadrons at Kuching, the capital of Sarawak. 'A' Company of 40 Commando, commanded by Major Peter 'Pug' Davis DSC, remained temporarily on board as the 99 Brigade Reserve, ready to be deployed as required anywhere in the area of operations.

'Pug' Davis was a distinguished early member of the Royal Marines Special Boat Service. Small of stature but with a bright and 'bubbly' personality, 'Pug' had earned a Distinguished Service Cross when, as a young officer in charge of a small flotilla of landing craft (assault) – LCA – he had led a brave mission to save Royal Marines who had been in danger on the island of Vis, off the Yugoslav coast, in 1944.

In deference to his nickname, the 'A' Company Group was known as 'PUGFORCE', which was deployed from the Ship on 17th December by Wessex helicopters into the village of Danau and, by this time, 'PUGFORCE' included elements of Gurkhas, Sarawak Rangers of the Malay Army and Iban trackers from Sarawak. The Group was re-deployed by helicopter and re-supplied to enable it to perform its task of 'rounding-up' the remnants of the rebel groups in various locations in Brunei State and the 5th Division of Sarawak. Over 300 rebels were captured and the helicopters brought back on board dozens of captured weapons, shotguns, rifles and parangs.

On 7th January 1963, 40 Commando was re-embarked and *Albion* sailed for Singapore with her Squadrons for a well-earned 'Run Ashore'.

(Postscipt: 'Pug' Davis died on 18th August 2011, aged 87.)

846 Squadron in Borneo

By Lieutenant Commander Peter Williams: Senior Pilot 846 Squadron (Whirlwind 7)

On 15th December 1962, the Whirlwind Mk 7 aircraft of 846 Squadron were detached from *Albion* into Brunei to help restore stability, not only for the Sultan of Brunei, but also in other parts of the 5th Division of Sarawak. Our tasks were a far cry from the work-up at Culdrose. We had arrived in the monsoon period and a lot of ingenuity was spent over combatting the hazards of the lightning, thunderstorms and torrential rain on our tented camp. Later on, a private long-house was built for us.

In mid-April 1963, 846 was moved from Brunei down the coast to Kuching in Sarawak to meet the Indonesian Confrontation threat in the First and Second Divisions, where it remained until late December '63, when *Albion* took us to Singapore for a jolly Christmas. At Kuching, the mixture was very much as before: recce, troop lift, CASEVAC, light cargo carrying, and general cabbying in and out of jungle clearings, but on routes very close to the Indonesian border. At last, the Squadron re-embarked in *Albion* on 2nd July 1963, just under seven months since our debut at Brunei. We spent six weeks away from Kuching, enjoyed Singapore and Penang and helped in the Fleet Operational Training Exercise (FOTEX 63), when on 19th August they said: 'Just nip back to Kuching for a week or two, would you?' The fortnight stretched a bit. We each had our two weeks 'R and R' at Singapore and went back to Sarawak to get fit again. Time, airframe hours and engine failures went by until *Albion* made a very special effort, for us, to go and get 225 Squadron RAF from Libya and put them into Borneo in early December. The engine failures, by the way, by-passed the ordinary mortals and selected the CO, LtCdr David Burke and myself, the Senior Pilot; someone up above obviously thought that we were the best people to deal with them.

In general our work continued to be pretty routine, with an unrelenting mixture of border and ambush insertions of our troops, resupply, command and civilian coordination, CASEVACs, roulments, inland recces, and coastal and river patrols working primarily with Royal Marines, Ghurkhas and the special SAS units. Throughout our time in Borneo we operated without crewmen, always single pilot and forever trying to stretch our meagre payload further than was really wise.

During the eight months based on Kuching the squadron operated throughout the 1st Division and with frequent detachments to Simanggang in the 2nd Division. At some point during the Kuching time, around 1st July I think, we were taken back to *Albion* because the RAF arrived! We operated with *Albion* around Malaya and Singapore for a short while, but then something went amiss with the RAF and we were once more recalled to the 'front line'.

On 12th December 1963, the Squadron pulled out, they said 'For good - unless a dire emergency happens'. We said: 'Good, Swinging, Lovely', and went off to have a lovely holiday in Hong Kong for a few beers and to reinforce some special border operations in the New Territories. During this very pleasant break at Hong Kong, the USS *Evans*, known as the 'Palm Tree Ship' in the Seventh Fleet, presented us, the 'Palm Tree Squadron', with a very healthy copy of our joint mascot which, even now, flourishes in a Singapore garden, living proof that hard liquor is the best fertiliser. Shortly after Christmas '63 things got a bit ugly in the far top right-hand corner of Sabah (formerly North Borneo) and we were shipped off and detached into a base at Tawau, working with the Ghurkhas in the Wallace Bay area and quite a distance along the border to the west. It took a while for things to settle down there but by April '64 all was pretty stable once more and the old 846 team were pulled out. A new team stayed on in Tawau for a while, with Lieutenant Commander John Stewart Jervis at the helm.

In recognition of the Squadron's virtually continuous operations over an 18-month period, 846 Squadron was awarded the Boyd Trophy for 1963.

Editor's Note. The following awards were made to 846 Squadron personnel:

Lieutenant Commander David Burke – MBE

Lieutenant Commander Peter Williams – Star Negara Brunei

Chief Aircraft Artificer Harold Corpse – BEM

Memories of 846 Squadron in Borneo

By Lieutenant John Hedges RN: Pilot 846 Squadron (Whirlwind 7)

We were the Whirlwind squadron in HMS *Albion* and were on our way to the Far East.

The ship left Mombasa on a Sunday morning, when we were told to proceed at best speed in an easterly direction. This was because we understood that (amongst other things) some insurgents had tried to take over the oil fields in the State of Brunei. On the way across the Indian Ocean the helicopters were fitted with machine-guns and we practised on a splash target towed behind the ship. As we got closer to Singapore it became clear that 846 Squadron would be disembarked to Brunei airfield in support of the Royal Marines, who had already been flown there.

Fig 7. *Albion* **proceeding towards Singapore 'with all dispatch' - one 846 Whirlwind on deck**

Being a Naval Squadron, we were not experts in the use of guns so the Squadron Commanding Officer, Lieutenant Commander David Burke, decided that only the pilots of the squadron would be armed. So we were duly trained to use the Sterling sub-machine-gun in case we needed to protect ourselves when we were in the jungle. Meanwhile the technicians in the Squadron felt very vulnerable and several made weapons to take with them. The ship berthed in Singapore the following Friday afternoon, took on Commando Brigade staff and sailed that night for Kuching, Sarawak, where we arrived on 14th December and, later the next day, 15th December, at Brunei.

846 Squadron flew ashore at Brunei with a lot of kit and as many groundcrew as we could lift. I managed to take the electrical officer and one other. The Whirlwind Mark 7 could not lift any more in that heat. As soon as we landed at Brunei airfield we started getting the kit out of the helicopters when suddenly there was a burst of machine-gun fire. We all dived for cover but there were very few places we could hide. Luckily one of the pilots was a Royal Marine officer (known to all as Biggles). He took charge of the situation and started ordering us about, trying to establish from where the fire had come. He told Dennis, our engineer officer, to move round to a different position to see what he could see. But Dennis was not armed and was doing his best to make the small rock he was behind grow into a much bigger rock - so Biggles was told in no uncertain manner to get lost. However, after a time and no more gunfire, we emerged from our hiding places only to find out it was an accidental discharge from the Royal Air Force Regiment. Our sailors soon realized the sense of the CO's decision not to arm them.

We pitched our tents on an open, flat piece of ground at Brunei Airfield and the next day, when the rains came, we realized we were pitched on a large mud-flat. We discovered that next to the airfield was a quarry, so we went and commandeered lorries, which we filled with shingle and then took a grader and a large, motorized roller to flatten the shingle out. This improved the camp considerably because the rains came at 4.30pm every day, which turned out be useful. We normally got back to the airfield by 4pm every day and would have a shower, which was in the open, wash the clothes we had had on all day and, without rinsing them, hang them on a line and then redress in the dry ones we had washed the day before. At 4.30pm the rains would pour down in torrents, rinse the clothes on the line, and the next day's sun dried them.

After we had been there a week a local architect arrived when I was Duty Officer and said that he had come to build us some better accommodation, which was to be a wooden hut with a corrugated sheet roof. He showed me the plans and I immediately said it was not big enough to house all the squadron personnel. So I told him to mark where I was standing and then walk away from me to give the length of the building and similarly to get the width. The first house I had ever planned which, when built, was enormous and could have housed two squadrons.

We used to fly a lot to a village called Bangar, which was a military base and various operations took place from there. On day I was tasked to collect a prisoner from an outlying base and take him back to Bangar. On arrival at Bangar I was met by one of our Petty Officer Technicians and I asked him to take the prisoner down to the prisoner compound and duly gave him my Sterling sub-machine-gun to march the prisoner there. On returning to me the Petty Officer said to me: 'Sir, how does this gun work?' Our ground crew were very resourceful.

One day I was flying with the Squadron CO. We took off from the airfield heading for Bangar. We had just reach a thousand feet when the engine spluttered and stopped. The CO immediately went into autorotation and we headed for a pineapple field, which luckily was quite boggy so it took our heavy landing safely, although we rolled on our side. The helicopter was recovered and, when the technicians drained the fuel, it was discovered to be half full of water. The 'sealed' Shell 44-gallon aviation fuel drums had been sabotaged and so we had to use a much more robust filter system when we refuelled from then on.

The Whirlwind Mark 7 was very underpowered for working in the heat and humidity that we endured. To carry the maximum load from the airfield to various destinations we often had to taxi out to the main runway to do a running takeoff like a normal aeroplane, to give us the lift to get airborne. Once we had burnt off fuel and unloaded our cargo, be it troops or stores, we were light enough to get out of the clearing we had landed in. As a general rule the Whirlwind could carry two fully-kitted-up Royal Marines or three Gurkhas.

In mid-April 1963 the squadron moved to Kuching, Sarawak.

KOYLI Lift

By Lieutenant Peter Woodhead RN Pilot 845 Squadron (Wessex 1)

I was tasked to pick up a troop of the King's Own Yorkshire Light Infantry (KOYLI) who had been deployed for some time in an inhospitable jungle area close to Kapit. My aircrewman was Chief Kentsbeer (KB) and we spent the outward leg reminiscing about a previous trip together when, on landing, the aircrewman started firing his SMG in response to some movement near the Landing Site.

We arrived at the KOYLI landing site (LS) to find more troops than we were expecting and, as we crammed them all in, it was clear I was well above the maximum take-off weight. As a fellow Yorkshireman, I was particularly sympathetic to the Troop Commander's plea to get them back together for a debrief and redeployment, so unwisely asked KB to remain at the LS and be picked up later. We briefed the troops on safety drills and, in view of my previous experience with KB, covered weapon safety. We took off on the limits and, struggling to gain translational lift as we fell off the LS, I was distracted by the troops passing up their weapons to me from the cabin. 'What are you F★★★★★★ doing?' I yelled at the Troop Commander on the intercom. 'I'm the Pilot not a F★★★★★★ Cloakroom Attendant! Take charge of your men and stay seated.' On landing at Sibu I gathered them together and gave them a hard time. 'You're a disgrace to the County', I told them. And then I took the Troop Commander, a young Subaltern, aside and told him what I thought of him. 'What part of Yorkshire do you come from?' I shouted at him. 'Well actually', he said, 'I'm from Tunbridge Wells!'

A 'Hostile' Fighter Attack

By Lieutenant Brian Skinner Royal Navy - Pilot 845 Squadron (Wessex 1)

The latter half of December 1962 saw a great deal of aerial activity between *Albion* and Brunei and Sarawak. We landed HQ 3rd Commando Brigade and 40 Commando at Kuching, initially at the three landing sites: 'Brown' at the Sarawak Constabulary Parade Ground, 'Green' at the Jubilee Recreation Ground and 'Yellow' at the Brook College Playing Field. I was briefed to use 'Green' site, where the stands rapidly filled up with locals come to see this great aerial spectacle, and I believe the same thing happened at the other sites, so altogether a very festive day for the locals. Although we could not hear them much with Wessex engines running, we could see our audience waving and grinning enthusiastically.

Fig 8. Assault Stations *Albion* 18 Dec 1962

We then steamed up to Brunei to land 846 Squadron at the airport and then nipped back and forth between Kuching and Brunei, putting troops ashore here and there and moving them from one location to another. 'A' Company of 40 Commando, which had remained on board in reserve for the initial assaults, was put ashore at Danau, south of Kuching.

One of the on-board activities in between sorties at this time was aircraft recognition, with sessions conducted by Chief Air Fitter Kentsbeer, (KB) - who led a multi-faceted life as volunteer aircrewman by day, Aircraft Recognition teacher in the evenings and aircraft maintainer by night. From 1962 to 1965 Indonesia received many types of aircraft – bombers, fighters, transports and helicopters, from the Russians. They also had a number of old World War 2 fighters left over from fighting the Dutch for their independence. We were particularly warned about the possibility of being attacked by Indonesian P-51 Mustang fighters which, although much slower than their jets, would make formidable threats to our helicopters should they decide to cross the border and interfere with our troop movements. We therefore studied carefully the black-and-white aircraft recognition diagrams of the Mustangs, together with the red pentagon on white background insignia painted on all Indonesian military aircraft.

On 18th December 1962, a wave of several Wessex was launched from *Albion* led, I believe, by Alan Hensher, the Squadron CO, to insert troops at an inland, grass landing site a few miles up the coast from Kuching. I was launched last from the ship and caught up with the rest, but was 'Tail End Charlie'. After landing the troops ashore, I lifted off for the return flight over the jungle canopy to the shore and then *Albion*. Hoping to catch up with the rest, I was still climbing when my engine revs began to oscillate. Mindful of the need to avoid the then Wessex 1 tendency for the revs to run up uncontrollably, I reduced speed to just below 60 knots and, switching to manual throttle mode, 'nursed' the revs to try and keep us in level flight until I could find somewhere to land safely. I radioed the CO and told him that I was continuing but would be late getting back. The other Wessex disappeared seawards and KB and I were left alone.

Thus we continued at about 100 feet above the jungle with no sign of any clearings whilst I, in manual throttle mode, tried to keep the engine revs steady. By and large, I was able to keep at this height despite the revs rising and falling slightly. I felt that we might make the beach at least.

After a while KB mentioned that he could see a fixed-wing aircraft heading straight for us, more or less up-sun. Glancing out, I saw this aircraft, which then began to dive straight towards us. Quickly, I passed my Sterling SMG and clips down to KB to supplement his own gun and said that if the fighter kept on I would bank to port at the last minute to swing the main rotors out of the way, to give him clear elevation to fire from the cabin door. KB acknowledged this and said: 'KB at the door in fighting posture, Sir!' I glanced out of the starboard window and saw KB's head sticking out of the aircraft sliding door with his beard flowing in the wind. I could see that he had a Sterling in each hand pointing aggressively at the oncoming 'bandit'.

Still grappling with the engine revs and just when I thought I would have to turn to port for KB to open fire, several things happened very quickly:

- Both KB and I recognised the aircraft as an Army Air Corps Auster.

- I shouted to KB: 'Don't shoot, it's an Auster!'

- KB shouted to me: 'It's a friendly, Sir!'

- The 'bandit' turned to port to pass by us, with the pilot waving cheerily.

- Somewhat shamefaced, we waved back.

Of course, an Army Auster was nothing like a P-51 Mustang but, in mitigation, it was diving down on us with the sun behind it!

That excitement over, we still had the engine problem and nowhere to land. However, there was a slight improvement in the rev oscillation and, when the beach appeared, I was glad to see that *Albion* was quite close inshore. I called Flyco and said that things were a bit better now and that I thought I could make it to the ship. I was cleared to do this and was told that they had prepared space for me to make a short running landing to avoid having to pull more power to hover. All went well and, with great relief, I 'greased' the aircraft onto the deck for a short run and stopped with the toe-brakes. The Squadron Engineer Officer (Lieutenant Nick Rowe) climbed up beside me, plugged into the intercom and asked me to tell him about the engine's behaviour. Fortunately, in support of my story, the engine revs were still fluctuating gently and, after a while, I was asked to shut the aircraft down and it was duly removed from the landing spot for more examination.

Neither KB nor I mentioned that we had prepared ourselves to try and shoot down an Army Auster. Of course, had the 'Bandit' proved to be a hostile fighter, we would have been poorly placed to defend ourselves after the initial spray of both Sterlings (in the unlikely case that he came that close anyway). Our only chance would have been to hug the jungle canopy and hope that the fighter had difficulty in hitting such a slow and low target; however, our ailing engine would probably not have condoned this activity and might well have given up and caused us to sink as gently as possible into the jungle canopy.

845 Operations from HMS Albion December 1962

By Lieutenant Brian Skinner (Pilot, Wessex 1)

Squadron flying operations into Borneo began on 14th December 1962. Between that date and 31st December, we landed troops at many places in Sarawak and Brunei. I personally carried out 16 sorties to Kuching, Brunei, Bangar, Labi, Lawas, Danauand Long Tengoa.

The initial landings were to the Kuching area delivering our Royal Marines. Our maps were dated 1945 and, although Kuching itself was quite well depicted geographically, the surrounding kampongs (villages) were not. Pre-flight briefing in *Albion* covered the routes to take and the codewords for the way points, and we marked up our maps accordingly. So, for example, we might be instructed for the inbound route to coast in at Point 'Sheila' at a height of 1000ft and for the outbound route to coast out at Point 'Judy' at 400ft. At 'Sheila', if flying in Wessex 'Kilo', one would radio the ship and report: 'Kilo, feet dry, Sheila' and, after delivering the troops, report: 'Kilo, feet wet, Judy'. By this means, the Ops Room in *Albion* could keep the plotting map up to date for all aircraft movements.

The coasting in and out points were given female names, at least to start with, whereas actual landing sites were named after colours.

Our Crewroom Flying Statistics Board recorded the number of hours flown by the pilots and aircrewmen for the month of December and shows that we all contributed roughly the same hours, with most of them accrued during the last half of the month during Borneo operations, and there was no let-up for Christmas.

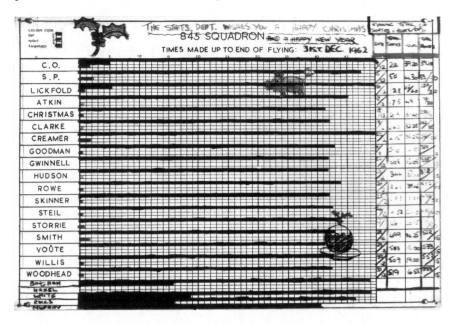

Fig 9. 845 December 63 Crewroom Flying Statistics Board

845's Detachment to Labuan, January 1963

From 845 Squadron Record Books

After operating from *Albion* daily since 14th December, it was decided that a detachment of our Wessex was needed ashore at Labuan Island, just across the bay from Brunei Town, to give closer support to operations in and around Brunei without the ship having to remain in the vicinity.

Lt Cdr Geoff Andrews (the Senior Pilot) led this detachment, supported by (amongst others) Dick Steil, Geoff Atkin, Peter Gwinnell, David Christmas, David Creamer and Nobby Hall (the Deputy Squadron AEO).

Fig 10. 845 Labuan Detachment Jan 1963

Launching from *Albion* on 7th January, they set up the operational site on Labuan Airfield.

In January 1963, during the early days of operations against the uprising in Brunei and whilst operating from our base in Labuan, a patrol of Sarawak Rangers in the jungle was reported missing, having failed to maintain contact with Headquarters. Searches were carried out without success as concern for their safety grew. Crews operating in their last known area were asked to be watchful. Some days later on 23rd January an 845 Wessex crew engaged on

Fig 11. 845 Dispersal Labuan January 1963

troop repositioning noticed an unusually small, red object above the otherwise green jungle canopy. With just enough time to investigate, they identified a small balloon on a piece of string. Its position was reported back to base and 2 Wessex were sent to investigate. Below the balloon a small clearing had been carved out of the trees and a log-pole landing pad had been made on the ground. This was in fact the lost patrol and the aircraft eased gingerly into the clearing one at a time and were able to extract the lost patrol and return them safely to base.

846 Disembarkation to Labuan February 1963

From 846 Squadron Record Book, courtesy of the Fleet Air Arm Museum

Back at Singapore, whilst *Albion* prepared for sea and embarked the 1/7th Gurkhas and the King's Own Yorkshire Light Infantry (KOYLI), the Squadron prepared both professionally and socially for a long absence from *Albion* disembarked in Borneo.

On Tuesday at 0745 *Albion* slipped and proceeded for Borneo to relieve two Army units and land the Squadron at Labuan.

Between embarking in *Albion* and disembarking at Labuan no flying was undertaken, as all efforts were concentrated on bringing the Whirlwind aircraft up to a state of maintenance that would permit the longest possible period of operation without component change or major maintenance. We also loaded the two RN 3-tonners, which we were taking ashore with us loaded with stores, spares and ground equipment; one of them was going to be turned into a mobile workshop.

The move ashore began on Thursday and was eventually completed by 0700 on Saturday. This was the first seaborne disembarkation we had done and it showed us and the ship how fortunate we have been in the past to have 845 Squadron's Wessex (with their heavier lift capability) to assist us. Our six 846 Squadron Whirlwind aircraft took off at 1000 and flew to Labuan airfield. The main party went ashore at noon by Landing Craft Assault (LCA) and by 1500 all that remained on board was a very small air party and the two 3-Tonners. Some difficulty was experienced in getting the 3-Tonners ashore; the strops were too long to lift the lorries clear of the deck within the limits of the ship's crane, the availability of the two Landing Craft Tanks (LCTs), *Ardennes* and *Agedabio* was limited as they were occupied in ferrying Army vehicles from the ship to Brunei and vice versa and also there were difficulties in putting the LCTs onto the ramp in Victoria harbour at night. Despite these difficulties, the two 3-Tonners were loaded into the LCTs and were ashore by 0700 on Saturday 9th.

Labuan airfield is on an island eight miles long by five miles wide. It was two miles from the only town of substance, Victoria, which is also the only harbour in the island. The runway was 6074 ft by 150 ft, with a bitumen surface. The RAF was operating Single- and Twin-engine Pioneers, Beverleys, Valettas, Hastings and, occasionally, Hunters and Britannias. The Control Tower had UHF, VHF, Eureka, NDB, a night-flying capability, AVGAS and AVTUR in bowsers.

The island itself was very attractive and surrounded by shallow waters, which gently caressed the long white coral beaches of the palm-fringed bays and coves. The whole island was covered in lush vegetation. Stark reminders of less peaceful times were the decaying remains of WW2 Australian LCAs, which still marred the gleaming sands of some of the beaches. Towards the North end of the island was Surrender Bay, where the Australians accepted the Japanese surrender of Borneo. The Imperial War Graves Cemetery tells its own story of the fierceness of that battle.

A large dispersal with a Pierced Steel Planking (PSP) surface was shared by the Squadron and three Valettas. 845 Squadron, a detachment from which had deployed to Labuan earlier, had put up marquees at the Royal Navy end of the dispersal. These provided a stores tent, aircrew briefing room, A.M.C.O. and Staff Office, and an Electrical Maintenance Shop. In the first two days a lot of hard work considerably improved the appearance and efficiency of the site.

The accommodation, whilst not being all we wished for, was satisfactory. The officers lived in the airport hotel, which was used by all services trooping in and out of Borneo and was shared with a voracious breed of mosquito. The ratings lived in long huts provided by the RAF in the main camp and also in tents alongside the dispersal. The food provided and cooked by the RAF was complimented by the Squadron ratings.

The Squadron was employed during this stay in Borneo moving troops, stores and supplies from fixed wing air-heads to helicopter landing zones, flying communication and reconnaissance with VIPs and CASEVACs to Brunei. This latter tasking gave the Squadron some of its most rewarding missions. On 8th February two aircraft went to Lawas in North East Sarawak to carry out a troop move. Lawas was used as an air-head into which the troops were flown by fixed wing with the Squadron, then flying them on to their further distances.

Floods!

By Lieutenant Peter Voute RN 845 Squadron (Pilot Wessex 1)

During mid-January 1963 Brunei and parts of Sarawak (especially around Marudi) suffered devastating floods. Food for the civilian population was in short supply so, on 7th January, our Wessex flew from Labuan to Brunei to embark sacks of rice for the flooded areas. In order to carry maximum loads, I remember being briefed that the aircraft were too heavy for vertical take-off so we were to taxi out to the main runway and carry out rolling take-offs. This was quite exciting as we staggered into the air at the end of the runway and, by the time we got to the Marudi area, we had used up sufficient fuel to carry out a vertical landing. Various sorties were carried out before we returned to Labuan to re-embark in *Albion* and then disembark to RNAS Sembawang on 21 January.

The Creamer Computer

By Lieutenant David Creamer RN Pilot 845 Squadron (Wessex 1)

By the end of October 1962, 845 Squadron, equipped with Wessex HU Mk1, the first single-engine, gas-turbine-powered helicopter produced for carrier-borne operations in the military support role, had been formed, trained, worked up and was ready for embarkation in *Albion* to depart the UK for the Far East on 1st November.

On 28th September the Squadron was subject to an O.R.I. (Operational Readiness Inspection) by a team from Flag Officer Naval Flying Training (Rear Admiral Percy Gick). The inspection was passed satisfactorily, but some doubts and concerns were raised as to the preparedness and ability of the crews to cope with the demanding aspects of operating in the tropical conditions and performance limitations that would be experienced in the hot-high-humid conditions that would be encountered, and which had not been experienced during the work-up in the UK. Careful planning would be required before each flight to ensure safe operations. This would require calculations of payload that could be lifted safely over sometimes long-range destinations to sites at various altitudes where aircraft performance would vary with the effects of high temperature and humidity, the number of troops to be carried, the weight of equipment or stores in the cabin and/or weight of vehicle, guns, or netted stores to be carried externally on the cargo hook. The navigation aspect would also have to be determined, i.e. the distance the load had to be carried, weight of fuel for that distance and also to return if fuel was not available at the destination.

All this information was available in the Pilot's Notes for the aircraft type, but it was presented in graphical form and took a long time to establish, even while the aircraft were still aboard the ship or at a shore base. However, once away from ship or shore base, any new sortie had to be calculated by the crew, mainly in the aircraft during flight and possibly in difficult or even hostile situations. These issues were further complicated by the need to address them when dropping or picking up troops and equipment at remote (hot) desert sites or jungle landing sites requiring steep descents into, or climb-outs from, to clear tall trees.

Since the Wessex 1 could carry a much great payload than its predecessor, the piston-engined Whirlwind 7, this was a new challenge for Commando helicopter crews.

With just one month left before embarking in *Albion*, serious thought was needed to find some way of alleviating these problems.

Having previously completed a tour of duty East of Suez in 848 Squadron in *Bulwark* flying the Whirlwind Mk 7, I had experienced a lot of these difficulties - particularly in Aden and around the Persian Gulf in temperatures of 100^0 F during the first Iraq incursion into Kuwait in August 1961 in temperatures of 120^0 F plus. When moving troops around the desert it was often necessary to land and disengage the rotor blades to avoid exceeding engine and transmission temperature limitations. During that time I was personally involved in the loss of an aircraft (fortunately with no casualties) by being overloaded with troops from the ship with lots of wind at takeoff and subsequently attempting to land at a mountain location in Borneo at altitude with no wind. With this experience behind me, I felt that I should try to think of a solution for the Wessex.

My aim was to display the graphical information from the Pilot's Notes on something that would be easy to use and small enough to be carried in flying overall pockets or navigation bags. Something along the lines of a Dalton navigational computer, circular with revolving wheels on either side.

With this in mind I took a copy of the Pilot's Notes home with me and, using an old *Weetabix* box (for cardboard), laboriously calculated results to provide a maximum take-off weight to give 180ft per minute climb as required - adjusted to height, and temperature at that height, with a headwind correction. This was presented on one side of the computer. The other side would be calculations for payload. Payload is a function of load to be carried and fuel required to cover the distance to the landing site, which would be more for long flights, resulting in reduced load. The results were displayed around the two rotating discs so that as one increased the other reduced, and vice versa. The fuel load was determined using fuel consumption of 700 lbs/hr at a cruising speed of 90 knots and making allowance for 300 lbs of unusable fuel. Once the load was established it could be readily displayed as the number of

Marines with their equipment (222 lbs each) or known loads: the Wombat (600 lbs), Mobat (1000 lbs) or 105 Howitzer (2,700 lbs). Other known fixed-weight loads such as Land Rovers, etc. could be pencilled in if required - or the whole load, carried internally in the aircraft cabin or externally, netted on the cargo hook.

This computer then produced the information required in seconds rather than the lengthy time it took to laboriously interpret the graphs from the Pilot's Notes. The *Weetabix* computer was shown to the squadron the next day and later checked and approved by the Culdrose maintenance test pilot. It was then sent off to the Admiralty for its consideration.

The Squadron embanked in *Albion* on 1st November 1962, one month after the O.R.I., and departed for the Far East. I was later summoned to the Dockyard in Singapore, where fine-tuning adjustments were made to the computer and the final display design decided upon. The compass, now known as the 'Creamer Computer', went into production but had not actually been issued to the Squadron until after I had returned to the UK. So I never had the opportunity to try it out in anger.

However, I am informed by Brian Skinner that the Creamer Computers worked well and were invariably carried in Pilots' flight holdalls. He said that it was a great piece of kit and served the Squadron well in the early months of Borneo and, even when pilots had gained more Borneo experience and could generally give a pretty good mental estimate of what could be carried, the Creamer Computer was always there as a reassuring second opinion.

As a postscript, I was later awarded the Herbert Lott memorial award for the princely sum of £25!

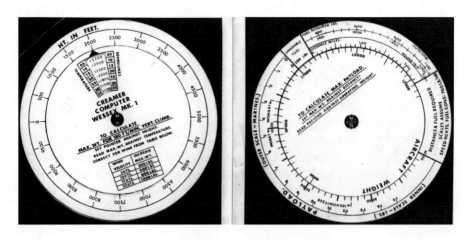

Fig 12. The Creamer Computer Front and Rear

Part 2

Indonesian Confrontation April 1963 to March 1964

845's First Detachment to Kuching, April 1963

By Lieutenant Brian Skinner Royal Navy - Pilot 845 Squadron (Wessex 1)

In April 1963, 845 Squadron was ordered to provide Wessex aircraft to operate from Kuching Airfield in support of military operations in the First Division of Sarawak. Accommodation for the Squadron Personnel was to be in two requisitioned bungalows on a hill just outside Kuching, one for the officers and one for the senior rates. The junior rates were quartered within the Royal Marines' camp. The bungalows had water and cooking facilities, but no furniture at all. I was detailed off by the CO to be the OIC Accommodation and authorised to go into town and purchase some furniture. I remember buying chests of drawers and small wardrobes for clothes storage and tables, benches and chairs. For sleeping, of course, we had our folding camp-beds and mossy nets.

Fig 13. 845's Bungalows at Kuching with Senior Rates on left, Officers on right and Private one in foreground

One immediate problem I had to deal with concerned the drainage in the Senior Rates' bungalow. Basically it was all bunged up. I needed a plumber! Someone told me that the Royal Marines sometimes had

55

qualified plumbers on their strength. I didn't really believe this but asked the Royals anyway. To my amazement, in very short time and on the same day, a Land Rover appeared with a Royal Marine who looked at the problem area and set to with spade and pickaxe from the vehicle and dug down to find where the blockages were. He was, in fact, a qualified plumber. He identified the blocked (and broken) pipe, cleared the blockage, repaired the pipe and tested everything. All worked perfectly now and our saviour saluted smartly and disappeared in the Land Rover. I have never, ever, come across such efficient and rapid plumbing service since – and with no call-out charge either.

I also had to arrange victualling, which our Squadron Hong Kong Chinese cooks and stewards prepared and served. I think that it was breakfast and supper only as we probably either had lunch in the Royal Marines' camp or were provided with bag meals.

One point, which troubled us a little in the bungalows, was that we were rather isolated up a hill and quite a long way from other habitation and any military support. We were not allowed to take any firearms off the airport and we felt a bit exposed, especially during the nights. Lieutenant Chris Grover Royal Marines was the Officer in Charge of *Albion's* Aicraft Control Team (A.C.T.), which deployed to set up remote landing sites with radio contact plus flares for night operations, to guide the Wessex in. More to the point, bungalow-wise, was that he and his team were fully equipped with their own Land Rovers, plus firearms and ammunition. Thus, when he asked if he and his team could join us in the bungalows, we accepted with alacrity. We then slept a little easier with at least some defence in each bungalow.

We managed to put in quite a lot of flying in the First Division of Sarawak on this deployment in support of the Royal Marines and began to feel comfortable with navigation right up to the Indonesian border – not always easy to recognise in the dense, green mountain ridges.

Long Semado – The Loss of Belvedere XG 473.

By Lieutenant Peter Voute Royal Navy - Pilot 845 Squadron (Wessex 1)

I was based at Kuching, Sarawak in early May 1963 with 845 Squadron. The Squadron was equipped with Wessex Mk 1 helicopters and was based there as a Forward Operating Base from HMS *Albion*. I cannot recall the exact number of aircraft but I believe it was a detachment of four.

Early on 5th May the Commanding Officer, Lt Cdr Alan Hensher, was ordered to detach two aircraft in the SAR role to Brunei as an RAF Belvedere helicopter was missing. The aircraft had taken off from Brunei during the afternoon of 4th May, *en route* to Long Semado airfield at the head of the Trusan Valley in the Fifth Division of Sarawak. It had its crew of three, three experienced and decorated SAS officers and one trooper, an official from the FCO and a civilian from the Borneo Company. They were also carrying two 45-gallon drums of AVPIN. This is a monofuel that was used to start the Gazelle Napier engines of the Belvedere and also the Wessex Mk 1. It was dangerous stuff.

Alan Hensher and one aircrewman (I cannot recall his name) were the lead SAR aircraft and I was detailed off to be the second, with CAF Kentsbeer as my crewman. We took 3 hours 45 minutes to fly to Brunei, via a refuelling stop at Bintulu. On arrival, we were rapidly briefed on the expected track of the Belvedere and set off to search. About two thirds of the way to Long Semado, we came across the crash site in thick, virgin jungle. It was a wide area of burnt-out trees, and at the bottom, I always remember, there was the shape of a Belvedere, but in aluminium powder. It was clear that nothing could have survived the crash and, if anyone had survived the initial impact, they would have been burnt to death when the AVPIN ignited. However, there was always the chance someone might have been thrown clear. We reported the crash site and returned to Brunei as darkness was approaching.

Early next morning, we launched with RAF Rescue teams on board both aircraft and arrived at the site. I recall CAF Kentsbeer saying over the intercom as we approached the site, 'Into the Valley of Death go the Wessex'!! Alan Hensher went in first and found that he was hovering at maximum power just above the jungle canopy. The rescue team tried disembarking using the winch but found that it was not long enough, so a rope was attached to the winch hook and then lowered. At the extremity of the winch, the Rescue Team transferred to the rope and then 'shinned' down to the site. I followed in the second aircraft, expertly conned by Chief KB, and remember very vividly being at

19,600 maximum compressor rpm as we disembarked our members of the Rescue Team. We circled overhead until they established communications and confirmed there were no survivors. We carried out one further sortie with stores for the people on the ground and then the third sortie that day was to search for a downed Army Air Corps Sycamore helicopter. We located it and thankfully the pilot was safe. Further sorties were carried out to the Belvedere site on the 7th and 8th, after which we flew from Brunei to Labuan and then embarked that evening in *Albion*, which was close off-shore.

After a restful and refreshing night in our mother ship, we returned to Kuching on 9th May via a refuelling stop at Bintulu. This was a sad mission which has, in some ways, similarities with the later loss of the RAF Chinook in Scotland in 1980, which was also carrying important intelligence experts.

Alan Hensher told me later that he had briefed the rescue team leader that if the helicopter began to lose height at maximum torque just above the jungle canopy he would have to cut the wire to avoid a further disaster.

Many years later I found out that the nine bodies had been re-interred at Long Merarap in the Trusan Valley. A memorial to those who lost their lives is located on the Memorial Wall at Terendak Camp, near Malacca, Malaysia.

TWO TALES ABOUT GURKHAS

By Lt Cdr Peter Williams, Senior Pilot 846 Squadron (Whirlwind 7)

The first tale centres on a long-range CASEVAC – well, long for an ageing and seriously unsophisticated 846 Squadron Whirlwind Mk 7!

The plea for help put an injured Gurkha some 70-odd miles south east of Kuching, somewhere on a river bank near the Indonesian border. Our maps of the area were from sketchy aerial photographs, with large areas shaded white and marked 'obscured by cloud'. 846 carried no aircrewmen and, with enough fuel for over two hours, just one pilot. After an uninspiring flight over ceaseless tropical jungle, with a few forlorn contours and the odd small river, fortune shined and just as 'abort' seemed inevitable the patrol appeared on a tiny sand bank.

Now the point of this tale is not the flight but about my admiration of Gurkhas.

Whilst the casualty and carer were being stowed aboard I looked around at the rest of the Gurkha team, who were all steadfastly watching in all directions for any rebels. Not once did any of them ever look around at the helicopter - very serious professionals. The return trip to Kuching hospital was less dramatic, being towards the coast, albeit in torrential afternoon rains and with much disquiet over the fading fuel-gauge. Happily the patient lived to fight another day.

Fig 14. 846 Whirlwind on CASEVAC mission

Many years later and to my surprise, I discovered that an MBE had been suggested for the rescue but the office wallahs back in Singapore thought it sounded like a fairly routine trip; just as well, really, or by the time I left Borneo I could well have been awash in pretty ribbons.

My second tale shows the lovely Gurkha sense of humour.

The scene has a lonesome Whirlwind with its faithful pilot pottering around many miles south of Simanggang in the Sarawak 2nd division. In an area too remote even for Ibans, and nowhere vaguely suitable for landing, so the Gurkhas would have to rope down on to a scrubby knoll. Not their idea of fun. However, all went well until the last man reached the ground when the renowned Leonides engine coughed and sighed and down came the helicopter in untidy fashion amongst the Gurkhas.

The reaction of the Gurkhas is lovely to record: 'If you were going to land anyway why on earth did you make us climb down that accursed rope?' I could not think of a good response, so I left them to it whilst I used the accursed rope to tie the remains of the helicopter to a tree stump to prevent it rolling down the hill.

The Gurkhas then gave up rebel-chasing for a while and kindly spent time ruining their kukris clearing the hilltop.

Sometime later along came one of the RAF's fine 'flying longhouses' (the Iban name for the Belvedere) and lifted the 'accursed one' back to Simanggang where, after much tender loving care, it made a full recovery.

Fig 15. 846 Whirlwind after unplanned landing

845's Detachment to Labuan, August 1963

By Lieutenant Brian Skinner Royal Navy - Pilot 845 Squadron (Wessex 1)

It was decided that once again a detachment of our Wessex was needed ashore at Labuan Island, just across the bay from Brunei Town. The CO was to lead this detachment and he informed me that I would be the detachment Senior Pilot. This turned out to be the first of many times that I found myself having to do more than just fly a Wessex on a mission with someone else doing the planning and briefing.

We launched from *Albion* on 18th August and set up our operational site on Labuan Airfield. We had some tents for Briefing, Admin and Stores and some camp furniture such as folding tables and chairs. Most importantly, I remember that we had an excellent large, paraffin-powered fridge that kept us going with cold drinks. Having set everything up on the airfield, we then made our way to our accommodation at the Airport Hotel.

We slept on camp-beds two to a room. We had been warned about the mosquitoes and so had been issued with a mosquito-net each. After the first night, I managed to obtain a second camp-bed, as a single one was too short for my 6ft 6in frame. I also obtained a second mosquito-net and contrived to rig the two nets over my 1½-length extended bed. This proved effective, although requiring careful entry into the bed and not too much turning over once inside, as it didn't take much for the whole thing to collapse upon me. Nevertheless, I did manage to avoid too many mossie bites during that detachment.

We fed in the hotel and the food was OK but not very filling, as I recall. One thing I do remember is that we asked the RAF for a vehicle to visit the town in the evenings. They could not offer us a car or Land Rover but did say that they had a spare water bowser that we could borrow. We accepted this kind offer and I was designated as the authorised driver. I have vague but happy memories of driving this vehicle, still full of water, for runs ashore into Labuan town. There were not many restaurants there but we seemed to visit a particular one quite often. The journeys back were always interesting, with 3 people in the driving cab and several others clinging onto the water tank by the fixed ladders. No one fell off as far as I can remember and we returned the vehicle, undamaged I am pleased to say, to the RAF (bless 'em!) at the end of the detachment with our grateful thanks.

Basically, we were supporting the troops at Brunei Town, some 30 miles South West from our island base at Labuan. We flew from Labuan to Brunei to pick up troops and take them on to more forward areas and bring them back again as required. At the end of the day we would return to Labuan for aircraft servicing and sometimes evening "runs ashore" as already described.

One day, I was in the Labuan Airport Tower briefing the duty staff about our known programme for the day and found that several RAF officers were gathered and looking out of the windows at a Hastings aircraft that was trying to start all of its four engines before requesting take-off for its destination (I think Singapore). The problem was that three engines started OK but the fourth, although it coughed encouragingly, kept dying. It was explained to me (as a lowly helicopter pilot) that this was a not unknown problem and it was possible to start a recalcitrant engine by going as fast as possible down the runway on the good engines and trying to start the other engine by the propeller windmilling in the airflow. 'A bit like running a car downhill in gear and letting in the clutch', I suggested. It was agreed that this was a not dissimilar process. The problem was that the runway was flat and of limited length. After that it was palm trees. I was assured, however, that this procedure could be done (just) on a runway of this length providing the pilot knows what he is doing.

As the aircraft taxied out to the duty runway, on three engines, the numbers of spectators in the tower increased, word having got round about his exciting attempt. I, of course, stayed to witness this event.

Having positioned the Hastings at the absolute limit of the downwind end of the runway, the pilot called for take-off and was given permission, with a 'Good Luck!' added. The aircraft trundled down the runway at a seemingly slow rate of acceleration and when about two thirds of the way down we heard the last engine begin to cough somewhat asthmatically. Just when we thought that it was not going to start, it finally fired and, in the nick of time, the pilot was able to lift off and clear the tops of the palm trees by a very narrow margin. Everyone in the Tower was pleased and relieved and the pilot of the Hastings was congratulated. As I left the Tower to return to our Squadron I saw the Hastings coming in to land to pick up its passengers or freight – without stopping the engines this time –a sensible decision!

The next two weeks were spent in moving troops from Brunei to more remote places such as Kampong Amoh and Labu. On 22nd August I was scrambled to Long Merrerap with Petty Officer Guppy as my aircrewman and, following several trips to build up troops there, I returned to Brunei with two prisoners on board on the 24th. There followed two more weeks of troop movements until we re-embarked in *Albion* on 9th September.

Albion steamed up to Hong Kong for a welcome break from Borneo and on the 17th we were carrying out border recces along the Hong Kong/China Border. I also had the opportunity to fly in an Army Auster for further area familiarisation. All good things come to an end, however, and on the 26th we were back off Borneo and I was flying equipment from the ship to Brunei and Labuan.

Belaga Detachment and Battle of Long Jawi

By Lieutenant Dick Steil Royal Navy - Pilot 845 Squadron (Wessex 1) Detachment Commander, Belaga.

The Enemy Attack. The attack on Long Jawi took place spasmodically throughout Saturday, 28th September. The enemy, (subsequently known to be led by Indonesian Major Muljono) were estimated to be up to 250 strong, of whom about 100 were Indonesian Kayan guides and bearers. They had infiltrated into the longhouses over the previous two or three days, managing to persuade the inhabitants, also Kayans, to keep quiet. On the day before the fighting broke out, a Captain of the 1st/2nd Gurkhas visited Long Jawi and spoke to the natives, at which time they all must have known the attack was imminent and many of the enemy must have been hiding in the longhouse, but no hint was given. This lack of co-operation was blamed upon the fact that the inhabitants of Long Jawi only moved from their border kampong just after the Second World War and still traded freely with their fellow tribesmen over the border.

The enemy first attacked the radio station, early a.m. 28th, killing one Gurkha and one Border Scout radio operator and burning the shack to the ground. The rest of the defence consisted of one platoon of Border Scouts and five Gurkhas. They were situated in the schoolhouse about 100 yards from the nearest longhouse, and on a small hill, thus overlooking the kampong. They came under sporadic fire, from rifle,

SMG, MMG and mortar, and they returned the fire for the rest of the day. Another Gurkha and one or two more Border Scouts were killed before the remainder retreated into the jungle; they had not been surrounded although with their numbers the enemy could easily have done so. Many of the Border Scouts were captured, two of whom escaped from the camp to which the enemy withdrew, but the Gurkhas made their way back to Belaga and Kapit. The enemy made no immediate attempt to follow up and were estimated to have lost four killed and several wounded.

The Initial Response. News of this battle thus did not reach Sibu until a.m. Monday 30th September, when two Wessex aircraft at Song were diverted to Kapit to stand by for troop lift. The remaining two at Sibu were put at half an hour's notice and then scrambled at 1230, proceeding also to Kapit with Lieutenant Colonel John Clements, the Officer Commanding 1st/2nd Gurkha Rifles. The four aircraft were turned round and refuelled by the skeleton ground crew with utmost despatch, for a maximum effort troop lift into Long Jawi.

Unfortunately, on start-up 'C' failed to do so, so with three aircraft we took in a platoon of 24 men, under the command of Major Mole, Long Jawi being 085 degrees from Kapit 75 miles. (See the following Article "Long Jawi Assault").

Follow-Up Operations. The following day, 1st October, the four aircraft moved from Kapit, where they had spent the night, up to Belaga airstrip, which was to be our operational base, with forty troops. These were later placed in two ambush positions on the Batang Balui, upriver from Long Jawi, the most likely escape route for the enemy. Interestingly, the only prepared landing site on the river which had been cleared by Border Scouts some weeks previously, was found to have been staked with poles 8 to 10 feet in length pointing vertically; this could only have been done by the enemy on their way in to Long Jawi, showing that they understood helicopter operations and could recognise an LS. A platoon was roped in to this site and it was that evening at dusk that this platoon carried out the very successful ambush of two longboats, all passengers, approximately 26, reckoned to be killed. One longboat sank and disappeared, but the other was wrecked on the far side of the river and from this a lot of interesting information and equipment was obtained.

The next few days consisted of flying up troops to Belaga from Kapit and Song and placing them in ambush positions. The platoons in ambush were re-rationed and, where necessary, re-ammunitioned. Further ambush positions were put in place down the Sungai Aput, another on the Batang Balui, and one on each of the suspected northern escape routes, the Sungai Linau and Sungai Kayang. All the inhabitants of Long Jawi had left by the 30th and moved down-river into other longhouses; some escaped Border Scouts were also in these as well as two casualties from the battle. The Border Scouts and casualties were lifted out and, on the 3rd, the Colonel and District Officer were taken around these Balui longhouses to talk to the locals, gain information, assure them that no further attacks were likely, and try to persuade the Long Jawi inhabitants to return. This they would not do; in fact, many of them believed that fighting was still going on there. It was that day, the 3rd, that Alan Hensher - the Squadron CO - had to call into Long Jawi before returning to Belaga with Border Scouts and others he had lifted out of a downstream kampong. On running in to the LZ he could hear the screams and wails coming from the aircraft cabin, and his crewman had great difficulty in controlling them.

Throughout this first week of Long Jawi operations we had been forbidden by the Colonel to overfly the Jalangai/Balui river junction, where the enemy camp was reported to be by the escaped Border Scouts, in order not to disturb them. The initial platoon put into Long Jawi was trying to follow up the enemy on foot and was finding it incredibly hard going. Eventually they came to a full stop when they were unable to cross the Balui. There were no clearings in the jungle, the only possible LSs being a couple of shingle banks on the Balui/Bahau river junction. The platoon eventually arrived at this point and was ferried across the river by two aircraft; both landing sites were extremely tight! A new platoon commander was put in and Major Mole lifted out.

Now came a brief period of re-rationing and generally sorting out the troops. The initial positioning had been done in such haste that the first troops available had been put where required just to get the ambushes in place. Now it was time to get the platoons together under their right commanders, etc.

On 12th October, Major Willoughby and his follow-up platoon reached the enemy camp. He reported that the enemy had left up to five days previously, leaving behind four graves, no doubt of their own wounded who had since died, and six to ten unburied bodies. These latter were unrecognisable due to decay, but it is reckoned they were the captured Border Scouts who must have been murdered before the enemy left the camp. This camp appeared to be where the main body was waiting to be ferried back to the Indonesian border by their five powered longboats. However, two of these were knocked out in the ambush, one was surprised by an Army Auster near the Balui/Aput junction and later seen abandoned, so that left two that got away and presumably did not come back. Thus, after a wait of nearly a week, they must have given up and started walking. Two days previous to the Gurkhas' arrival at Jalangai, the first ambush platoon up the Aput had a contact with two enemy, of whom they killed one, but the other escaped. They were presumed to have come from the abandoned longboat.

The extremely weary follow-up platoon was then pulled out of Jalangai and replaced by fresh troops, who continued the trail south along the Balui.

All this time, Long Jawi was being built up as a Gurkha Company Headquarters, with reserve troops and rations being flown in whenever possible.

Fig 16. Some of the Staff at 'RNAS Belaga'

On 14th October the 'Royal Naval Air Station Belaga' was honoured by the visit of Brigadier Glennie and other high-ranking officers of COMBRITBOR's Staff, including Group Captain Dennis, the Air Task Force Commander. They spent some time on the airstrip trying to sort out our main problem of where to put our aircraft to allow both RAF Twin Pioneers to land and air-drops to take place, as our only sites were on the runway or by the DZ. It was a busy day on the airfield that day and it was soon appreciated by the Brigadier that for us to move our aircraft to allow for each operation was highly wasteful and most impracticable. The problem was solved later by signal, the Twin Pioneers being ordered to wait at Bintulu and be called in when the strip was free, until such time as our new dispersal, to be built by the Gurkha Engineers, was completed. The reason for the Twin Pioneers landing was to pick up the parachutes for re-use, without which the RAF air-drops, and consequently this operation, would have come to a grinding halt.

Also on the 14th we were to put in two 'long stop' ambush positions at the boat stations at the top end of both the Balui and Aput. These boat stations mark the uppermost navigable reaches where those going over the border, usually traders and such-like, leave their boats and have to walk over the watershed that usually marks the border before picking up another boat at a similar station on the other side. The Balui platoon went in at the boat station as planned. Unfortunately it was not realised until three days later, when the Aput platoon gave their position as being virtually on top of another, but could not find the latter, that they must have been put in the wrong position. The leader of the formation that had put them in had returned to Sibu and, what with bad weather delaying the search, the appalling maps which not only gave no detail but on which even the main features were hopelessly inaccurate, it was a further couple of days before we located them five miles down the Sungai Kliong, a tributary of the Aput which at the junction appears a far larger river, the Aput almost disappearing under the canopy of trees. We winched them down a power-saw and fuel from 100 feet up - the full extent of the aircraft's winch-cable - and were then able to lift them out and put them into their proper position. It was while winching the saw into this site that a tree the troops had been cutting fell, carrying away the winch-cable and hook. Fortunately the aircrewman had noticed the troops below scattering, surmised that something was amiss, and gave the 'go up!' just in time. The pilot only felt a small, sharp jerk to the aircraft and no damage was done. It required five aircraft to pull 22 troops out of this position, the trees being very high, the valley steep, and the LS small, but luckily this was the only occasion, due to visiting aircraft, that we had five available for a lift!

Another lift which demonstrated the limits to which we were operating was pulling 24 men out of the Sungai Kajang ambush position. The distance 70 miles direct, the height of LS amsl 2,000 feet and the temperature 26 to 27^{0}C. The platoon had to be moved out in one as it was unacceptable to leave a small group of men in a position which could be attacked. At this height and temperature, with 850 lbs of fuel each aircraft could lift 8 men, with 950 lbs they couldn't and with 750 lbs they couldn't get back to base. This made no allowance for adverse weather conditions, however, and on the above occasion there was a large thunderstorm near the airfield which necessitated two aircraft, with insufficient fuel, putting down at Long Linau for the night, being refuelled and flown back next morning.

Apart from these occurrences mentioned in detail, the majority of the day's flying consisted of re-rationing platoons, changing personnel from Kapit, Long Jawi or Song, building up Long Linau, and stockpiling rations there and at Long Jawi. These were the mundane but necessary trips.

In the first fortnight two civilian childbirth CASEVACS were taken from Belaga to Kapit. The second one unfortunately died in the aircraft from loss of blood due to haemorrhage.

On 17th October the platoon on the Balui, upstream from the Aput junction, reported advancing mortar fire. This continued throughout the day and the mortar fire closed to 800 yards. The platoon waited in ambush but no further contact was made.

On the 19th, just prior to the lift-out by five aircraft of the 'lost' platoon from Sungai Kliong to the Bungai Aput boat station, one aircraft had landed at a platoon position 2 miles east of the Aput/Kliong junction to land some small stores, and it was here just thirty minutes later that three enemy walked into the ambush. One was killed, two were wounded and ran. However, they dropped all their gear and weapons, which included a .30in Browning MMG plus a belt of 800 rounds of ammunition. Had they been able to get that weapon into position, the five aircraft troop-lifting up the river valley would have been very poorly placed! On following the blood trail of the wounded enemy, the Gurkha platoon discovered a trail used by 80-odd men leading up the Aput valley. This platoon then continued the follow-up and the platoon at the Aput boat station was reinforced with the platoon from the Sungai Linau, and formed a 50-strong ambush right across the valley. Thus the remainder of the raiders were sandwiched. Their only hope was to cut across country, before reaching the boat station, in which case there would be no chance of intercepting them, the station being only five miles from the border and that area being steep jungle with no LSs. At the time of my departure, on handing over the Belaga Detachment to Lieutenant Commander Digby Lickfold on 23rd October, there was no news of any contact, but the sandwich was getting progressively thinner!

Operating Conditions. The greatest drawback to operations in this area was the weather. The valleys were invariably full of cloud, often down to ground level until mid-forenoon. Then late afternoon, from 1500 onwards, the thunderstorms started building up. The weather deteriorated noticeably during the three-and-a-half weeks of the Long Jawi campaign, presumably due to the approaching NE monsoon, and the flyable period of the day was getting shorter and shorter, sometimes down to three-and-a-half hours from 1130 to 1500.

The terrain itself was incredibly rugged. It consists mainly of ridges, 2,000 to 3,000 feet high, running east and west, but with the occasional mountain range rising from 4,000 to 6,000 feet. These were almost invariably, if not always, covered in cloud. On occasions when flying south from Belaga mid-forenoon, one would be above cloud for up to 25 minutes before descending into the Balui valley, which was usually clear.

The range which most affected our operations was just over halfway from Belaga to Long Jawi, i.e. 25 - 30 miles South East of Belaga. This was a ridge eight miles long, 3,700 feet high, with 4,000-foot mountains at the western end. The ridge stretched east/west across our most used track south. As this area was so uncertain and, as nearly happened on two or three occasions, one could get caught with the ridge and mountains in cloud, low on fuel after a long sortie down the Balui or Aput, it was decided to build an emergency LZ on the Balui/Bahau plateau to the south of the range. The plateau, being 2,500 feet high, had patches of fairly small scrub, with the occasional bare, sandy patch. It was on one of these that we put a platoon of Gurkha Engineers, who cleared a site which then took three aircraft easily. It was marked by Blue, Yellow and Red parachutes and was situated 3 miles and bearing 300° from Nawai Falls, the latter being an easily recognised feature on the edge of the plateau.

Another feature of these operations was the range involved. Most platoons were put in at a range of 60 to 80 miles. To get a platoon in in one lift invariably meant overweight running take-offs from the Belaga airstrip. The fairly standard payload was eight troops plus kit (200 lbs each) plus 1,800 lbs fuel, the airfield temperature being 30 – 34°C with never more than five knots of wind. The LSs used nine times out of ten were shingle banks in the rivers. These were usually quite good but unfortunately sometimes disappeared when the rivers rose after rain.

Although the trees were high and the valleys sometimes steep, one had usually a good entry and exit lane along the river. Heights of the sites varied considerably, from 80 feet amsl at Belaga, to 800 feet at Long Jawi and over 2,000 feet amsl up the Sungai Kajang.

The LSs cut out of the jungle by the Gurkhas invariably started as a vertical 'tube' through the trees, sometimes 140 to 150 feet long, just wide enough to fit one Wessex all the way down with perhaps 5 feet to spare all round; however, considering the equipment they had, usually just machetes and kukris, and the size of the trees, they did very well, and eventually the word got round that we needed an approach and exit lane.

Tasking. All tasking of the aircraft was done by the Colonel or one of his officers. The normal routine was that after flying I should go to TAC HQ in Belaga, give a debrief on the day's flying, clear up, if possible, any doubts as to the positioning of platoons, etc., then get briefed on the tactical situation, followed by a rough requirement for the next day's flying. The detailed requirement was brought down to the airfield by a Gurkha officer, then he, or later a REME Staff Sergeant who spoke Gurkhali, would fly in the lead aircraft whenever possible to organise the troops on the ground, loading and unloading, etc. He would then lift off with the last aircraft. This system worked extremely well and, except for special tasks, e.g. winching, obviated the need for aircrewmen. It also showed the officer how difficult it was to navigate and so prevented any scenes if any platoon was put in not quite the right position! This didn't often happen.

Maps. As mentioned earlier, the maps of the area were almost useless. The main rivers were marked, but sometimes quite inaccurately. Very few of the myriad small rivers were shown. The mountain ranges, depicted occasionally by hachuring, were completely inaccurate except for the spot heights. There is not much one can mention about the maps as they were 90% blank, white paper and they even had Belaga airstrip two miles out of position and on the wrong side of the river!

Communications. On the whole, communications were generally good. UHF Air/Ground range was very limited owing to the terrain, but HF contact could usually be maintained, if not with Belaga, with either Sibu or Kuching. Unfortunately both the ground troops, in HQ bases, and the Army Air Corps Austers only had VHF. It would have been particularly useful to be able to communicate with the Austers and for them to be able to lead us into a new LZ. It would have been much more efficient to have an Auster searching for a good river LZ than three or four troop-laden Wessex doing the same thing. We tried this co-operation on two occasions. First, on taking the platoon up the Sungai Kajang, the Auster went ahead to orbit the spot which he had previously recced; however, although we gave him 15 minutes start, his 15 knots less cruising speed and, for safety, following the river (flying singly), and our going direct (fuel!) meant that we got there well before him, had orbited and found the LZ before he arrived on the scene. On the second occasion we tried carrying an Army A.41 VHF set in the left-hand cockpit seat of a Wessex, but although we could speak to the other aircraft before starting up, once our electrics got going they completely obliterated any screening the set might have had and nothing could be transmitted or received.

Our ground communication was operated very efficiently, by *Albion's* Aircraft Control Team of 1 Lieutenant, 1 Corporal and 2 Royal Marines, who also controlled visiting Twin Pioneers, Single Pioneers, and air-dropping Beverleys and Hastings.

Maintenance. The aircraft were normally parked on the airstrip, where they were refuelled by hand pump or 'Zwicky' pump from 44-gallon drums. A certain amount of flexible servicing operations could be done to enable us to keep each aircraft three or four days. They would, as major servicing items came up, be returned to Sibu, whence an exchange aircraft would come. Thus with the four aircraft, reduced to three after the first fortnight, we had, on the average, one changeover daily. The total maintenance team at Belaga was only twelve, including the initial five - who arrived, as did the pilots, with only what they stood up in! Chief Air Fitter Measures, with this small team of his and the Kayan labour force who assisted refuelling, did extremely well in keeping the aircraft flying whilst working in these conditions of extreme heat, humidity and dust. The fuel came (arrived by daily Beverley drop) from Labuan, dropping 30 to 35 drums each time. This was just about the amount consumed, so no stockpile was achieved; in fact, on several occasions we were down to two or three drums but the *Beverley*, the only one too I believe, never let us down and we never actually ran out.

Domestics. The ratings and the A.C.T. officer lived in one of two long atap bashas on the airfield. It was reasonably waterproof and comfortable. The other basha was occupied by transiting Gurkha troops and, after the threat of airborne invasion during our first week at Belaga, the Airfield Defence Platoon, who also had slit trenches dug in various commanding sites. These bashas had been built by the SAS and were in situ on our arrival. The officers would sleep in the Belaga Town Dispensary - which had ten comfortable beds and no patients - they were all immediately CASEVACed! This arrangement required quite a pleasant longboat ride for twenty minutes, morning and evening, and was not without its thrills either, especially at night with the frail boat doing twenty knots and the river full of tree trunks and lesser logs.

Food consisted mainly of 'Compo' rations, once again air-dropped, but supplemented by the occasional fresh fruit and vegetables sent up from Sibu and fresh meat, venison or pork, as provided by Kojan or one of his fellow Kayan hunters. All that it cost us was our used engine-start shotgun cartridges! In charge of the galley and all cooking arrangements - cooking over an open wood fire -was Petty Officer Ben Hazel, an Aircrewman P.O.A.H., who did exceptionally well in keeping all bellies well-filled considering the facilities he had. In this way he contributed greatly to the high morale and good humour of those on detachment.

Water was obtained from a nearby stream by the Kayan labour force, and this stream was also used as bathroom and wash place for all ranks and, coming down from the 1,500-foot ridge, was beautifully cool and refreshing.

The routine worked was basically as follows:

0700 Hands turn to, BF and refuel aircraft Maintenance operations as necessary

0730 Officers' longboat leaves Belaga for airfield

0800 Aircraft ready for take-off

0830 - 0900 Breakfast

1030 & 14-30 Tea and Snacks served on completion of Flying Lubricate and cover all aircraft

1730 - 1800 Evening Meal

1815 (approx) Officers' longboat leaves airfield for Belaga

The ratings were told that they could change round with one of their counterparts in Sibu or Kuching at any time a seat in an aircraft was available. One or two did after a fortnight but the majority, having settled in, were happy to stay on.

Except for me, the officers changed over every three or four days. This fitted in well with the daily aircraft exchange and, unlike myself, I think most officers enjoyed the Belaga Detachment in small doses only!

Statistics. From the scramble on 30th September to the time I left Belaga on 23rd October, 284 hours had been flown in 189 sorties.

The total troops lifted was never fully counted, but the count for one day during the lifts up from Kapit and positioning of ambushes was 120. That was with four aircraft and each lift being between fifty and seventy miles, and this was by no means exceptional. For the record, in the above period I flew 72.30 hours in 41 sorties.

Long Jawi Assault

By Lieutenant Brian Skinner Royal Navy - Pilot 845 Squadron (Wessex 1)

On 27th September 1963 I disembarked from *Albion* to join 845's detachment at Sibu in the Third Division of Sarawak and, although I was not to know it then, I would not be based in the ship again.

At the end of September the 1/2nd Gurkhas, who were protecting the Third Division, were becoming concerned that the radio station at their forward outpost at Long Jawi had failed to check in for several days. Intelligence had also been received that a large party of Indonesian troops had crossed the border into Sarawak and could be somewhere near Long Jawi. The Battalion Commander, Lieutenant Colonel John Clements, requested that troop reinforcements be moved up from Song to Kapit to be ready to deal with this incursion when more reliable information was received. Accordingly, on 30th September, four 845 Squadron Wessex, led by Lieutenant Dick Steil, with myself, Peter Voûte and one other pilot whose name I cannot recall, flew from the Squadron's main base at Sibu and lifted troops from Song and Bangkit to Kapit and shut down there in readiness to lift the troops in as soon as possible. Whilst we four pilots were being briefed by the Colonel in a bungalow on stilts at Kapit, two Gurkha soldiers appeared, supporting a Sarawak Border Scout between them – who seemed to be asleep or unconscious. All three were exhausted and somewhat dishevelled.

The Gurkhas (both Signals Radio operators) saluted and reported that they had been on duty at Long Jawi three days before when they were attacked by a sizeable force of Indonesian soldiers. The small Gurkha garrison had put up a stiff resistance but they were heavily outnumbered. Forced out of the radio post, which had been set on fire, these two soldiers and the Border Scout had managed to escape and commandeer a canoe to paddle down the rivers towards Kapit. The journey took over 48 hours and they paddled and portaged their canoe non-stop and with almost no food. After listening carefully to the report, Lieutenant Colonel Clements told the soldiers that they had done very well and must now go and rest. The Gurkhas saluted smartly again, wheeled about and, still supporting their unconscious Border Scout comrade, left through the door. When the door closed there was a loud crashing noise and we all leapt up to see what had happened. Opening the door we saw that the Gurkhas, having done their duty in reporting the enemy, had relaxed and, totally exhausted, their bodies switched off and they fell down the steps and were all asleep on the ground.

Having given orders to look after this brave trio, Lieutenant Colonel Clements ordered an immediate assault to Long Jawi. We all manned up the four Wessex, loaded as many troops as we could lift and started up. The Gazelle engine of one Wessex failed to start, however, and so only three aircraft lifted off from Kapit, watched by the unfortunate Lieutenant Peter Voûte, pilot of the non-starter. At that time, the climb out from Kapit with heavily-laden helicopters was quite difficult as a large hill stood in the way; later the top of this hill was lopped off to give an easier climb out.

The flight to Long Jawi took about one hour and, on arrival, we could see how the village had been ransacked by the invaders. Several buildings had been burnt down and quite a few dead bodies were lying on the ground. Lieutenant Colonel Clements, in the lead Wessex piloted by the flight leader Lieutenant Dick Steil, wanted his Company Commander to lead the assault as we did not know whether the village was deserted (as it appeared to be) or whether the enemy were merely lying in wait to open fire on our troops as they landed. It turned out that the Company Commander was in my aircraft. It was decided that I would make a very low and fast approach to the village and set the troops down quickly in some long grass some 100 yards from the village. I would then clear away as fast as possible, keeping very low, to allow the other two aircraft to follow in and discharge their troops.

Accordingly, I made my approach as low as I possibly could with my aircrewman (CAF Kentsbeer) lying on the deck with his head out of the door to give me a running report on how much ground clearance I had and, also, if he saw anybody firing at us. The aircraft began to shake a bit as I was just about to tell the aircrewman to stand by to start jumping the troops out when I descended to about 5 feet above the very long reeds covering the ground. The aircrewman somewhat breathlessly said that, led by the Company Commander, all the troops had trampled over his prone body and jumped out when the height was 10 feet or more and were now advancing through the long reeds towards the village. I quickly turned to port and made a speedy low-level departure as the other two aircraft followed and discharged their troops.

In the event, the village was deserted as the enemy had moved on (taking several villagers as hostages/load-bearers) and the uncaptured villagers had not yet returned to their homes. However, much damage had been done to this remote village and a large party of 'bandits' was now at large. The task now was to find and neutralise them; this took some time but was eventually achieved.

Later, it was established that early on September 28th (the day that Malaysia was officially established) Long Jawi had been attacked by 100 Indonesian soldiers and 100 guerrillas with up to 300 porters and longboats, led by an Indonesian Army officer, Major Muljono. The ensuing gun battle had killed two Gurkhas and three Border Scouts. I believe that 5 Indonesians were killed then.

Footnote. On 28th March 2005, John Bulision of the British Executive Service Overseas (BESO) visited Long Jawi and laid a wreath there in honour of these two Gurkhas and three Border Scouts who died in the defence of Malaysia.

Further Operations from Belaga Airstrip and the Move to Nanga Gaat.

From a report by the late Lieutenant Commander Digby Lickfold Royal Navy – Senior Pilot 845 Squadron (Wessex 1) Detachment Commander, Belaga.

Continuing the Hunt for the Enemy. By 23rd October 1963, on which day I assumed command of the Belaga detachment from Lieutenant Dick Steil, the pattern of military operations had settled down after the very successful ambush on 19th October at the landing site 2 miles east of Aput/Kliong Boat Station. It was not known which routes the remaining enemy were taking and consequently new sites in tactical positions had to be found; meanwhile, existing ambush positions had to be re-supplied. The most likely route for a retreat was thought to be via the Aput River to within a few miles of the border, and then a short march over one ridge to the enemy headquarters at Long Nawang.

Throughout October the meteorological conditions over the entire area were bad and appeared to be steadily deteriorating. Cloud base of 500 feet over the airstrip until 1000 every morning was normal. By 1200 most valleys were cleared, but hilltops remained in clouds. By 1430 steam-like clouds from the tree-tops began ascending to meet the cloud base, often leaving less than a fifty-foot gap. Landmarks were never visible and the only sure way of finding the position was to have a pilot leading who had previously been there. The maps provided were totally inadequate- several large rivers were not even marked and there were large areas with no contour information in which there were high mountains. By piecing together information from all the pilots, a picture of the entire area was obtained; however, pilots new to the area needed about ten days flying before becoming sortie leaders.

During October the 1st/2nd Gurkhas received many instructions from headquarters to cut down on Wessex flying hours as the supply of fuel by air drop was likely to dry up if one Beverley went unserviceable or if the monsoon really set in. Evidently the entire Far East stock of 40-foot parachutes had been utilised in supplying Belaga with fuel. The military commander was unable to comply with this requirement if he was to continue the pressure on the retreating enemy. For this reason it was decided to move to another base, if one could be found. The main requirement was that the new base must be able to be supplied with fuel by some other means than air. A preferable but not essential secondary requirement was that a clear flying route to the forward base of Long Jawi should be available.

There was a high sickness rate among the troops and hardly a day went by without one or two Gurkhas being evacuated by air with fever. On several occasions special flights were undertaken to evacuate dangerously-ill civilians to the Methodist hospital at Kapit. I had been informed by the doctors at Kapit that on two occasions the patients would have died if it had it not been for the prompt action by our helicopters. An example of this was a boy of 12 years who had a spike through his kidney and was unconscious through lack of blood. He was flown from Long Jawi to Kapit in failing light and, after an operation, recovered.

During this period various new sites were developed, for example the Aput boat station. Despite constant requests by the military the RAF felt unable to drop rations, let alone fuel at Long Jawi. This meant a very long radius of action to the Aput without diversion and the operational payload reduced by the requirement to carry full fuel. In case Belaga should ever become weather-bound whilst aircraft were on operations, several emergency landing sites were cut.

By 31st October it was suspected that the remaining enemy had slipped back over the border into Indonesia. Austers continued reconnaissance on the northern rivers, Darum, Lindu, Kajang and Murum. From information and rumours reaching the military, another enemy incursion was expected down the Linau. Patrols were tactically positioned by helicopters near Punan villages and river junctions. There were no landing sites available and, as the river was flooding, no shingle banks either; consequently, the only way to unload troops was to hover as near the river bank as possible and make them jump. An aircrewman was essential to throw out the packs and stores and, if the site was chosen carefully, the water was not too deep to inconvenience the troops.

The major maintenance for all aircraft at Belaga was carried out at Sibu. However, some rectification action had to be carried out locally, and on one occasion a team from Sibu carried out an engine change on the strip at Belaga.

Kayans were employed at Belaga primarily for recovering the air-dropped stores and fuel. However, they soon became well versed in other tasks and it was not long before they were carrying out most of the loading and fuelling of the helicopters, thus relieving the Squadron personnel of much hard work.

Turning to our domestic arrangements at Belaga, despite the most primitive conditions morale was always high. The perpetual sand flies, mosquitoes, heat, humidity and tinned food sometimes resulted in short tempers, but at no time was discipline impaired. The moment an operation was on hand all ratings turned to cheerfully without orders. The local Military Commander helped greatly in keeping up interest and morale by informing the detachment of latest intelligence and how the operations were progressing.

Ratings lived in a basha on the airfield which leaked during the regular storms; a plague of rats had to be combated without poison (which had gone bad on receipt). Fresh rations, enough for one day, arrived by air drop every ten days, NAAFI stores such as beer and cigarettes arrived less frequently.

Several ratings and one pilot fell ill with a fever which fortunately lasted only 24 hours. Medical facilities were non-existent except when the Battalion Doctor from Kapit was visiting Belaga. All washing and drinking water was obtained from a stream a quarter of a mile from the airfield; this stream had been medically cleared by the military and was the only luxury at Belaga. Victualling and cooking were put in the charge of a Petty Officer Aircraft Handler and a Naval Airman Aircraft Handler, neither of whom had previous experience in cooking.

Consequently, Belaga was not entirely suitable as a base because of the problems of air supply and because the airfield itself was likely to be closed in by bad weather.

Operations from there were hampered by the inadequacy of maps, though this was largely offset by the experience of the pilots. It was believed that air photographs of the Third Division existed, but these were not made available at that time.

The living conditions at Belaga were not really satisfactory and, though the limits of endurance were not tested, probably a month would have been enough for most people after which the rotation of personnel would have been necessary.

I would like to mention some particular names, whose willingness and devotion to duty helped in keeping the operation under way. All pilots under my command showed an excellent fighting spirit and, despite trying living conditions and flying long hours, they were always willing and eager to get airborne and get stuck in to the enemy. P.O.A.H. G.J.H. Hazel contributed much with his cheerfulness and ability to get on with the local Kayans. C.A.F. K.J. Measures did wonders with turning round and refuelling aircraft as well as running the servicing. Corporal O.J. Cotterell, with two Marines, kept constant day watch on HF radio and his Royal Marine training was invaluable in improving the domestic arrangements in the camp. Relations with the 1st/2nd Gurkhas, both officers and men, were excellent and a fine spirit of co-operation was always evident. Our ratings, comparing the conditions in which the Gurkhas lived and fought, found little reason to complain of their conditions.

Nanga Gaat Operations. The move to Nanga Gaat from Belaga was completed on 1st November. A week previously Lieutenant Geoff Clarke with C.A.F. Measures and P.O.A.H. Hazel were sent in to organise aircraft sites, fuel, accommodation and cooking facilities, clear up any difficulties and hire local labour. A Corporal and three Gurkha Engineers helped by blowing up trees and clearing tree stumps to allow four aircraft to land comfortably. By the time the full detachment arrived, conditions were such that aircraft were used immediately on operations without having to settle in.

After the intensive military operations following the Long Jawi raid, companies, platoons, sections and even individual soldiers were often mixed up in the various positions. For one week our aircraft were used to sort out these troops into logical areas. For example, a whole company was lifted into Long Jawi which then became responsible for all positions on the Balui and Aput rivers. Troops already along the Aput and Balui were lifted out and taken to their own company headquarters, which might be Belaga, Nanga Gaat or Kapit.

Based at Nanga Gaat, it was realised that our helicopters could not only cover the previous area of the Long Jawi/Aput/Balui but also guard the whole of the southern border from the headwaters of the Gaat to the headwaters of the Balui. By allowing a stock of fuel to be built up at Belaga we could cover the north eastern rivers from there, operating on a daily basis and returning to Nanga Gaat at the end of the day.

Three major factors now influenced helicopter operations for the better:

The RAF consented to drop fuel at Long Jawi.

The route from Nanga Gaat to Long Jawi was always open through a gap in the mountains even in the worst weather.

Constant supply of fuel by longboat meant the Squadron was supplied independent of weather or air drop.

Although in theory the monsoon was supposed to be getting worse, the weather actually improved and throughout November and December operations went ahead without being hampered. The occasional thunderstorms, although violent, were localised and could often be by-passed.

Aput Boat Station Operations. I had reported to the brigade in October the presence just across the border from the Aput Boat Station of a large clearing with buildings which, to my inexperienced eye, looked like a military camp. By carefully checking the map I was certain this clearing straddled the border and most of it (about five acres) was actually on our side. It was not until late November that a foot patrol sighted this clearing by telescope and eventually it was discovered to be evacuated - however, several other large clearings in the vicinity were clearly in use by several hundred Indonesian troops. Mortar and artillery firing was heard and a radio station sighted; men partaking in exercises, football and PT were also seen. At this particular section of the border the Dutch and British maps were at variance by about seven miles. The Dutch maps showed the whole enemy complex to be on our side of the border whereas the British maps showed all but the area mentioned above on theirs. The watershed was the obvious border, but in this section it was a flat-topped ridge of several miles width with no water flow either side.

It was assumed that this area might be used as a base for another large scale infiltration, so an observation post was set up. Long Jawi Landing Zone was improved to eight helicopter standard so that a large forward base was available, fuel stocks there were increased and other precautions taken.

Once all the troops of the 1st/2nd were organised into their respective areas, small patrols were constantly being relieved by fresh troops who in turn had to be supplied at regular intervals. 'D' Company at Belaga and 'A' Company at Long Jawi with all their outlying patrols, were entirely dependent on helicopters for all movements. 'C' Company at Nanga Gaat was reinforced and re-supplied by boats and helicopters. Six small patrols of SAS were positioned in hitherto unexplored areas in the headwaters of the Murum Danum, Kajang and Linau - they went in with five weeks' rations and were withdrawn on 18th December in time to fly back to UK for Christmas. Six new SAS patrols were taken to the Baleh, Entuloh and Mengiong rivers to act as listening- and watching-posts along the known passes from Indonesia into the southern area.

The introduction of the Helicopter Despatch Service (HDS) had provided a logical method of changing over aircraft at Nanga Gaat for servicing at Sibu. The maintenance at Nanga Gaat was again confined to turnround and daily inspections, and rectifications.

In this area of the Third Division, rotary, hand-fuel-pumps were placed at Kapit, Belaga and Long Jawi and, later, a further one at Nanga Gaat. On normal operations which required operating all day from Belaga or Long Jawi, a small party of one supervisory and three junior rates was landed at these sites to turn round aircraft during the day, returning to Nanga Gaat on the completion of operations. If space allowed in the initial lift, the *Zwicky* pump was taken and saved much hard work in hot conditions.

Domestic Arrangements at Nanga Gaat. At the beginning of the detachment it was not known how long it would last, and frequent personnel changes necessitated by the 'R and R' programme stifled any enthusiasm for work on long-term projects to improve conditions.

However, once the 'R and R' period was over it was possible to man Nanga Gaat entirely by volunteers. As soon as the news came through that 845 Squadron would be staying at Nanga Gaat, everyone set to with a will to make the place as pleasant as possible.

Recreation space was built with a 'village pub' atmosphere of beer and darts and a refrigerator was provided. Fresh rations were obtained from Kapit. A pig farm and chicken farm were started and, perhaps the most important of all, film shows were instituted four nights a week.

The river was the principal washing facility and, at that time of the year, rainwater could be collected in sufficient quantities for those who did not favour the river. Drinking water, which was always scrupulously sterilised, was obtained from a small stream.

At a forward base such as Nanga Gaat the presence of a Sick Berth Attendant (S.B.A.) was obviously essential and the prolonged period of operations without any medical advice on the spot was a great worry. During this period all medical work was carried out by two Squadron pilots.

Eventually, S.B.A. Wood and S.B.A. Harrison were loaned in turn from 3 Commando Brigade, and the Squadron's own S.B.A. followed. All these proved to be of great value.

An immense variety of medical work was carried out at Nanga Gaat, including the stitching of very severe wounds and frequent injections. The presence of an S.B.A. definitely contributed considerably to the morale of the detachment.

The lack of good communications between Nanga Gaat and Battalion Headquarters at Kapit sometimes resulted in confusion - particularly as the net was operated in Gurkhali with the added hazard of translation errors at either end.

Aircraft HF communications fell short of the reliability required for this sort of operation. This was partly due to the difficulty of keeping the sets themselves working perfectly, partly due to electric storms and dawn and dusk interference, but primarily due to the overloading of the net.

There were six ground stations operating on the Helicopter Air Support Frequency (H.A.S.) and a great deal of traffic was passed ground station to ground station. On one occasion continuous ground station traffic jammed-out an aircraft endeavouring to transmit a distress call.

Looking at personnel, A.A.1.J.W. Salisbury was the Senior Rating. His conscientiousness and cheerfulness when working on aircraft were an example to all. P.O.A.H. Hazel continued to work cheerfully as the 'Camp Buffer', in charge of all locally-employed Ibans and the fuel hoist. E.A.2. Denham took over all NAAFI management, as well as spending long hours at Long Jawi or Belaga turning round aircraft. All junior ratings also worked willingly and it would be wrong to pick out any particular one. Pilots were constantly changing; however, once settled in, they were nearly always sorry to leave. Lieutenant G. Grover, Royal Marines, and his team of Marines were always efficient whilst on operations and entered right into the fine spirit of the camp. Lieutenant Grover was later relieved by Sub-Lieutenant Canning, who continued the good work.

In conclusion, from all points of view operationally and domestically, Nanga Gaat proved to be a much better helicopter base than Belaga. The detachment could have continued to operate from this base indefinitely if required.

My Nanga Gaat Memories from October 1963

By Lieutenant Geoff Clarke RN (Pilot Wessex 1, 845 Squadron)

During October 1963, as military operations penetrated further and further into the centre of Borneo, it became necessary to establish a Forward Air Base to reduce the hours spent in transit flying from the coastal region. An initial recce was made from Sibu to determine the practicality of establishing a base on land belonging to Chief Temonggong Jugah at the confluence of two rivers, which was a site easily defended with rivers on two of the three sides. The site was very hilly with a good many large trees, but it was considered possible to level off five or six landing platforms. This was discussed at length with the infantry on the ground, who would also share these facilities, provide security and the manpower to build accommodation and clear the site of trees.

I was selected to be in charge of a small ground party to supervise preparations of the site by military personnel, including a detachment of the 1st/2nd battalion of the Gurkha Rifles. There were only three of us in this small party and, due to pressure of aircraft hours, we went by river in a native dugout canoe powered by a big outboard motor. The landing site was known as Nanga Gaat, some 100 miles upriver from Sibu.

Fig 17. Tun Temonggong Jugah (centre) flanked by Ken Measures (left) and Geoff Clarke (right).

The Jugah's site had a fairly modern bungalow as befitted a very important local chief. He very kindly gave permission for the three of us to live in the basement of his bungalow while the Gurkha engineers built Basha accommodation for squadron and army personnel. The site was very rough and most of the work of levelling the helicopter pads had to be done by hand. My colleagues were CPO Ken Measures and PO Ben Hazel. Ken was one of those practical people who took everything in his stride, and Ben Hazel was a man of great personal initiative, stronger than an ox (he was a Fleet Air Arm Field Gun Crew member). He was soon hard at work, assisted by the Gurkha engineers, making a long ramp up which fuel drums could be pulled from the river to the landing site.

Fig 18. Embryonic Fuel Drum Ramp

Fig 19. Ben Hazel's Chicken Coops

Ben Hazel amazed the locals with his remarkable collection of tattoos. On his back was a graphic picture of a hunt in full cry - you can imagine where the fox went to earth! Ben Hazel also built a whole series of chicken coops and amazed the locals by achieving a far higher rate of egg production from the local jungle fowl than the locals reckoned was possible.

We spent several nights sleeping under Jugah's bungalow, which would have been ideal if only his chickens had not decided to roost in a tree just outside the building. These birds insisted on having their dawn chorus at about 5 am. We decided after two nights of disturbed sleep to deal with the problem. Ben Hazel got hold of some plastic explosive and bugged the tree with numerous small charges. I seem to remember that we got Jugah's permission and he thought the idea was quite funny. Accordingly the following evening, when the birds had settled to roost, there was a series of explosions which very effectively cleared the chickens and we enjoyed our beauty sleep undisturbed thereafter. Meanwhile, advance parties of army personnel were beginning to arrive, including a Major from the Greenjackets. He was a very fastidious officer who insisted on having his own private basha. Like all the temporary buildings put up by the army this was made of bamboo, with the floor level about six feet from the ground to avoid being flooded while the river was in spate. It so happened that the area accommodation was grazed by a herd of cattle who, in the night watches, would go under the bashas to scratch their backs on the supports. This didn't matter for the larger buildings as they had so many supports to keep them up, but the Major had insisted on his own des.det.res, which was much more flimsy. During the night watches, the cattle got underneath 'The Laurels, Nanga Gaat' and turned the Major into a military version of 'Rock-a-by-baby'. In the morning he got hold of Lanting, the herdsman, and gave him the most imperial dressing-down, ending with the grand finale 'and what's more, Lanting, your cattle have got **** holes like TRUMPETS'. He then stomped of in high dudgeon. After that the cattle were fenced off. The work in clearing the site proceeded apace, with Chief Measures keeping a watch on the Gurkha engineer's activities. The result was, from memory, that we had about five landing pads. Large posts were driven into the ground at each side, to which aircraft could be lashed to minimize the risk of them sliding off the pad in the very heavy rain, which occurred quite frequently.

Fig 20. 845 Squadron's Air Base at Nanga Gaat

One aircraft, which had not been sufficiently well secured, did slip off its pad during a heavy downpour. It ended up with a tree trunk embedded in its nose and was clearly unflyable. It was decided to take it apart and fly individual components back to the ship for re-assembly and repair. A small team of helicopters was made ready, including an RAF Belvedere. The intention was to fly the stripped-down fuselage under the Belvedere. I was detailed to lift the main gearbox and rotor-head off the fuselage and then proceed back to *Albion*, which I succeeded in doing. Not so the remaining loads. The aircraft lifting the engine got into difficulties and had to jettison it almost after lift-off. The Belvedere took up the fuselage and all the spectators heaved a sigh of relief as it headed up towards the ship. However, their optimism was short-lived as the fuselage, which was hanging underneath the Belvedere on a long strop, began to swing violently. The pilot was not able to correct the swing and released the load over the jungle when only a quarter of a mile from Nanga Gaat. It was not long before the pale green, quilted lining to the cabin of the Wessex was *de rigueur* for clothing the smart set of local Society.

Nanga Gaat airbase was quite difficult for flying operations. The standard approach meant flying south up-river and then turning sharply to the west over a small ravine. The ravine still contained some magnificent jungle trees, including one goliath about 150 feet high. Living up to my green credentials, I vetoed the felling of the tree. Pilots were instructed to use this marker as a pivot for their turn for their final heading before landing. More on this tree later.

Fig 21. Bird's Eye View of Nanga Gaat

One of the attractions of these Borneo operations was that, due to the very basic radios in the aircraft, communications between our main base at Sibu and various forward airbases such as Nanga Gaat were virtually non-existent, so Detachment Commanders worked directly with the local military command on all operational matters. We just got on with it! The flying was mostly very enjoyable and sometimes quite exciting. We had to operate at the very limits of performance of the aircraft, particularly in the jungle-covered mountains when inserting or withdrawing patrols. It was not unusual to have an altitude of 5000 feet at a temperature of 30°C, conditions which combined to create the worst possible situation for a helicopter's performance. I well recall flying with Lieutenant David Storrie Royal Marines, when we were recovering a patrol that could only be reached by hovering in the jungle canopy and picking up the troops one by one using the aircraft winch at full extension (125 feet). As the last man came off the ground the aircraft began to lose height, and the only thing we could do was to put the nose forward and fly off down the mountainside with the unfortunate last man being dragged through the branches. He then had to be winched up into the cabin with the aircraft in forward flight. He looked somewhat surprised when we got him on board the aircraft. Mission accomplished!

One of the greatest problems at Nanga Gaat was to provide the very large amount of fuel required for the helicopters. We made attempts at supplying by river, and Petty Officer Ben Hazel's Field-Gunning experience came in handy. He designed a ramp up which it was intended to pull the 45-gallon drums from the foot of the riverbank. Unfortunately the ramp was too steep to make this practical, so we had to resort to flying in fuel as an under-slung load to start with. A certain amount of fuel was also lifted by helicopter from river craft and deposited by each landing pad. Other supplies were flown in, or to a limited extent purchased from local people. In addition to his chicken coops, Ben Hazel also constructed a couple of pigsties to provide more fresh food.

Nanga Gaat was always a busy place and was principally used for deployment of troops and recovery of patrols. We only had very primitive maps, which were derived from aerial photos. These had large, blank areas when cloud cover obscured the ground during mapping. Aircrew got the lie of the land and navigated mostly by river, which provided most of the few landing sites that were clear of trees (on the inside of river bends). One interesting employment of the helicopters was to use fixed forward-firing machine-guns to provide what the army called "prophylactic fire" over the jungle canopy, the idea being to drive the enemy patrols into an ambush set up by friendly troops. Quite by chance there were Indonesian troops in the precise area where we fired into the jungle, and a few were killed. The psychological effect of this episode was considerable, as the enemy troops thought we had some secret method of seeing through the trees. Neil Burns-Thompson, who took over from me as a detachment commander at Nanga Gaat a few days after this event, had his hands tattooed by the locals with the marks of a warrior, because they thought he had been the one who had killed the enemy troops. He still has these tattoos to this day.

Among the abiding memories of the Borneo Operation are the grandeur of the unspoiled jungle, the friendliness of the local people, the very challenging but often exhilarating flying and the satisfaction of working so well with the army units, who always appreciated the can-do approach of the Fleet Air Arm. We became a very close-knit team and I think everybody realized that they were having the best time of their lives.

Fig 22. David Storrie (holding baby) and Geoff Clarke on right

One last anecdote:

As a lover of trees I had stopped the Gurkha engineers from cutting down the particularly fine jungle specimen mentioned earlier, which was growing in an awkward position for the approach to the landing site. Shortly after take-off on my last trip back to Sibu there was an enormous explosion which lifted this tree several feet into the air, and it fell down into the ravine above which the aircraft flew on their final approach. I always regretted that tree and hope its demise didn't affect the fabulous Rajah Brooke butterflies which lived in the area where the tree fell.

Nanga Gaat - The Start

By Lieutenant David Rowe RM 845 Squadron (Pilot Wessex 1)

Having been through the Brunei Rebellion with 845 Naval Air Commando Squadron (as we were called then), subsequent flood relief and operations elsewhere in Borneo's Second Division, in Oct 1963 I was back in Kuching, whilst we had a flight based at Belaga in the Third Division, in support of 1st/2nd Gurkha Rifles who were setting up ambush positions to catch the retreating Indonesian incursion into Long Jawi. It soon became clear that long-term operations from Belaga were not feasible, mainly due to the problems caused by resupply of fuel by air drop.

I subsequently moved to Sibu (Third Division) in support of the Gurkhas and on 1st Nov 1963 landed at Nanga Gaat, the confluence of the Baleh and Gaat rivers, 120 miles upriver from Sibu. The Rajang River was the only means of transportation and the nearest township was Kapit, some 30 miles downstream. Nanga Gaat was an old logging camp and the rural home of Temonggong Jugah anak Barieng, the paramount chief of the Ibans (Sea Dyaks), the fabled head-hunters of Borneo. Jugah had served in Tom Harrisson's irregular force during World War II, operating against the Japanese, for which he was awarded an MBE and a gallantry medal. He later became a Malaysian Federal Minister, and was granted the highest honorific title of Tun.

A fellow pilot in 845 NACS, Geoff Clarke, had proceeded in advance to Nanga Gaat by boat up the Baleh from Sibu with a detachment of Gurkha Engineers, to prepare the site for use by helicopters. A substantial amount of explosive was used to remove the trees to provide clear spaces for, initially, four Wessex helicopters. The explosive also removed some of the glass windows in the Jugah residence, which we had to replace! We flew in from Sibu with four aircraft at midday on the second day of clearing operations.

The accommodation for the ratings was a long atap basha, which had been used by seasonal logging labour. Having been unoccupied for some time, it was full of spiders, snakes and scorpions! The officers' accommodation was a small, airless room underneath Jugah's house, with little or no privacy. The washing and latrine facilities were non-existent – thankfully the river was nearby! Adjacent to the squadron's camp was a company of 1st/2nd Gurkha Rifles who, in true Gurkha style, had made themselves very comfortable. As they provided the guard force for the Forward Operating Base, there were no comments made! Tasking for operations was done over a HF link with Morse key back-up! Secure radio traffic was done in Gurkhali, a trick taken from the USMC Navajo 'code talker' signallers in World War II.

We started from scratch, concurrent with flying operations, to establish a more comfortable lifestyle. We had no electricity, no heads (toilets), no potable water, no cooking facilities, and no medical support. As the sole Royal Marine, I found myself plunged into 'living in the field' activities and I was most fortunate to have an outstanding Petty Officer, Ben Hazel, who later qualified as an aircrewman, who had been a butcher and fishmonger in civilian life. I immediately appointed him 'The Buffer' and the naval armourer was given the task of being the 'santan man' in charge of all waste, including human. As we did not have any cooks on the Squadron complement – we were, after all, meant to operate from a Commando Carrier – I found that my skills were stretched culinary-wise and, using the 'compo' rations that had come with us, I produced a varied menu of curry and rice – and curry and rice! Later, I relented and, for those with weaker stomachs, produced a generic stew.

As the fuel was being brought up-river by boat, I rapidly interviewed a selection of local labour, in my very basic 'kitchen' Malay acquired when the Squadron lived in bungalows at the 7½ milestone in Kuching earlier in the year. There was no budget for hiring labour (some 30 in total) – or indeed the purchase of supplies to improve our living conditions (there was later). As we refuelled the helicopters to full capacity each night in case we had to evacuate, and then defuelled to meet operational tasking, there was plenty of contaminated fuel. With a ready market for JTP 4, we were able to build up a sizable kitty to pay wages and purchase food from an entrepreneurial Chinese trader who had set up shop on the base. Additionally, our 'Buffer" constructed henhouses and pigpens, which we stocked with purchases from the local longhouses, fattening them up until slaughtered. We also were able to purchase the occasional wild boar – thankfully dead – but this had to be eaten in short time as there was no refrigeration.

Fish was also part of our diet. In conjunction with the local penghulus (chiefs), I organized a weekly fishing party – never in the same place – using a *Scott's Porage Oats* tin and four pounds of plastic explosive. Harpoons and tridents were formed out of six-inch nails, heated and hammered using my trusty Primus stove from my emergency pack. I recall that I was severely castigated by the Commander of 99 Gurkha Brigade, Brigadier Pat Patterson, for using 'unsporting' tactics to secure our catch! I tactfully refrained from commenting that I had brought my fly rod with me and had introduced the dry fly to the Rajang!

News of our arrival quickly spread up both rivers and soon we were holding sick parades on an almost daily basis for the local tribespeople. With no formal medical training available beyond basic first aid, triage was basic. Our 'Buffer' took the most basic ailments, with more serious cases passed on to me where, using 'The Ulu Dresser's Guide', a relic of colonialism and the White Rajahs, I was able to carry out a series of basic stitching and lancing procedures, including using local anaesthetics. More serious cases were sent down-river to the cottage hospital in Kapit, by boat or helicopter. I recall one horrific incident where a young boy had been accidently shot in the head with a spear gun (powered by old inner-tube) and he was flown out with the spear sticking out of both sides of his head; amazingly, he survived!

Shortly after arriving and establishing the base, I took over command of the Detachment. We improved the accommodation, built the famous 'Anchor Inn', made showers using solar-heated oil-drums, potable water, a galley (with a real cook and now a paraffin refrigerator!, dining hall, a sick bay (with SBA), slit trenches and long-drop latrines. Yet flying remained our *raison d'etre* and I note that my flying log book shows a total of 160 hours for the first three months and I know that other pilots logged even more air time, as base duties tended to keep me on the ground. CPO Ken Measures and his team of groundcrew were exceptional in their maintenance of the aircraft under the most basic conditions and I do not recall any mechanical failures during my time at the Gaat.

Thus, the legend of the 'Pirates of Nanga Gaat' was born (and embellished!). I was 23 years old when I took over command of up to six aircraft and 80 personnel. Before I left some six months later, Tun Jugah adopted me as an honorary son, a singular honour. The Borneo

Confrontation was the last of the colonial wars, a unique and rewarding experience of which I am proud to have been a part.

Fig 23. Tun Temonggong Jugah and adopted son - David Rowe

At the end of a subsequent tour with 845 Squadron ('Commando' had been eliminated from the title!) in the Far East (and many hours in the air with Ben Hazel), I was able to revisit Nanga Gaat, Kapit and Sibu. Much had changed and much has changed since, but the memories and camaraderie remain.

845 Operations at Kuching October to December 1963

By Lieutenant Brian Skinner, Pilot 845 Squadron (Wessex 1) Detachment Commander Kuching.

Following the initial Long Jawi assault on 30th September 1963, I spent a week in fairly hectic flying from Belaga with troops and ammunition during the Long Jawi follow-up operations by the 1st/7th Gurkhas. On 8th October I returned to Sibu and then spent another week in flying from there to Song, Mangai and Bankit. On 15th October I landed back at Sibu after my fifth sortie of the day and was told by the new Squadron CO, Lieutenant Commander 'Tank' Sherman, that he was sending me on down to Kuching straight away to be the Squadron

Detachment Commander there. Grabbing all my kit I took off again and flew down to Kuching, and assumed command of the 845 personnel and aircraft there.

Albion had landed three more aircraft of 845 Squadron on 1st October at Kuching and, on the 12th, returned and landed the remaining three together with one F.I.R., so now the whole Squadron was ashore. Also, to provide support for 845 and 846 Squadrons, the whole of the ship's A.E.D. was also landed at Kuching and established on the airfield as a 'Chacon City'. However, at this time it was also decided to withdraw the whole of 846 Squadron for a period of Rest and Relaxation in Singapore. 845 Squadron now became responsible for the entire helicopter support of the 1st, 2nd and 3rd Divisions of Sarawak. On 28th October, two Wessex were detached from the Kuching detachment to Simanggang. The disposition of the 13 Squadron aircraft therefore became: 3 aircraft at Belaga, 3 at Sibu, 2 at Simanggang and 4 (plus one F.I.R.) at Kuching.

From 1st October onwards, there was great activity to set up the Squadron's and the ship's A.E.D. facilities on Kuching airfield. We were situated on the opposite side of the runway to the ATC tower and the RAF facilities. Tents were erected to serve as Operations Room and Pilots' Crewroom, A.M.CO., Stores, Junior Rates' Crewroom, Ground Equipment and Inflammable Stores. Accommodation was provided by 40 Commando Royal Marines; the Officers in the Officers' Mess, Semengo Camp, the Senior Rates in the Sergeants' Mess and the Junior Rates in two huts in South Camp - mostly in Bashas.

The main tasks of 845's Kuching Detachment at that time was to provide deeper maintenance on the Wessex aircraft than was possible at the more forward bases and also to provide operational sorties as requested by our Tasking organisation at HQ 3rd Commando Brigade, which was situated in Kuching. The Brigade Commander was Brigadier Barton Royal Marines.

Semengo Camp, just outside Kuching, was a well-organised (and defended) camp consisting of basha-type huts. There was excellent victualling with Royal Marine cooks and good washing facilities with showers. All quite luxurious compared with what we had been used to recently at Belaga and Sibu. I shared a basha cabin with Peter Voûte and remember the morning when we were woken by a radio announcement from the next- door cabin that 'President Kennedy has been assassinated'. Peter sat bolt upright in bed and exclaimed: 'It must be the Russians – this means war!' Fortunately it wasn't quite as drastic as that.

It was decided that the terrorist situation had deteriorated to the extent where a direct attack on Kuching airfield was possible and, therefore, some degree of defence organisation within the Squadron was required. A series of deep trenches was dug around the dispersal and tented area. The A.M.C.O. tent was fortified with an exterior wall of sandbags and designated platoon headquarters in the event of an attack.

A small, emergency platoon was formed with an Officer-in-Command, Petty Officer and twelve ratings. The purpose of this platoon was to back up the airfield defence force of Royal Marines and RAF Regiment in the defence of the aircraft, dispersal and equipment.

The tasks of the Kuching detachment were, firstly, to provide a main maintenance base for the whole Squadron ashore in Borneo, including the Sibu detachment and forward bases; secondly, to provide Wessex support for the 1st Division and, thirdly, to back up the Simanggang Detachment in the 2nd Division if necessary.

A considerable number of hours were flown in support of troops in the 1st and 2nd Divisions throughout the period of the detachment. The multiple border incursions in the 2nd Division at that time required the rapid movement of troops and ammunition as the Indonesian border was quite near, thus allowing enemy forces to pop over the border, create some mayhem and then retreat rapidly back into Indonesia. I led four Wessex operating from Simanggang on 25th October during an interesting 3-day war conducted by the 1st/10th Gurkhas between 24th and 26th October. Sixty flying hours were expended carrying troops, ammunition, CASEVACs, prisoners and enemy corpses. It was during this period, when 2 Wessex were shut down at Selepong, that firing broke out 100 yards from the aircraft. The aircrew were deprived of the chance to fire their SMGs, however, as a platoon of 1st/10th Gurkhas beat off the enemy. Support for this operation entailed several night landings at Simanggang airstrip, where a satisfactory 'T' of gooseneck flares was provided. My aircrewman for these three days was, once again, Chief Kentsbeer, in whom I always had the greatest confidence.

On one sortie, a Major of the 1st/10th asked to fly with me in the left-hand cockpit seat. We were searching for likely exit routes for the incursionists and, when we found a likely spot, the Major produced a captured mortar bomb and was about to strike the rear primer on the dashboard cover of the aircraft. I managed to stop him in time to prevent damage to the aircraft, so he hit the primer with his hand and threw the bomb out of the window with a twisting action. We saw no indication that this *ad hoc* attempt to hit back at the enemy with one of their own mortar bombs worked!

When 846 Squadron returned from Singapore on 28th October it was decided that 845 Squadron should continue the task at Simanggang indefinitely, as terrorist activity was widespread in the 2nd Division at this time and the lift capacity of two of 846's Whirlwind Mk.7 aircraft was considered insufficient. A detachment of two Wessex was despatched to Simanggang under the command of Lieutenant Dick Steil.

We were visited at Kuching by Vice Admiral Sir Desmond Dreyer, Flag Officer Commander-in-Chief Far East Fleet (FOCINCFEF), who went down very well with both officers and ratings with his warm, friendly and understanding manner. At that time he was coordinating all of the Commonwealth Naval Forces in their resistance to Indonesian incursions into Malaysia, which meant that he was commanding a third of the Royal Navy as well as Australian, Malaysian and New Zealand ships and aircraft.

Fig 24. Vice Admiral Sir Desmond Dreyer chatting to Senior Rates whilst Detachment Commander looks on

Fig 25. Charwallah (left) and Admiral

The Admiral also chatted to our local 'Charwallah', who had set up his tent in our Squadron area and dispensed food and drinks throughout our working hours. When we knew that we were going to close down at Kuching in the middle of December and transfer to Sibu, we told him that we had appreciated his services but could not tell him where we were going for operational reasons. He said nothing but, when I arrived at Sibu just before Christmas, there he was all set up on the airfield with his tent and goods and doing a thriving trade. He greeted me cheerfully with a knowing look and vigorous handshake. How he got there with all his equipment remained a mystery, but I assumed that he must have come by boat up the River Rajang.

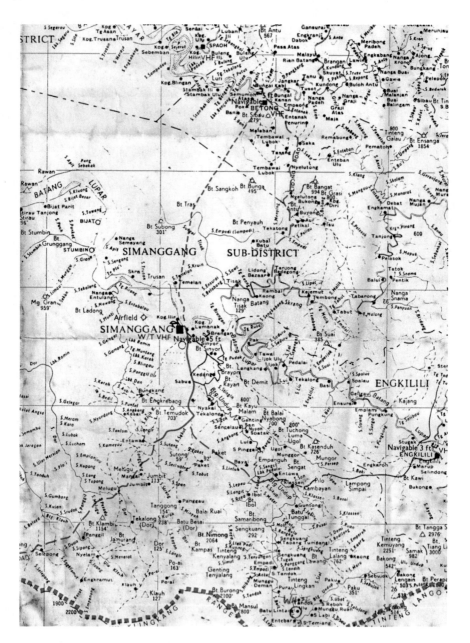

Fig 26. Map of Simanggang Area from the South China Sea to Indonesian Border

846 Squadron nominally took over responsibility for all helicopter support in the 1st Division, aided by two Belvederes of 66 Squadron RAF when available. Nevertheless, 845 Squadron Kuching Detachment was often asked if one or more Wessex could be provided for

CASEVACs, urgent troop lifts and VIP trips for the 1st Division. All except a very few of these requests were met, often with the maintenance team working at high pressure for long hours to prepare aircraft. Our detachment also remained the main aircraft support base for all of the Squadron aircraft.

The stores backing provided by the ship's A.E.D. proved excellent. Many times, often in the middle of the night, the stores opened to provide components urgently needed for aircraft at Sibu or Nanga Gaat, and which had to be placed on an early morning flight. The workshops - radio, electrical and mechanical - which were set up in the Water Works at Kuching, provided first-class facilities and support and their help was greatly appreciated by all detachments of our scattered Squadron.

Very often, Borneo Airways were used to fly vital stores and components between Kuching and Sibu. They often carried items for the Squadron without charge and at very short notice; their help and dedication cannot be too highly praised.

During this period I was asked by the Brigade Commander to provide a platoon to march in a formal parade in Kuching. It was important that we did field a platoon because, if we did, the Royal Marines, who were by far the most numerous of the military units, could march at the front of the parade as part of the Royal Navy contingent. If we did not parade, the Royal Marines would have to march behind some Army units, which took precedence over the Royals in the absence of any Navy contribution. Accordingly, 845 provided such a platoon and the whole parade went off very well. There was even a band to lead us.

On another occasion, two Wessex were scrambled at 1730 to carry Marines of 'A' Company, 40 Commando to assault a small settlement near Tanjong Datu, which was reported to be in the hands of the enemy. A beach landing was made and the Marines stormed the village, meeting with no resistance but recovering useful documents and arms. Extensive follow-up operations revealed that the enemy had retreated over the border shortly before the Wessex arrived.

A good deal of flying was carried out for 'A' Company of 40 Commando in troop re-deployment and stores build-up. This sub-unit proved extremely pleasant and efficient to work with.

Many CASEVACs were carried out, withdrawing injured personnel from forward positions and landing them at Police Headquarters, adjacent to Kuching General Hospital.

Units which received initial helicopter troop drills included 'C' Squadron, *Queen's Own Irish Hussars*, 70 Battery, *Royal Artillery*, 1st/10th Gurkha Rifles; 2nd/10th Gurkha Rifles and 5th Royal Malay Regiment. In addition, continuation training for 40 Commando was given.

A lot of maintenance was carried out at Kuching to meet the primary task, which included several engine and tail-rotor gearbox changes, 2 main gearbox changes, 2 main oleo changes, 16 main rotor-blade changes, and many starter and injector changes. Much work was done in searching for and remedying oil and hydraulic leaks, and many compressor washes executed. In the middle of November the tie-down base was declared usable and, from that day forward, there was always an aircraft on the base, either carrying out post- engine-change runs or having strange faults investigated such as reported lack of power, or excessive pressures and temperatures at high power. Great credit was due to all maintenance personnel who worked at Kuching during this period, in view of the natural disappointment that might have occurred when the maintenance crew saw aircraft after aircraft on which they had worked hard to bring up to scratch whipped away to another detachment, and a further unserviceable machine presented in lieu.

One day, we noted that the RAF had hoisted quite a large RAF Ensign on 'their' side of the runway. I felt that we needed to emphasise that there was also quite a large RN contingent present. This was important, as some of our visitors and prospective passengers arriving on the other side of the runway had difficulty in first finding us and then crossing the runway to get to us – which required ATC permission. I made enquiries with 3 Cdo Brigade HQ and we were quickly provided with a white flagpole, which we duly installed on our side of the runway, and ran up the White Ensign; at least people could now see where we were!

Relationships with RAF Load Control (on the other side of the runway) were generally satisfactory, with one notable exception. For a scheduled H.D.S. flight back to Sibu via Simanggang, we duly passed details to Load Control of the size and weight of our own stores to be embarked. Just before take-off, some extra stores arrived from Load Control with a detailed manifest which indicated that the total weight of stores ('ours' and 'theirs') was just under the maximum that the Wessex could carry. I accompanied the pilot for this sortie to the aircraft for his pre-flight inspection. He just happened to be my CO, Lieutenant Commander 'Tank' Sherman, who had flown down the previous afternoon for a visit to us and 3 Cdo HQ. We thought that the stores looked pretty bulky inside the cabin, but the manifest was quite clear as being within our limit. The CO then started up the aircraft and ground-taxied out to the runway for a running take-off – normal procedure to avoid blasting sand and dust around by a vertical take-off. We noticed that the aircraft took a very long time trundling down the runway before getting airborne and, even then, seemed to take quite a while to gain any height.

The CO telephoned me after he arrived at Sibu and asked me to investigate the loading, since he had very little power in hand after he got airborne and for half of the flight he could not exceed 60 knots, whereas the normal cruising speed was 90 knots. I went across to the Load Control unit and discovered that they had not allowed for the RN stores that we had reported, and so they had used up all of the possible weight with 'their' stores only. They admitted that it was their error and apologies were tendered – which I accepted - and we had no further loading problems.

A staggered programme of R and R for the Squadron as a whole was executed from Kuching. Personnel joined the detachment from Sibu a few days prior to their R and R date and their places at Sibu or Nanga Gaat were filled by those who had completed R and R. Great difficulty was experienced with getting personnel to Singapore, as the Squadron had no priority for these R and R flights and was thus always last in the queue for air transport.

However, through the perseverance of Lieutenants Voûte and Hudson and the good offices of Staff Sergeant Lewis of 'Q' Movements, 3 Commando Brigade, nearly everyone in the Squadron managed to fly to Singapore for an average of ten days R and R. The considerable effort involved in successfully running this programme was considered well worthwhile as a change of location to RNAS Sembawang, and the opportunity of improved runs ashore in Singapore was very welcome to all. Most of us had been ashore in Borneo for several months.

I was keen to get to Singapore for my own personal R and R on 2nd December, because I had arranged to marry my fiancée, whom I had not seen for 13 months and who was flying out from UK for the planned nuptials, optimistically arranged for 6th December. However, since we had the aforementioned low priority on the RAF Hastings flights from Kuching, and following careful enquiries on my likelihood of getting a flight not being very encouraging, I hitched a lift to Singapore aboard a RNZAF Bristol Freighter.

The Kuching detachment re-embarked in *Albion* over a three-day period from 14th to 16th December after being relieved by 225 Squadron Royal Air Force, with Mark 10 Whirlwinds.

HMS *Albion's* Air Engineering Department at Kuching

By Lieutenant Commander Ken Shattock Royal Navy, Ship's AEO HMS *Albion*

Since the disembarked squadrons would be without A/E, L and Radio workshop support, the ship's workshop personnel were moved ashore into Kuching in October 1963. Some members of the Supply department were also included in the move. The ship also provided some members of the Communications department for all disembarked personnel to deal direct with Singapore and, when applicable, to the UK.

A Royal Marine staff officer was directed to find suitable accommodation. The final choices were the local brewery or the local waterworks. To the dismay of all, the selection was the waterworks. After a couple of days the workshops were operational and providing on-the-spot support to the squadrons, including splitting engines for examination.

The members of the Supply department also provided very competent support in the ordering of aircraft and other necessary equipment.

The squadrons and the AED were also allowed to recruit local labour, all with the appropriate Dayak tattoos. One group walked all the way from the Hose mountains to 'join Queen Victoria's Iron Birds'.

There are further anecdotes in which the reader may be interested. The ship's AEO was visiting Belaga owing to the unserviceability of two aircraft of the flight there, each with the same defect. No spares were available. What was required were a couple of asbestos joints for the air compressor on each engine. A trip was made to the bazaar longhouse in Belaga village, some distance from the landing site, to look for suitable jointing material. Amongst the bazaar fruits and nuts, a piece of Klingerite steam jointing was found. It was found that this item had been in the longhouse since approximately 1863, when Rajah Brooke used to travel upriver in his small, steam-driven launch, which could be disassembled to allow it to be carried past rapids. The two aircraft were made serviceable using the packing, and a successful 'stop' was then put in on a river, preventing Indonesian troops infiltrating further. Later, the company in the UK which manufactured the packing was informed of the incident.

A humorous anecdote concerned the occasion when *Albion* had been on station for the period of nine months, when it was expected that the ship would be relieved by the other Commando Ship, *Bulwark*. Unfortunately this was not possible, and the ship's company were told that they would have to stay on station for a further nine months. There were no RAF helicopters to replace the Navy squadrons. The Belvedere aircraft brought to Borneo by *Albion* had proved unsuitable for combined operations, and remained on the ground. The morale in the ship and squadrons fell but, after a short while, Navy humour took over.

845 Overview October to December 1963

By Lieutenant Commander G.J. 'Tank' Sherman (Commanding Officer 845 Squadron, Wessex 1)

I assumed command of 845 Squadron from Lieutenant Commander Alan Hensher on 7th October 1963. On that date the Squadron had a total of nine aircraft ashore. Six of these were supporting operations in the Third Division of Sarawak based on Sibu, the remaining three being based at Kuching in the First Division.

At this time the battle of Long Jawi follow-up action was in full swing and four of the six aircraft in the Third Division were operating in support of this from a forward base at Belaga. As most maintenance was still being carried out at Sibu, one aircraft was changed over daily from Sibu to Belaga, proceeding up-river early morning and down-river late afternoon. Thus, quite frequently, there were five aircraft used on operations during the day from Belaga. The daily aircraft run also proved very useful in moving troops, stores, Squadron personnel and CASEVACs.

The Sibu area at this time was, fortunately, very quiet and routine troop movements were taking place by boat. However, one aircraft was normally available after about 1000 each day, by which time the servicing required on the aircraft down from Belaga the previous day was complete.

All Squadron aircraft needing major servicing or component change were, as far as possible, kept at Kuching, where 845 Squadron was initially only committed to one aircraft at 15 minutes' stand-by. At that time 846 Squadron was meeting the requirement of a pair at stand-by at Simanggang in the Second Division and also the major stand-by at Kuching with an RAF Belvedere back-up if a heavy lift was required. 845's main requirement in the 1st and 2nd Divisions was producing a heavy-lift stand-by on the frequent occasions on which none of the three Belvederes was serviceable.

On 12th October, *Albion* returned to Kuching and landed the remaining three aircraft of 845 Squadron, together with one F.I.R. and also the whole of the ship's A.E.D., to provide support for 845 and 846 Squadrons. At this time it was decided to withdraw the whole of 846 for a period of Rest and Relaxation in Singapore. This threw a very heavy strain on 845, as the Squadron now became responsible for the entire helicopter support of the 1st, 2nd and 3rd Divisions with the somewhat unreliable assistance of three Belvederes. By now, the Squadron load had reduced to three aircraft at Belaga and remaining aircraft were distributed as follows: 3 at Sibu, 2 at Simanggang and 4 at Kuching.

The overall requirement of 75% serviceability could have been met easily had the Squadron been concentrated at one location, but operating from four locations an average of one hundred miles apart made servicing a constant headache due to the total inadequacy of the Squadron ground equipment and the spares availability. Due to the very hard work of the Squadron personnel, the unfailing co-operation of

Borneo Airways in carrying stores not on their manifest and without charge, and last, but not least, the Army Auster, which seemed to be forever flying from airfield to airfield with our dynamic-flushing rig, an average of 79% serviceability was maintained. However, there were days when simultaneous, unscheduled unserviceabilities at different locations brought the Squadron below target figure despite all efforts. The principal problem throughout this whole period was the unreliability of the starting system. One aircraft, 'E', failed to start for ten days despite changing ten injectors, seven starters and every other component in the starting system.

In the meantime, operations from Belaga were throwing a very heavy strain on the RAF air drop capability. Belaga operations were entirely supported by fixed-wing air drops and the fuel requirement alone averaged forty barrels a day. In this connection the excellent work of the RAF Beverley Squadron deserves mention, as its crews dropped with extreme accuracy almost regardless of weather, and often throwing in a morale-boosting present, such as daily newspapers or a box of oranges on their own behalf.

To ease the strain it was decided to move the Squadron's forward operating base to Nanga Gaat, the junction of the Gaat and Baleh rivers and home of the paramount chief of the Ibans, the Temonggong Jugah. At the time there was nothing there except a timber mill and the Temonggong Jugah's bungalow and, furthermore, not even room enough for one aircraft to land. The principal advantage, however, was that the base could easily be supplied by river, thus releasing the RAF air drop capability for other tasks.

Immediately after moving to Nanga Gaat, however, it was discovered that Belaga itself could have been supplied by river. Everyone at Brigade had stated that this was impossible but, typically, the only people who had not been asked were the boatmen at Kapit. Fuel was then regularly supplied to Belaga by river as it was still used as a refuelling base. However, Nanga Gaat proved a very much more pleasant place from which to operate than Belaga, as it was nothing like so dusty when dry and muddy when wet. Another advantage was that the Temonggong Jugah had a 240-volt generator and, although this had not worked for six months when the Squadron arrived, it was soon repaired and film shows became the high spot of the social life of the Baleh valley.

As a result of the RAF being freed from the Belaga air drop commitment, they were able to carry out air drops at Long Jawi. This gave 845 Squadron the twofold advantage of being relieved from supplying Long Jawi itself and having an additional refuelling base for operations in that area.

846 returned to Kuching on 28th October. However, it was decided that 845 should keep the Simanggang stand-by in view of the increased activity in that area. 845 therefore retained the Simanggang detachment until relieved by the RAF on 16th December.

However, 846 did relieve 845 of most, but not all, of the flying commitments from Kuching, which was providing the main maintenance base for the Squadron with both A.E.D. backing and the very valuable tie-down base being available. The tie-down base was ready by the second week in November and was in almost continuous use after that. The Kuching detachment did a very good job during this period, as they had all the hard work of the Squadron's most troublesome aircraft without being closely associated with the glamour of operations or, indeed, the satisfaction of high serviceability as, no sooner was an aircraft fully serviceable, than it was removed from Kuching to an area with a more immediate operational requirement. Nevertheless, 845 did continue to provide CASEVAC support in the Kuching area, as well as troop movements in the 1st Division, some VIP flights and the training of Malay troops in helicopter drills.

With the RAF taking over in the 1st and 2nd Divisions from mid-December, 846 Squadron and half of 845 Squadron re-embarked in *Albion*. It was decided to leave the 3rd Division to 845 Squadron; accordingly five F.A.E., plus one F.I.R aircraft were left ashore, the F.I.R. only to be flown in an emergency. With the five aircraft the aim was to keep a serviceable pair at Nanga Gaat and a serviceable pair at Sibu, with the fifth aircraft available on H.D.S. days. On the whole this was achieved, apart from the last weekend in December.

It is worth mentioning here the difference between the RN and RAF methods of assessing helicopter effort. If, for example, the RN on the H.D.S. run took off from Sibu with ten troops and landed at both Song and Kapit for loading/off-loading small quantities of stores before delivering the troops to Nanga Gaat, the return would show ten troops lifted in one sortie (i.e. from first take-off to engine shut-down). However, the RAF counted each touch-down as a new sortie and would, therefore, claim thirty troops in three sorties.

Neither method really showed the effort required, as the distance was not brought into it. Obviously, one hundred troops could be moved far quicker over the fifteen-mile radius typical in the Second Division than over the one-hundred-mile radius typical in the Third Division. Yet another factor was the variation between landing sites; whereas 845 Squadron aircraft frequently lifted twelve troops out of good landing sites, a payload as low as three troops was sometimes found necessary such as at a very difficult landing site at a height of 3,500 feet above the upper Linau on a hot afternoon.

The only true representation of effort was the actual hours flown on troop lift operations, as it could be safely assumed that on all troop lifts and operational stores lifts the maximum available payload, dictated by either aircraft all-up weight considerations, or the vertical performance of the aircraft under the existing conditions, was actually utilised.

Although most VIP flights entailed specific flights by Squadron aircraft, on all occasions the fullest possible use was made of the flights by ensuring that the full payload of the aircraft was utilised by troops or stores needed *en route*. During this period the Squadron carried twelve VIPs of one- to four-star status.

Only on CASEVACs was the full payload of the Wessex not utilised. In view of the shortage of doctors and medical orderlies, such flights formed an essential part of the Squadron operations. These flights undoubtedly saved lives, as well as serving to maintain the morale of supported units.

The health and spirits of the Squadron personnel were excellent and it was considered that the prevailing scale of operations at the time could be continued indefinitely with adequate stores backing.

Simanggang Detachment October to December 1963

By Lieutenant Dick Steil Royal Navy - Pilot 845 Squadron (Wessex 1) Detachment Commander, Simanggang

On 28th October 1963, 2 Wessex of 845 Squadron left Kuching for Simanggang, in the Second Division of Sarawak, some 75 miles to the East of Kuching, to form the Simanggang detachment and to operate in that area in support of the 1st Battalion, 10th Gurkha Rifles, which at that time provided the security force for the Second Division.

Only two pilots went initially, and six maintenance rates. Of these it was planned to change one pilot and one or two of the ratings every few days with those at Kuching, only myself as Officer Commanding the detachment and the senior maintenance rate, an A.A.1., remaining permanently.

Shortly after our arrival on the 28th we took Colonel Burnett, 1st/10th Gurkha Rifles, and Brigadier Barton, 3rd Commando Brigade, on a tour of inspection of the company and platoon positions. These VIP tours were to become quite regular on this detachment! The main trouble in this area was along the Simanggang to Serian road, of which some 30 to 40 miles ran within 2 miles of the Indonesian Border, the latter being a steep escarpment 800 feet high, the high ground being enemy territory. The rebel bands were making lightning raids on the road; they shot up a bus, killing a schoolteacher before going on to nearby longhouses, Selepong, 10 miles south of Simanggang, being the favourite target. After a raid it would take the rebels approximately 45 minutes to get back up one of the many well-defined tracks and over the border. Thus, unless our troops happened to be right on the spot, their reaction had to be extremely swift to get an ambush in on the track to cut off the rebels. Our aircraft were therefore put at 10 minutes' notice during daylight hours and stand-by platoons were held at readiness in the company headquarters ready to be picked up by helicopter and roped in to a cut-off ambush position on the appropriate track as near the border as possible.

This very organisation was put into practice two days later on the 30th when, at 6 a.m., the Selepong longhouses were raided by a band estimated to be 15 to 20 strong. The police field force platoon returned the fire, killing one rebel, then radioed the alarm. Both Wessex tookoff, but had to pick up troops from the company base at Pantu, about 20 miles further down the road, so time was pretty short. One platoon was roped in to the border end of the most likely track - there were three or four possible tracks at that location - and the other landed on the road by the longhouse to search the surrounding countryside. Two Wessex sitting on this rather narrow road caused quite an unusual traffic problem, especially when two scout cars drew up as well! We lifted out the dead rebel, a Chinese, strung, as usual, by his ankles and wrists to a pole and wearing only a very tattered jungle-green shirt, and landed him in Simanggang town on the road by the Police Station for immediate identification. This was also partly as a deterrent to any locals (and many came out to watch) who may have planned to cross to the other side, as this one, slung on his pole, was not a pretty sight; half his head was missing and there were lines of bullet holes across his body.

When no contact had been made by p.m. that day, it was decided to drop dummy parachutists (FREDs), with their time delay 'battle-noise' kit, along the border. This, it was hoped, would keep any remaining rebels in and allow them to be rounded up by our troops. It is believed that this was the first operational drop of FREDs since World War 2, and the noise they produced was very realistic. Unfortunately it also confused some of our own troops in ambush positions, who did not know whether it was attacking rebels or not. Sadly, no further contact was made with this band of rebels.

Information now came in warning of a raid coming over the Eastern border of the Division, to the East of Jambu, the company base in that area, and the next two days were spent deploying platoons to various outlying longhouse LZs in the Ulu Ai.

Two days later I proceeded to Kuching and Singapore for 10 days R and R, Lieutenant Geoff Atkin coming down from Sibu to take over the detachment in my absence. All was quiet on my departure; however, the 2nd Battalion of the 10th Gurkha Rifles was just moving in to take over from the 1st. This changeover was completed by the time I returned on the 15th and the operational situation was still very quiet. The only flying done was occasional troop re-deployment and replenishment, CASEVACs, and a brief tour for the Colonel and Resident (the Diplomatic Officer in charge of the 2nd Division), 2nd Division. A third pilot had joined the detachment by this time, enabling us to have an officer on the ground at all times to deal with any emergencies.

On 22nd November a platoon of Gurkhas was pulled out from Sungai Sawa, in the South East corner of the division, and a dozen police Field Force landed to proceed further up-country in order to recover the body of one of their number killed in an ambush some ten days previously. He had been buried on the spot, and his relatives now wanted the body, or at least the head, back. Luckily the Field Force stayed the night in the Longhouse at Sungai Sawa because, as transpired later, an Indonesian force had been watching the Gurkha withdrawal from a nearby hilltop and had decided to raid that night as a result. They either had not noticed the Field Force or considered them no opposition, and raid they did. For quite a long period during the night they mortared and shot at the longhouse; the Police returned the fire and so kept them from closing in. A follow-up platoon was sent after them next morning, but they had gone back over the border, leaving behind one dead. As this latter had half his face missing it was thought that he had got in the way of one of his own mortars. He was brought out on a pole next day for identification.

As a result of this the Colonel tried several 'ruses' to try to fool the enemy; we pulled troops out from border positions without trying to conceal the fact, whipped them round to a nearby LZ low-level, then made them walk back. Instead of taking them direct to an LZ we would take them in low-level to a nearby one and again make them walk. Alternatively, we did the reverse of the first one - troops that had been in some time were removed surreptitiously and re-positioned, hoping the enemy would believe they were still there. Unfortunately, these imaginative activities met with only limited success.

Badau, a fairly large Indonesian kampong just over the border from Lubok Antu, was continually having air-drops, with considerable movement seen there and reported, and on one occasion two 'Hound'-type helicopters were seen orbiting. Information was continually being received of troop build-ups there and of imminent attacks but, although the reception committee was always ready, they never came.

Another popular invasion area was that to the south west of Selepong, where the border was only two miles from the main road; information was continually being received of troops massing for attack; we would then fly in ambushes, only to be told a couple of days later that the enemy had withdrawn for further training!

General Walker (COMBRITBOR), Dato Fenner and some of their staff arrived on 28th November for a tour of the area. The rest of the month was quiet except for a certain amount of troop re-deployment and re-supplying.

December started off in the same vein, with purely routine flights in support of the troops. However, on the 6th, a reliable source of information stated that a party of fifty strong was mustering on the border South of Selepong and would be carrying out a concerted attack on one or more longhouses in the area within the next four days, the attack probably coming at night. As a result of this the Colonel obtained more air support in the shape of a Twin Pioneer, and the following plan of action was inaugurated. On receiving the 'go', the Army Air Corps Auster (also based at Simanggang) would takeoff, fly to the border and illuminate the appropriate tracks with flares; the Twin Pioneer would then, guided by the Auster and the flares, drop 'FREDs' along the border to keep the enemy in. Finally, we would appear with a platoon in our Wessex aircraft to be roped in, again by the light of flares, to an ambush position on the track. B.A.S.O. back in Kuching unfortunately looked up the book and found that all Wessex pilots were out of night-flying practice so should not participate. This we quickly corrected by night-flying from the airfield that night, but then it was found that the same applied to the Twin Pioneers, so they were recalled. This 'stand-to' lasted for four nights. Information came through later that the force had indeed been ready to come over, but had got wind of the fact that we were ready for them and had decided against it. Although this suited the politicians admirably, it was highly frustrating for us.

It was on the 7th, after discussions with the Colonel of various means of stopping enemy raiding parties getting back over the border, that I decided to try Bren LMG firing and grenade dropping from the aircraft cabin. With the Adjutant 2nd/10th Gurkha Rifles and his Bren mounted on sandbags in the back, I took off and carried out various strafing runs along the river bank down the Batang Lupa. This was quite accurate and, despite the small arc of fire, could be quite effective along a track. Similarly the grenades, with a little practice, could be dropped fairly accurately. However, I was later informed by Brigade Headquarters that armed helicopters were not, at present, to be used.

On Monday 9th the Border Scouts based at Enkilili Training Centre came to the airfield and carried out roping- and troop-drills. They proved surprisingly adept.

Seven Indonesians were captured to the north of Saratok on 11th December and it was requested that we should bring them in as soon as possible for questioning. This I did, picking them up from Roban where, after half an hour's wait, my main wheels had sunk a good foot into the local football pitch. There had been another band of rebels, all armed, a few days previously, who, heading back to the border from the Third Division, had been led by their Iban guides into a Simanggang coffee shop and kept talking whilst the security forces were informed. For this neat piece of work the guides picked up 1,000 Malaysian dollars!

'RNAS Simanggang' paid off on 16th December 1963 and handed over to two Whirlwind Mk. 10s of 225 Squadron, Royal Air Force. Unfortunately, whilst on our handover tour with one Wessex and one Whirlwind, the latter was recalled to be grounded and they were both still so grounded that afternoon when we finally departed and re-embarked in *Albion*. I understood their difficulties were, happily, only short-lived.

Operating conditions were, on the whole, very reasonable. The land was mainly flat with ranges and isolated hills rising out of it, occasionally up to a height of 3,000 feet. The border to the south and west of Simanggang was clearly marked by the Klinkang range and generally followed hilltops or ridges of high ground over the rest of the area. The worst terrain was to be found to the east of Lubok Antu, in the Ulu Ai and Ulu Mepi area; here it was very hilly and, although the hills were seldom over 2,000 feet, the valleys were steep and, if forced down by bad weather, quite difficult to get out of.

The weather was also reasonable, but low cloud and thunderstorms could form and move with incredible rapidity. This was made clear to me on one occasion when, having landed some troops in an LZ at the bottom of a valley near the border in the Ulu Ai, a thunderstorm came up the valley completely sealing off the way I had come in. Visibility was down to fifty yards in rain, so I went out the other way and only just managed to clear the cloud forming on the hilltops and got round the storm without going over the border. On another occasion two aircraft were troop-lifting into Jambu when, on the last run, the site was in the centre of a heavy rainstorm. Visibility on this occasion was about 300 yards but my wingman, Lieutenant Neville Hudson, had his windscreen-wiper fail and his visibility as a result was less than fifty yards. Having eventually found the LS, I dropped my troops, picked up Neville Hudson's aircraft orbiting clear of the storm and, with him in very close formation, led him in. Luckily this particular site was on top of a 600-foot ridge.

One great advantage of this area over, for instance, the Third Division, was the openness of the country. Most of it was secondary jungle or scrubland with large areas of old and new cultivation. This made single-aircraft operation over most of it quite feasible. Ranges too were relatively small; Simanggang being centrally placed in the Division, the furthest points of the border were not much more than forty miles away. This meant that with 1200 lbs of fuel our aircraft could reach any part of the area within half an hour with ten fully-equipped troops onboard.

Tasking was done daily by the Colonel commanding the battalion in the Second Division. He had his HQ in Simanggang Police Station and there, at 0830 daily, he would hold a meeting at which, amongst other things, the flying tasks were discussed. Details were finalised between the Adjutant and I and, at the end of the day, a SITREP sent down to the Kuching detachment for inclusion on their SITREP Signal.

This organisation, being the RN way, and B.A.S.0., (in Brigade HQ, Kuching), being basically RAF, did not always agree. B.A.S.O. wanted all trips to be authorised by him before they were carried out; as this was obviously impracticable over such ranges something had to be done and eventually *Albion's* Commander (Air), acting as mediator, paid us a visit and sorted out the problem. He also eased B.A.S.O.'s worry about the hours being flown by the Wessex at Simanggang which, for some reason, had become exaggerated down the line.

The Communications Control hut, such as it was, at Simanggang, was run by an RAF Flight Sergeant and one SAC, who manned the VHF, Civil HF and A.43 (UHF) set. One Royal Marine from *Albion's* Aircraft Control Team manned the Service HF net under the call-sign 'Regent'.

Although the UHF set was a bit short-ranged, probably due to the aerial situation, the cover provided by this and the HF set was quite adequate. In some areas Simanggang could not be raised on HF but Sibu or Kuching could, so messages were relayed.

The map normally used was that made up for the Security Forces based on the Four Miles to One Inch War Office map, with the contours coloured and all LZs marked and numbered. However, after a couple of weeks' flying in the area no map was needed, the features being quite distinct and easily recognisable.

The team of six maintenance rates, headed by an A.A.1., did all Front Line servicing and could deal with any minor faults. An aircraft was exchanged with one from Kuching every two or three days, depending on the amount of flying, for the larger maintenance operations. For major unserviceabilities, the necessary personnel and equipment had to be flown up; the Squadron being split four ways through half of Sarawak at the time, there just wasn't enough equipment for everyone to do all of their own maintenance. The ship's Air Department, with all its stores, was ashore in Kuching over this period, so the system worked very well. In fact only once during this detachment did we have an unserviceable aircraft necessitating a spare part to be flown up.

Fuel was provided in 44-gallon drums from Kuching, brought up by either road or river. The RAF motor pump did sterling service, and it even had a pressure-fuelling nozzle which allowed us to refuel with engine running.

The Squadron ratings lived in the British Other Ranks mess in the Gurkha camp and seemed quite satisfied with their lot. The only problem was meals; the Gurkha mealtimes, except for supper, were unacceptable to us as it meant sending everyone off the two miles from the airfield into camp at 1000 for breakfast and this invariably clashed with the flying programme, so an early breakfast was organised. Lunch was usually cooked up by the ratings themselves on the airfield from the stock of 'Compo' held; their mess provided only soup and biscuits for that meal.

The officers lived in the Gurkha Officers' Mess where, of course, one could get a meal or drink at any time of the day or night, so there was no problem there.

During this period our two aircraft flew for a total of 185 hours 40 minutes in 148 sorties. We lifted 12 CASEVACs, 14 VIPs and approximately 2,000 troops.

This detachment, with the rest of the Security Forces in the area, had to be on the alert all the time. In fact, during the above period very little action took place, but all leads and information had to be followed up and acted upon. With the area being so small and with all the main centres so close to the border, any infringement had to be dealt with immediately, otherwise this 'hit and run' type guerrilla warfare could easily have panicked the locals, or at least frightened them sufficiently to stop them giving the information upon which the Colonel so much relied.

Any troop movement by air in this area was obviously very difficult to achieve without it being seen by or reported to the other side, thus they could soon tell if a planned attack had been compromised. This accounted for the small amount of action, but at least it achieved the ultimate aim of keeping the peace.

Operations from Sibu August to December 1963

By Lieutenant Commander G.J. 'Tank' Sherman (Commanding Officer 845 Squadron, Wessex 1)

845 Squadron first arrived at Sibu on 19th August 1963 when the Senior Pilot, Lieutenant Commander Digby Lickfold, flew in with six Wessex 1 aircraft and commenced operations in the Song area straight away.

The Senior Pilot had arranged with Mr Seal, Head of Civil Aviation in Borneo, that the Squadron should use some Public Works Department airfield Bungalows allocated to Civil Aviation but not in use. As a Wardroom he was able to secure the airport manager's bungalow situated most conveniently right alongside the airport building, as the manager preferred to live in the town.

Initially, meals for all the Squadron were arranged in the airport bar while the Senior Pilot arranged for a dining basha to be built. The original quote from P.W.D. was for six thousand Malay dollars, which expenditure was not approved by Brigade. However, the Senior Pilot, acting on his initiative, managed to secure free prison labour and had the whole job done for eight hundred dollars.

By the time of my arrival on 7th October it became obvious that there was a long-term requirement for helicopters in the Third Division of Sarawak, whichever Service provided them, and that the time was ripe for improving facilities to a long-term standard.

P.W.D. proved most helpful in re-painting and generally repairing the five fourth-class quarters allocated to the Squadron ratings and, with a small financial backing from Naval sources and a lot of enterprise on the part of the occupiers, the living conditions were made very pleasant.

On return of the ship I obtained approval to land the Squadron's own Cooks and Stewards and set up the Officers' bungalow to reasonable Wardroom standards.

From early October 1963 Sibu remained the principal operational headquarters of the Squadron, as it had proved possible to keep in touch with all Squadron detachments from there. After 17th December, when 845 Squadron Kuching Detachment re-embarked in *Albion*, Sibu became the main maintenance base of the Squadron.

For continued operations at Sibu a new dispersal was needed clear of the civil aircraft pan, a tie-down base was desirable as well as undercover maintenance shelter. All these tasks were taken in hand, and were completed before the end of January 1964.

Conditions at Sibu from every point of view now became workable, if not ideal, and the Squadron needed only a starter bay and a radio workshop to be able to operate for prolonged periods without support from the ship.

During the period from 7th October to 3rd November 1963 there was no operational flying in the Eastern area of the Third Division, so that the main Sibu task was to service aircraft for operations from Belaga and, later Nanga Gaat. Sibu also provided the H.D.S.

On 3rd November, 2nd/10th Gurkhas were relieved by the 1st/7th Gurkhas. Owing to the short time factor allowed for this changeover, and the requirement to keep patrols at operational strength up the

Bangkit and Katibas rivers, all troop movements up-river from Song were made by helicopter and the changeover programme completed in two days. The Song and Sarikai movements to Sibu were made by river. The changeover programme was upset by a last-moment decision that Sibu airport could no longer be used by RAF Beverley aircraft.

Shortly after the battalion changeover, operations started in the 1st/7th area.

The first of these was Operation 'Richard Todd'. This started when a report came in of eight armed Indonesian troops in the area about 30 miles South of Sibu. During the next week considerable movements were carried out by helicopter in an endeavour to catch these men but, unfortunately, we always seemed to be a day or two behind them. The Indonesians were eventually tricked and captured by Ibans and taken into Simanggang in the 2nd Division. Interrogation proved that this was the band we had been chasing and follow-up action enabled the arrest of several C.C.O suspects and the discovery of weapon caches.

Continuous patrol activity in the upper reaches of the Katibas and Bangkit rivers and searches for tracks between the rivers were carried out. These patrols served a second purpose as there was now a large number of landing sites available for reinforcement of that area or if a cut-off operation after an enemy incursion were ever required. This was very important in this primary jungle area which, hitherto, did not offer as much as a winching site for distances equivalent to a week's march or more on the ground.

Despite extensive operational activity, the Squadron found time to enjoy a traditional Christmas. The Season was opened by delivering Father Christmas (P.O.A.F. Pearson) by winch to the Children's Ward of the local hospital on 23rd December, after which the helicopter landed and shut down. Half an hour later Father Christmas took off to be delivered in a similar fashion to the police padang, where the Squadron gave a party in the police canteen to the 78 children from the local Methodist Children's Home. This party proved a great success, the sailors proving as adept as ever at amusing children. The party included games playing, 'party pieces' by the children themselves, Gurkha Pipers, enormous tea and a film show. However, the high spot was undoubtedly Father Christmas arriving by helicopter with his bag containing a present for everyone.

Father Christmas was called out twice more on Christmas Eve - first to the police party for their own children, and then to the Island Club for the children of members. As ever, 'traditional' arrival from the sky was employed.

The aim of not flying Christmas Day and Boxing Day was, in fact, achieved. Two helicopters were kept at 15 minutes' stand-by during daylight hours, but were not required. Traditional Christmas morning rounds were carried out, and at 1000 the Squadron cake, most generously provided by *Albion*, was cut by Mrs Rosemarie Skinner, the recently-married wife of my Sibu Detachment Commander, Lieutenant Brian Skinner.

Fig 27. Mrs Rosemarie Skinner cuts the Cake

A rum issue was made from the ship's Welfare Grant. The Commanding Officer's prize for the best decorated bungalow was presented to L.R.E.M. Coates, the Leading Hand of the mess of 8 Bungalow. At 1900 the Squadron Junior Rates sat down to a first-class Turkey Dinner in the Airport Bar, which had been borrowed and decorated for the occasion. The Senior Rates had their Christmas Dinner at 2000 in their own bungalow.

Most of the Squadron ratings were asked out at some time over the Christmas period and the general consensus of opinion was that a good time was had by all.

On Boxing Day normal flying resumed with the H.D.S. run to Nanga Gaat.

Sometimes, however, things didn't go so well. On Saturday 28th December, Brigadier Barton Royal Marines visited Sibu to say goodbye to the units under his command in the Third Division. 845 Squadron at Sibu had two nominally-serviceable aircraft and a third A.O.G. for a number of items. However, on daily aircraft inspection, 'N' was found in need of a tail-rotor change and, on start-up, 'M' developed an oil leak. At Nanga Gaat there was one aircraft that would not start and the other two were fully committed on a troop lift so that there was no possibility of assistance from that end.

On completion of the tail-rotor change on 'N' ('robbed', i.e. removed from the FIR aircraft which was already classified as AOG and awaiting spares.), a requirement for a troop lift arose and the Acting Colonel of the 1st/7th was able to persuade Brigadier Barton that this was more important than his own trip. In the meantime, work continued on 'M'.

Finally, 'N' completed its troop lift and was turned round for the Brigadier's much-delayed trip up-river. However, on start-up the starter oil seal split, producing an unacceptable oil leak and another delay.

Unfortunately, the Brigadier's time factor was such that he had to return to Kuching without being able to visit the 1st/2nd Gurkhas or Nanga Gaat. This was the first time that an 845 Squadron commitment had not been met in Borneo.

To complete the saga, 'N' finally left for Nanga Gaat at 1700, and 'M' was finally run and declared serviceable at 1930. However, the next morning, 29th December, 'M' refused to start until 40 starter cartridges had been fired. At 1400 on 30th December, having made its point, it gave no further trouble. Altogether, between 0730 Saturday and 1400 Monday, the team worked for nearly 30 hours, most of the time in blazing hot sunshine to get 'M' going, a first-class example of the tenacity and hard work of the maintainers to which the Squadron owed its serviceability.

At the start of the New Year, the Squadron was back to five out of five F.A.E. aircraft serviceable with the F.I.R. a 'Christmas Tree' – an already unserviceable aircraft from which parts are removed to fit to other aircraft.

846 Squadron in Tawau, Sabah

By Lieutenant Keith Simmons RN (Pilot, 846 Squadron Whirlwind Mk 7)

In January 1964, having been alongside in Hong Kong for Christmas and the New Year, *Albion*, with 846 Squadron embarked, sailed for Tawau in the most southern part of North Borneo (recently renamed as Sabah).

A recent incursion by Indonesian forces had resulted in a battle with 3rd Royal Malay Regiment at Kalabakan and there had been several casualties. The Indonesians had dispersed into the jungle and were now a threat to Tawau, the third largest town in Sabah. The 1st/10th Gurkhas had been flown in from peninsular Malaysia and 846 Squadron was disembarked to Tawau to support them.

Fig 28. 846 Aircraft at Tawau

The Squadron was accommodated in a tented camp on a sports field with an adjacent bungalow acting as the Wardroom with two cabins (bedrooms) for the CO, Lt Cdr David Burke, and the S.P., Lt Cdr Peter Williams.The remaining officers slept in two-man tents in the bungalow garden. At one end of the lawn a large screen was erected to show the films that occasionally reached us from HMS *Terror* in Singapore. Thus evolved the traditional Sunday night cinema to which expat locals were often invited. On one occasion we wished to invite a plantation manager and his wife, Noel and Mary Hanson, who lived on Muratai estate some ten miles away and were only contactable by telephone, which was not working. On the way back from a day at a Forward Operating Base in Kalabakan, I flew to the estate with an invitation card in a message bag - the smallish, canvas type with a lead bar sewn into the bottom hem to give it some weight.

The house was surrounded by trees, mainly rubber, with a track leading to it. Having circled once with no reaction from Noel and Mary, I flew up the drive and got the aircrewman to drop the bag on a small lawn at the front of the house. Five seconds after release there was an 'expletive deleted' from the back - the bag had gone straight through the roof! Another circle but nobody appeared. I returned to base and waited in trepidation for three days until Sunday evening. The Hansons appeared with a large bill for roof repairs and then smiled, saying that it had been relatively easy to deal with. The bag had dropped into the amah's room onto her bed, but luckily she had been out, otherwise the incident might have been a lot more serious.

Fig 29. 846 Briefing at Tawau: CO (Cdr David Burk) seated with paper, SP **(Lt Cdr Peter Williams) kneeling**

Operation Hadrian's Wall

By Lieutenant Brian Skinner RN (Pilot 845 Squadron Wessex 1)

On 6th January 1964 a report was received from a 'source' that a kotak (fishing vessel) with about 26 of Indonesian Military Forces -Tentara Nasional Indonesia (TNI) - and Sarawak Chinese bandits embarked, had landed at Tanjong, Sedi on 3rd January. This party was said to be led by Suhaili, a troublemaker of Sarawak origin and leftish ideals. He had proclaimed himself 'Military Governor of West Kalimantan', and had been recognised as such by Ahmad Zaid, the Indonesian Defence Minister.

It was thought that the kotak might try to return to Indonesia for a second load of terrorists. I took off from Sibu in Wessex 'J' at 1600 to R/V with the coastal minesweeper HMS *Puncheston*, with the task of winching down Lieutenant (O) Geoff Thompson RN (Forward BASO) to brief on the kotak's probable escape route. However, the weather was extremely inclement and heavy rain and fog out at sea precluded the R/V. The mission was aborted after 40 minutes searching in the R/V area, no radio contact was achieved. *Puncheston* did, in fact, intercept the kotak later that night off Kuching, and escorted her into the Sungei Sarawak.

On 7th January 'C' Company of the 1/7 Gurkhas was moved to the Paloh village area by boat, leaving Sibu at 0800. I was flying Wessex 'N' lifting 'A' platoon from Binatang to a cut-off position on the South side of Paloh Island. The LS was intended to be the site of a disused airfield, but when the aircraft arrived there was nothing there but paddi, so the troops were jumped down on the driest ground available.

'A' Company was then lifted by Wessex into stop positions on the North West side of Paloh. The enemy were now reported to have split into two parties of 15 and 8 men. The smaller party had been led to a small island called Pulau Loba Balei, and told to wait while their guide (a loyal Melanu) went to see if the way was clear. 50 men of 'C' Company then assaulted this island using launches. After an intense battle fought in the dense mangrove swamp of the island, where visibility was seldom more than five yards, four enemy were killed and three captured. Two Gurkhas had been wounded and one enemy had escaped.

Lieutenant Commander Digby Lickfold hovered over the mud-flats and boats and removed the two wounded Gurkhas and two wounded enemy to Sibu hospital.

The remaining enemy fugitive was picked up two days later in poor condition by Ibans.

It was now reported that further kotaks were due to leave Indonesia for the Paloh area at one week intervals. 'C' Company was deployed on Paloh to await the next arrivals.

On 8th January the platoon which had been landed in the paddi at the supposed disused airfield (see map) was withdrawn from Belawai, to which they had made their way, and landed at Binatang. Two Wessex were used, with me flying 'N' and PO Guppy as my aircrewman, each aircraft making a double trip.

Various reports of Suhaili's whereabouts were received on 10th January and troops were moved around by launch to investigate. A loudspeaker aircraft broadcast invitations to surrender in Indonesian over the Paloh area.

On 15th January I was airborne again, this time with CAF Kentsbeer as my aircrewman, carrying a tracker dog and handler from Sibu to Sarikei and returning via Binatang to collect 3 NCOs for briefing at Sibu. After briefing we returned to Binatang and shut down to await the order from the OC 1st/7th Gurkha Rifles to move 11 Platoon. The plan was a three-pronged attack on the supposed enemy camp on the West coast of Paloh Island (see map). 'A' Company and one platoon were moving in from the south and south east respectively and the Binatang platoon was to be air-lifted in from the north when the other two units were in position. This order to move never came, however, for at approximately 1530 the bandits in question were captured by Police Field Force on the Rajang, a mile up-river from Sarikei. This included Suhaili. They had stolen a boat from the lighthouse keeper at Tg. Jerijeh.

Our two Wessex standing by at Binatang then proceeded to Sarikei and brought back the most important of the prisoners (Suhaili and Corporal Arifin of the TNI) to Sibu for interrogation. They were landed, together with their escort, on the Memorial Ground, where a large crowd had gathered to catch a glimpse of the bandits, especially the so-called 'Military Governor'.

The operation was a resounding success; the entire enemy were either killed or taken prisoner and all the arms except one SMG were captured. The enemy intention (to train guerilla fighters in the 3rd Division) was completely frustrated. The wide publicity that the operation received in the press served to underline the success of the Security Forces and to discourage further attempts of this nature. No further kotaks sailed from Indonesia thereafter.

Fig 30. Landing Important Prisoners at Sibu

In all the operation consumed 20 hours 15 minutes flying hours in 19 sorties.

An extract from the official Army report of the operation is given: '845 Squadron helicopters undoubtedly saved the lives of the two seriously wounded Gurkhas and the two Indonesians. They would have died if they had not been evacuated straight to hospital that evening.'

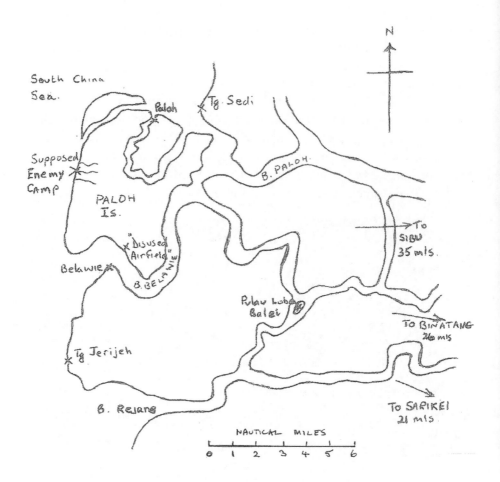

Fig 31. Sketch Map of Operation Hadrian's Wall

First Naval Wife in Borneo

By Lieutenant Brian Skinner 845 Squadron (Wessex 1)

When I joined 845 Squadron on formation at RNAS Culdrose in April 1962 I might have expected to do a normal tour of about 18 months in the squadron and then, after some leave, be appointed to another flying job. On this basis, I might have been expected to be back home round about October 1963.

I first met Rosemarie in June 1962 and decided that this was the girl I wanted to marry. Knowing that we were due to sail for the Far East in *Albion* in early November, I realised that there was no time to waste. I therefore proposed to her (in a Morris Mini-Traveller during a gale on Poole Harbour Quay) in August 1962, she accepted and we managed to get the message across to both families that the wedding would have to wait until I returned from the Far East towards the end of 1963.

As Borneo events were to dictate, however, there was no hope of returning to UK for an end-of- year marriage and so we concocted the idea of Rosemarie flying out to Singapore and myself managing somehow to get back there from Borneo for a wedding in the Naval Base Dockyard Church and a reception in *Albion*, if she was in port or, as a fall-back venue in RNAS Sembawang. In the event, the ship was due to be in Singapore for the first week in December 1963 and I had persuaded my Squadron CO (by now Lieutenant Commander Tank Sherman) to let me hand over my detachment at Kuching, which was due to be wrapped up soon after anyway, and fly to Singapore just in time for a wedding on 6th December. He also granted me some R and R leave to have a honeymoon in Malaya before returning to duty at Sibu, which was the main 845 base in Borneo.

There were a lot of risky ifs and buts about this wedding happening as planned but, despite all odds, everything did so happen. I had booked a passage from Kuching to Singapore in an RNZAF Bristol Freighter on 3rd December and was biting my nails as a torrential rainstorm hit Kuching and it was getting darker. This storm had struck very suddenly just as the incoming passengers from the Kiwi aircraft were disembarking. Passengers and crew legged it to the nearest tent for shelter, leaving the front clam-doors open. A fair amount of rain entered the aircraft and ran down towards the rear of the cabin before the front doors were closed. However, after the storm had passed the crew opened the rear side doors and the trapped rainwater poured out onto the tarmac. So that was all right then; we duly took off and made it safely to Singapore.

In a couple of hectic days I found my fiancée (who had flown out by Comet Mk 1), got a special marriage licence, confirmed that the Best Man (Peter Woodhead) and Tank Sherman (who was to 'give Rosemarie away') had also both flown back from Borneo in time, confirmed the church details with the Dockyard Chaplain and *Albion's* Chaplain and gave the *Albion's* Wardroom staff *carte blanche* over the reception (no time for anything else). Pru Thompson, wife of

Lieutenant Stu Thompson of 845 Squadron, kindly agreed to be Matron of Honour. On the eve of the wedding, I attended a ship's function representing Tank, as he had insisted on taking my future wife off somewhere to 'get better acquainted with her' before giving her away at the wedding the following day. 'Trust me!' he said.

Accordingly, on 6th December Rosemarie and I were married in the Naval Base Dockyard Church and, due to the photographs taking rather a long time, arrived back at the ship to find the reception in full swing with everyone having a good time. We joined in and enjoyed a splendid party. Later in the evening we caught the midnight train to take us up-country to the Cameron Highlands for the honeymoon. Alone at last, we thought, but no! Just as the train was pulling out from Singapore station about 20 of our wedding guests, including Tank, Peter Woodhead (Best Man), Peter Voûte and others, joined us in the buffet car, all very jolly by now and all without train tickets. The stately progress of the train to Johore Bahru enabled us to have a few nightcaps with them before they all got off at JB; several were all for staying with us for the honeymoon, but the Best Man somehow managed to get them all off the train so we then really were alone and steamed (yes steamed) steadily North at 20 mph.

Fig 32. Dec 6th 1962 Matron of Honour Pru Thompson, Groom, Bride, Best Man Peter Woodhead

After the honeymoon we returned to Singapore and Rosemarie was expecting to try and find some teaching or secretarial job whilst I flew back to Borneo to resume my 845 duties as Detachment Commander at Sibu until Their Lordships decided to send me back to UK. However, Tank Sherman had other ideas. He saw no reason for Rosemarie to languish alone in Singapore and so had arranged for us to borrow a bungalow just down the road from the airport at Sibu whilst the owner (Head of the 3rd Division Public Works Department) was on a month's leave. There were rules forbidding Army and RAF wives from accompanying their husbands to Borneo as it was a War Zone, but nobody had said any such thing about Naval wives. Accordingly, we flew together by Singapore Airways to Kuching and then by Borneo Airways Dakota to Sibu.

Rosemarie was the first 845 wife in Borneo and, as the only woman with the Squadron, was a popular choice for many roles - such as decorating the dining basha, cutting the cake on Christmas Day and presenting prizes. She also got a job as secretary to the Sarawak Psychological Warfare Team in Sibu, which produced propaganda leaflets to let the Chinese people in the 3rd Division know that we were the goodies and that the Indonesians were the baddies. Having run off these leaflets, they were air-dropped from our resident Army Air Corps Auster piloted by Captain Tim Dean, and further details of the work of the Lower Rajang Psychological Warfare Team are given in a separate report.

Fig 33. Captain Tim Dean AAC strapping in Rosemarie Skinner for leaflet drop

Tank Sherman had appointed me as his Detachment Commander at Sibu, which left him free to visit our detachment at Nanga Gaat and also to visit Brigade HQ at Kuching and *Albion* whenever she appeared. On 29th January 1964, I was required to accompany him to *Albion* to collect stores and spares and to update the ship's staff on our activities. We took two aircraft, with Tank flying one and myself the other. We had to remain on board overnight and return to Sibu the next day.

This on-board night stop meant that I had to leave my new wife alone in our borrowed villa down the road from the airport. There had been reports of suspected but undetected bandit incursions into the 3rd Division and so it was prudent to take defensive measures, especially for outlying staff. Accordingly, I found myself teaching Rosemarie how to load and fire a Sterling sub-machine-gun, with particular instructions to 'hosepipe' horizontally at the (bandit) target rather than trying to aim specifically at the centre of the body – the weapon being inherently inaccurate. She did not seem too keen on this procedure but went through the motions of the (non-firing) practice. Just before sundown, after I left, she gave the houseboy an early release and locked up the bungalow carefully. Shortly after she heard what sounded like several rifle shots from nearby. She poured herself a strong double whisky, retired to bed and wrote me a letter saying that it had been a fantastic and eventful short marriage which she had enjoyed very much. The loaded Sterling was under the bed, 'hidden' as usual under my dressing-gown. The following morning she awoke to a bright sunny day with a slight hangover and was pleased to see me when I returned in the afternoon. The 'rifle shots' turned out to be the rubber-tree seed pods shrinking at sundown as they cooled after a particularly hot day and giving out an audible crack.

After a month, the bungalow owner returned and Rosemarie and I were taken in by the 3rd Division Head of Police, Roger Edmunds, and his wife June. His large bungalow, on stilts, was nearer to Sibu town and usually guarded by armed Gurkha sentries – whose barracks were just opposite. This gave us increased night-time protection as well as the opportunity to hear various Bollywood-type Gurkha films from across the road.

One night Roger and I attended a mess dinner at the Squadron mess bungalow at Sibu airport, together with the 3rd Division Resident, the District Officer and the CO of the 1st/7th Gurkhas – Col John Clements. It was a very convivial affair and afterwards we all retired to our various abodes and slept soundly. Sometime during the night, an Indonesian transport aircraft flew very low over Sibu and dropped anti-Malaysian propaganda leaflets. None of the mess dinner attendees heard the aircraft but the 1st/7th Medical Officer was having trouble sleeping and was sitting up by a window in his basha and clearly saw the aircraft, which he identified as an Indonesian C11 Hercules. The leaflets failed to deploy at all and so the next morning were easily picked up still in their bags.

Rosemarie continued to work for the Psychological Warfare Team until the middle of March 1964 when we both flew back to UK.

Report on the Work of the Lower Rajang Psychological Warfare Field Team

By Rosemarie Skinner (845 Squadron Naval Wife)

The following report describes the aims and achievements of this team, of which I was a member from January until March 1964, and is reproduced with only minor clarifying amendments to show what efforts were made during Confrontation in 'Hearts and Minds' work.

Purpose and Aims

The Lower Rajang Psychological warfare Field Team was called into being with a limited purpose. The main aim was to attempt to persuade the uncommitted mass of the Chinese people living in the Lower Rajang area to understand what the Government is attempting to do and to take an active part in the struggle. A subsidiary aim was to function as a pilot organisation whose experience could be used if similar teams were created in other parts of the country. It was clearly understood that there would be an intensive effort for one month to produce leaflets and similar propaganda material sufficient to last for two or three months altogether.

What was Accomplished

A small organisation consisting of six people was formed on 6th January 1964 and, after 23 days, produced the following:

A series of 9 leaflets, aiming first at establishing trust in those who read them and, later, urging readers to supply information through P.0. Box 5000. This series was air-dropped over a period from 20th January to 4th February.

A second series, of 7 leaflets, continuing the work of the first series and, in addition, attacking the SFA, were due to be dropped over the period from 18th February to the end of March.

A series of four posters, 3 of which might not be suitable if Confrontation were brought to an end.

Drafts of 6 leaflet illustrations, also suitable for newspaper cartoons.

Arrangements were made for an advertising slide for use in the cinemas to be prepared in Kuching. It asked the public to use P.O. Box 3000.

A number of people were approached who could be relied on to give reports on the reception of leaflets and the views of the public on what they contained.

In addition, 20,000 leaflets were produced on a duplicating machine in our office as an emergency measure for the Paloh operation. This was followed by another 20,000 printed leaflets the next day.

Three news flashes were arranged for the Foochow broadcasts to intensify attention to the leaflets. Projects were planned for using outside broadcasts as a supplement.

A considerable increase in interest among the public was noticed. Almost all the leaflets in town areas appeared to have been gathered up.

Many children collected them, as with cigarette cards. Adults were seen reading them and reports appeared in the See Hua *Daily News*. In addition, one or two individuals in Sibu expressed appreciation of the interest shown by these leaflets in the future of the Chinese Community. Chang Ta Kang came to say that he had been waiting for an opportunity to thank us for the way in which the information for the Chinese Community was being put across. It looked, therefore, as if the first aim of the first leaflet series was achieved. A final assessment at the end of the campaign was to be attempted by the officer then in charge (after I had left).

The Organisation

The organisation consisted of the following people, whose duties were as described below:

| Mr K.G. Robinson | To allocate and supervise work. |

	To initiate projects.
	To obtain information and write it up.
	To decide timing of projects.
	To obtain clearance for project.
Captain Kyte	To submit ideas.
	To criticise projects.
	To advise on military implications.
	To assist in written work.
	To supervise administration of air-drops.
Mr Simon Lao	To be responsible for organising the printing and distribution of our materials.
	This includes:
	knowing the channels to be followed,
	advising higher authority of the
	dates for release,
	arranging for posters to be put on view,
	arranging for slides to be shown.
	To assist in assessing results of projects completed through "listeners".
	To assist in obtaining information for projects and advising on them.
	To be responsible for payments and expenses.

	To be responsible for inventories.
Mr Lo Syn Jin	To advise on "slant" of material.
	To advise on wording of originals.
	To translate prepared material.
	To build up library of productions and sources of information.
	To read daily the "See Hua Daily News" and "Brilliant Lamp".
	To keep a file of press cuttings.
Mr Hasbi B. Suleiman	To advise on suitability of ideas for drawing.
	To interpret ideas in drawing.
	To advise on layout of pamphlets.
Mrs R. Skinner	To organise filing system.
	To do correspondence.
	To keep a diary.
	To keep calendar of proposed action.
	To organise supply of stationery.
	To record trunk telephone calls.

An office, about 22' by 18', was provided in the Hock Hua Bank building adjoining the Information Office, Sibu. It was found necessary to have six tables and two typewriters, but duplicating facilities were provided by the Information Office. The room was cleaned by the Information Department office boy and he also delivered our mail. Relevant stationery requirements were provided by the Information Department.

It was found desirable to open files under the following titles:

Leaflet Dropping Programme

Ideas

Leaflets: First Drafts

Leaflets: Final Drafts (with English translations)

Posters and Illustrations

Extracts from Sibu Newspapers

Press Cuttings

General Correspondence

Journal

Useful information

Personnel

Record of Trunk Telephone Calls

Reference Books

Stationery File

Recommendations

a) It was strongly recommended that, if other teams were to be started, they should be in close association with the office of another department. In Kuching or Sibu this would perhaps best be the Information Office but, elsewhere, either the District Office or the Development Office would be most convenient.

b) A population map should be started at the earliest possible opportunity, as it was essential to know where people of a particular race lived and in what numbers. Unless this was done, accurate instructions could not be given to the pilot as regards the quantities to be dropped at a particular place. We had to be content with approximations as follows:-

Chinese population

Sibu Urban:	22,585	Sibu Rural:	29,349
Binatang	12,590	Sarikei:	14,760

Total: 79,284

It was not intended, however, that large numbers of leaflets should be dropped on towns because the people in the towns could read the contents of the leaflets in newspapers, and the leaflets were more easily retrieved after the drop than in jungle areas. Pilots were provided with a trace indicating the most important areas in which leaflets should be dropped. Working on a population of 60,000, we printed 100,000 leaflets. This was by no means a heavy concentration but, on occasions, such a concentrated programme did require the use of more than one aircraft.

It was found that the first leaflet series was too concentrated, with two different sets of leaflets in one drop, and two drops a week. It was felt desirable to have a large number of leaflets in considerable variety at first, in order to make a greater impact, but the second series would be more in the nature of a 'topping-up', with only one leaflet drop per week.

It was recommended that, in future, teams should have very clear-cut instructions as to the extent to which they should assist in the production of leaflets for active military operations, if at all, as such operations were likely to over-tax their resources and should probably be dealt with by a different organisation.

In setting up a team, it was desirable not to have all the members arriving on the first day, because it took a few days before there was sufficient work for everyone. The artist did not need to arrive until the 4th or 5th day and the representative from the broadcasting department could not usefully take part until the work had reached a fairly developed stage, with dates and times already worked out - probably towards the end of the second week.

It was found useful to keep a daily journal recording decisions taken and progress of work.

It was suggested that considerable heightening of interest, for a small expenditure, could be achieved by introducing some element of chance and gain into the leaflet, as with our A9, in which the leaflets were numbered and 100 of them, when produced, would entitle their owner to claim a cash prize.

It was considered very important that a stenographer should be a member of the team if it was intended that the team should work at high pressure for only a short time.

The priority for aircraft *vis-a-vis* leaflet dropping and other operations or tasks should be laid down by higher authority from the start.

The Final Stage

After Mr K.G. Robinson's retirement from the team it would be headed by Captain Kyte, who would make any necessary additions or adjustments to the second leaflet programme and ensure that the material prepared was dropped at suitable intervals. Also, that the posters, when printed, were distributed in such a way that they would be seen by the largest possible number of people. When he also retires from the team, the machinery would be kept running by Mr. Simon Lao, who would also continue to make reports on the reaction of the public, both to the DIVEC and to the Advisory Committee on Psychological Warfare in Kuching. When the entire programme was completed, the organisation would then be disbanded.

Postscript:

It has been described earlier that Indonesian aircraft dropped anti-British leaflets over Sarawak. One of these is shown verbatim (i.e. uncorrected) overleaf.

Dear Countrymen,

Tenku and Ninkang, the puppet of the imperialist' have shamelessly boasted, "Malaysia will bring liberty, equality, fraternity and prosperity to the peoples." After one year's trail, the fact proved their boast to be

---

worthless lies.

The persistence increase of taxes, the constant raise of the price of the goods and the rapid fall in the price of the local products make people poorer. Peoples are strugging desperately against poverty and this is their promised prosperity.

The Chinese valued and honour their language. But, under the Reactionary Governemnt, the Chinese Secondary Education is at edge of
extermination. We can be sure Chinese Primary Education will face the same fate.

The imperialist is strengthening and increasing the mobility of the military forces to curb the movement of anti-colonialism, We are at the mercy of the rapacious soldiery. They plunder and persecute the kind and innocent peoples and thus make them miserable and unberable. But the most serious and dangerous menace is the destructive war which is underplotted by the calculative puppet. If the war broke out, neither we nor our properties can be saved.

The Reactionary Governement never stop persecuting the kind and innocent peoples. They threnten and arrest-thes, put them into prison and torture them. Under their ill treatment, Wong Yan Jen, a youth of bright future is tortured to death. Recently other fifty detainee were stealthy removed to Malaya for more inhuman treatments. We can easily imagine the grief and nightmare this caused to the families of these sufferers. We are only human, with blood and flesh, our feeling is not numb. How can we bear this cruelty and unjest

Now, the puppet is schemeing other dirty plot----the force soldiering under the pretence of serving our country, urge us to fight against one another, to protect the puppet and to die for Tengku and Ningkang, while we are sheding our blood and mourning for our lost, the Reactionary Government will stand, and go on oppressing us and make our life a misery. Why keep quiet and wait for disasters. It is high time for us to go into action. Let us unite and oppose their persecution, oppose force soldiering. To hell with their "National Solidarity Week". Don't take part in their dirty acts. We must not be used by them.

We will only serve our own peoples. We must crush the domination of imperialism. We will defeat them and send them to the grave, just as the peoples of Vietnam and Cuba have done. Since the imperialist only deprive our liberty, eguaiity, fraternity and prosperity, we will fight for them ourselves Victory belongs to us. Unite and fight for it.

We are,

Your loyal sons and daughters.

These are the dry facts. I particularly remember that our office, with its internal wall with huge windows, made us feel like goldfish in a bowl, particularly on Fridays when Ibans, with their intricately-tattooed faces, pressed their noses against the glass. They had come to collect their wages from their employer, a logging company.

The greatest excitement was skimming over the jungle in the Army Auster, piloted by Tim Dean. My job was to throw out the coloured leaflets wherever there were longhouses. I don't think I was much good at it as it required quite a hard throw downwards to clear the fuselage. Anyway, I won't be asked to do it again!

Nanga Gaat Activities in early 1964

By Lieutenant David Storrie R.M. (845 Squadron Pilot Wessex 1) Detachment Commander Nanga Gaat)

Command at Nanga Gaat changed three times during January 1964, with Lieutenant Commander Digby Lickfold in charge from the 1st to 20th, Lieutenant David Rowe RM from the 20th to 23rd, Lieutenant Dick Steil from the 23rd to 29th, and then myself from the 29th onwards.

On 28th January came the announcement, from President Sukarno of Indonesia, of a ceasefire which would come into effect from that date. This made no difference whatsoever to the type of operations that had been going on during January, and did not alter the vigilance and counter-insurgent moves, until something more concrete was announced. The Officer Commanding West Brigade, Brigadier Patterson, emphasised the need to prevent any surreptitious incursions into the Third Division by a band intending to lay low until British troops moved out, and then start the carnage. This, then, set the pattern of operations.

There were no contacts with the enemy in the Eastern part of the Third Division during the month, and our helicopters kept up continuous support for the patrols in the location.

The Commanding Officer of the 1st/2nd K.E.O, Gurkha Rifles, Lieutenant Colonel John Clements, made a tour of his widespread company locations to discuss the tactical situation and to get first-hand information of the areas from the Company Commanders. Our helicopters allowed him to visit everywhere he wanted, and enabled him to formulate his plan of campaign. Note that 'Goorkha' is the correct spelling for the 2nd King Edward's Own Regiment. The other three regiments which continued to serve in the British Army following Indian independence in 1947 were the 6th Queen Elizabeth's Own Gurkhas, the 7th Duke of Edinburgh's Own Gurkhas and the 10th Princess Mary's Own Gurkhas. At the time of Borneo Confrontation each of these four regiments consisted of two battalions, the 1st and the 2nd in each case. For the sake of consistency in this book the Editor has decided to refer to all four regiments as 'Gurkhas', with apologies to any ex-Goorkhas that may read it.

The Companies were to send out patrols in their area to get a good idea of the terrain, to investigate local reports of tracks, and to ensure that no fresh tracks appeared which might indicate the entry of a large enemy band whose intention was to avoid detection and wait until vigilance had waned before striking at a base.

As a result of one such patrol in 'A' Company area, the escape route to the south of the Sungei Aput used by the Long Jawi raiders in September 1963 was discovered.

A troop of the SAS numbering twenty men was attached to the 1st/2nd to assist them in their task of watching such a large border area. Although basically controlled from Brunei, this troop was under the operational control of the Battalion, which was a new departure for the SAS, who always considered themselves as 'lone wolves'.

The SAS were split into patrols of three or four men, and flown into positions on the upper Baleh River, with the task of following rivers flowing from the high border ridge, and to investigate known and possible entry routes. This proved successful, and they brought out valuable information as to whether such a route was feasible, or impossible, and limited the 'unknown' down to definite routes, thus easing the situation for the planning team in the event of intrusion reports in that area.

All but one of the Baleh patrols were withdrawn, in the latter part of the month, and repositioned on the upper reaches of the northern rivers, the Kajang, Linau, Danum and Plieran. The landing sites in this area had all been cut by previous SAS Patrols with the exception of the Plieran, where there was none. These rivers rise in high plains at 2500 to 3500 feet above sea level, which seriously limited the Wessex 1 aircraft performance when required to go into difficult sites. In order to prevent long journeys from a fuelling base to these locations to drop only two men who, with 14 days provisions and weighty Bergen rucksacks could give a payload of 700 lbs, we would ferry the patrol of 4 men to an easy landing site in the vicinity of the patrol area, and the aircraft could then split the load and ferry it with two short trips.

The object of these Northern patrols was to contact the Punans, the primitive hunting peoples of the interior, who knew no borders, and to gain their confidence and use them as an advance listening-post of possible enemy intrusion from that quarter. The Linau patrols were very successful in contacting a large party of Punans in their area, and we flew in a large supply of 'goodies' and medical supplies on the 'hearts and minds' charge bill.

It had originally been intended to keep these patrols supplied by RAF air drop, but this was changed and became an 845 Squadron commitment.

The supplies were uplifted from Belaga and flown to the very small landing sites which these patrols were able to clear. Frequently the only way of getting the stores in was by winch from a high hover.

However, the SAS attached tins of rum with notes saying 'God Bless the Navy, we don't know what we would do without you!' to the winch cable, which made us realise that we were appreciated.

While the use of small patrols such as the SAS is fine from the military point of view, it imposed a difficult situation when the time came to pull them out of position. A patrol of 4 men had great difficulty in clearing a good site in primary jungle with merely machetes, and perhaps some plastic explosive. However, these were experienced men, and generally made a good job of building wheel platforms on uneven or marshy ground.

Some of the Gurkha patrols made very good landing sites. The best were on ridges and spurs, as these generally had thinner vegetation on top and, when the trees were cut away, the ridge provided a good entry and exit route, which generally obviated the use of a towering take-off which was so typical of the valley or river site. Ridge and Spur sites were also generally easier to find due to their height.

However, the basic difficulty was the lack of saws and axes, which were in such short supply, and machetes and Kukris made little impression on the teak of the forests. Plastic explosive was of some use, but the trees were so interwoven with vines that one tree would remain upright after having its base blown, until its supporting tree was blown, and so on. Also, very few Gurkhas were trained in demolitions, and plastic explosive was heavy.

It became essential for these patrols to carry No 80 (White phosphorous) and 83 (Coloured smoke) grenades, and Verey pistols with which to signal the position of the landing sites to the searching helicopters. Our briefing would be that a patrol had set off from a known landing site on a bearing of 195 degrees and estimate its position as G.R. 567345. With the inaccurate maps and very rugged terrain, the problem of finding these patrols was great.

Searching for lost patrols with the 1:150,000 maps that we were using presented pilots with unnecessary problems and wasted hours. Three helicopters had to search for two hours to find a patrol south west of Long Jawi on a map which was shown to put the main river, the Batang Balui, 4½ miles too far north than in reality. This naturally put the patrol out of position by 4 ½ miles, and made our job doubly difficult. It was extraordinary that, after a year of operations in this area, there was not one accurate topographical map, and 6,000 foot mountain ridges were ignored.

The pilots got into the habit of drawing in high contours on their blank maps, which were collated in the Operations Room at Nanga Gaat, and the information was passed to the Gurkha Intelligence Office. As there was only one Auster in the whole of the Third Division, we could expect no help in reconnaissance in the East.

January saw a gradual worsening of the weather, and it promised to last until the end of March. The monsoons increased in number from the south and north east, and gave nil visibility in the rain and very clear line of sight out of it. However, as the rainfall increased, so the mist and cloud formed on the hills until the vast rain-clouds were formed again. The mist hung around after the late afternoon and night rains until the middle of the next morning, and cut down our operating time.

This adverse weather did have an effect on our operations when working in the area of the northern rivers, which were between 45 and 60 miles from the nearest refuelling base of Long Jawi. The possibility of returning to Long Jawi from a trip to the Pliora to find the base in the middle of a monsoon shower made it politic to carry at least one extra quarter-hour's fuel, and this did cut down the payload by

200 lbs.

Although we were unable to control the weather, we had streamlined the Operational Tasking. The next day's task was passed by the Squadron Operations Officer, 'Kingfisher', on the Gurkha Command Net at 1730, and confirmed at 0800 on the day in question. For important and complicated tasks, either the Battalion Intelligence Officer (IO) would come up to Nanga Gaat to discuss it, or 'Kingfisher' would go down to Kapit to discuss it there. During this meeting a forecast of tasks could usually be given.

Personalities came into this and it was most important that the tasks should be worked out by people who knew each other, and not solely on the fly and via the impersonal HF radio set. The reason why the Long Jawi counter-moves went so smoothly in the previous October was that Helicopter Commanders and the Unit Intelligence Officer could work out their mutual problems in personal contact. It was, therefore, important that 'Kingfisher' should be someone who had some idea of helicopter and aircraft operations, and that he should have had the job for a reasonable length of time to maintain continuity. In this respect, Sub-Lieutenant Canning did an excellent job, and when he had become familiar with all the peculiar problems of operating in this area, he proved to be a valuable asset. His departure was a loss to the organisation and it became necessary to have a pilot to stand off flying for a week to do this job, which was wasteful and did not allow continuity.

The aircraft were now beginning to suffer from a year of standing in the open, often in appalling weather, and with alternate doses of hot sun and rain. The electrical and pressure instruments were particularly affected. However, the maintenance team under A.A.1 Salisbury and, later, under A.A.1 Mills, kept the machines flying and never lacked in their enthusiasm or industry.

The Gurkha Engineers heard our plea for a water point, and started constructing a drinking-water point and a shower 'basha', which proved a great boon as the river was now continually swollen and muddy from the monsoon rains.

We were suffering from the seasonal influx of flies, which coincided with the harvesting of the padi. This necessitated constant spraying of all possible breeding places. The Elsans (very desirable detachment items) were a great help in preventing flies in the 'Heads' area.

Fresh food came up from Kapit on the HDS aircraft or by the Gurkha ration-boat. However, these could not always be relied upon and we had our fair share of

Compo rations to fall back on.

The newly-modified aircraft with machine-guns arrived at Nanga Gaat on 23rd January. We thus had a defensive and offensive weapon system, together with the SS11 air-to-ground missiles. For hand- held weapons, we now had four Self-Loading Rifles (SLRs) and eleven Sub-Machine-Guns (SMGs) at the location which, together with the Marine Signallers' personal weapons, enabled nearly every man to have a weapon. Although there was no zeroing kit, each man received weapon instruction and had fired it on the short range.

Detailed orders for action in case of attack on the location were produced, with the priority of getting the aircraft away with as many ground personnel as possible. In the event of take-off being impossible, then each man had a defence position within the framework of the company defence.

To mark the Squadron's 21st birthday on 1st February, after tasking was completed, we gave a little display using three aircraft, which included some formation flying and one aircraft doing some precision manoeuvres. The Gurkhas and the locals seemed to enjoy it, and it set the pace for the evening's festivities. Lieutenant Rowe, PO Hazel and NAM Edkins prepared a fabulous set of buffet dishes, one of which was a suckling pig, for the party in the Anchor Inn, our 'pub' at Nanga Gaat. We invited Major Mole and his Gurkha officers and SNCOs, all old friends of the Squadron. A tremendous night was had by all and, as the party nearly coincided with the departure of 'C' Company 1st/2nd Gurkhas from Nanga Gaat to take place on 6th and 8th February, Major Mole produced a bottle of Champagne, and we exchanged one White Ensign for the 'C' Company flag, which was then hung in the bar. It was a pity that so many of the people who had been at Nanga Gaat for the previous three months could not be there, but they were remembered.

Living and operating in the field at Nanga Gaat seemed to bring out the best in all of us. Everyone at Nanga Gaat pulled their weight and the ground crews, galley staff, armourers, SBA and 'Base Staff' did everything that was asked of them, and more besides. It was even noticeable that some people who in other circumstances had been the cause of some concern, had blossomed out and did extremely well.

The setting-up of the Sick Bay proved fully justified. SBA Saunders did a first-class job and treated over 1,000 cases. The presence of a competent 'Doc', as the SBA became widely-known, greatly improved the morale of all rates at Nanga Gaat and lifted a great weight off the mind of the Detachment Commander. There was also a saving in aircraft hours as some sick, who would otherwise have had to be air

CASEVACed, could now be treated by the SBA.

In summary, January saw the Squadron continuing to give maximum effort to the infantry unit which we supported. An Order of the Day as issued by Major Mole, Officer Commanding 'C' Company 1st/2nd K.E.0. Gurkhas, gave a tribute to this, and it was warmly received by the Squadron personnel.

Operation Sabre Tooth

By Lieutenant David Storrie Royal Marines - Pilot 845 Squadron (Wessex 1)

Lt Col Jim Fillingham, CO 2nd/10th Gurkha Rifles, the commander in the 2nd Division of Sarawak, had planned a raid in response to the attack on the southern border of his TAOR. A patrol of 'A' Coy 2nd/10th had been ambushed by Indonesians on the steep slope of the border. The Battalion planned the raid by 'A' Coy to destroy the enemy camp on the ridge overlooking the 2nd Division, with direct support from field artillery, the 76mm guns of armoured cars (with their rear wheels in a ditch in order to get extra elevation).

Also, I believe for the first time in combat, two Wessex of 845 Squadron would fire wire-guided SS 11 missiles at a large cave near the top of the cliff just below the 'enemy camp' and which was thought to be an enemy OP. These firings were to be done at the same time as the approach was being made by 'A' Coy along the top of the ridge.

The two missile-armed Wessex had two 'Aimers' - the 'expensively trained in Paris Storrie' and Wing Commander Phillips, who was the senior RAF Air Commander in Kuching and who had admitted that he had been a trained SS 11 aimer in Aden with the Twin Pioneer aircraft as the platform.

In the early morning of 31 March 1964, I was in Wessex 'E', piloted by Lt Geoff Clarke, and the Wing Commander was the aimer in the second aircraft piloted by Lieutenant 'Cosh' Kennard. We flew in at about 1000 ft above ground level for the two aircraft to launch the missiles in sequence.

Fig 34. 845 Wessex 1 loaded with SS 11 Missiles

I went first and fired my missile which, after the initial flight in the direction of the target, turned vertically downwards and 'attacked' the ground below. A malfunction which, considering that the missiles had been stored in poor conditions for years, was not surprising!

The second aircraft fired in turn and I think its first missile went in the right direction. I fired 2 further missiles, which hit or were close to the target. I believe that one of the Wing Commander's missiles also malfunctioned.

These missile firings, combined with the armoured cars' artillery support, allowed the Gurkhas to capture and destroy the enemy camp, which had been vacated by its inhabitants before they were assaulted.

I note from my Log Book that I also fired 2 further missiles later that day after the first sortie, and that these were fired from the aircraft piloted by 'Cosh' Kennard.

I also carried out quite a few air-to-ground machine-gun sorties during that whole period.

A Night CASEVAC

By Lieutenant Commander G.J. 'Tank' Sherman (Commanding Officer 845 Squadron, Wessex 1)

Just before midnight on Monday, 2nd March 1964, I was shaken by my Sibu

Detachment Commander – Lieutenant Brian Skinner – who had answered the phone call from the Gurkha Battalion HQ at Sibu to say that their detachment at Song, about a hundred miles up-river from Sibu, had radioed to say an Iban tribesman was very seriously injured. Could we get him to hospital?

I went to the radio and asked the Gurkhas: 'What is the weather like at Song?'

'It is clear.'

Experience told me this was highly unlikely. The local climate had only two dependable features: there was very little wind, and low cloud blanketed the whole country every night.

'Can you see the stars?'

'No. We can see no stars.' As expected: total overcast.

'Is it raining?'

'No. It is not raining.'

'Can the man wait until the morning?'

'No. He will die by then.'

I balanced an unknown tribesman's life against the very real risk of taking a helicopter a hundred miles inland over unmapped cloud-covered terrain and then back out to Sibu. There was no way of knowing how bad the weather was. Cloudbase at Song might be five hundred feet - or fifty. And it was likely to get worse as the night went on.

'Will he die anyway?' I asked.

'We do not think so if he is rescued now.'

'OK. Expect us in about an hour.'

Five minutes later Brian and I, with A.A.1 Robjohns in the cabin as our Aircrewman, were airborne in drizzle and, finding the cloudbase lowering rapidly, I decided to abandon the direct route to Song and fly up the river. So began the most nerve-racking trip of my life. From the left-hand seat Brian was operating the landing lamp to keep the beam on the edge of the river, to give me a view of the approaching twists and turns and also an idea of our height above the water. As a second pair of eyes, he was also able to alert me to oncoming hazards such as overhanging tree branches and river obstructions so that I could concentrate on keeping in the air. Before long the cloudbase was touching the 200ft trees lining the river banks and, for the best part of an hour, we felt our way up-river in almost total blackness between water and cloud, alleviated only by the landing lamp, and watching out on the right bank for Song to appear.

The visibility at Song was so bad we would have missed it had they not heard us coming and waved flaming torches in the mist. This was the Gurkhas' idea of 'clear weather'! I crept in and landed in the Padang in front of the school.

I was unsure if I could face the journey back - until a doctor climbed into the cabin and told me on the intercom that he would be travelling with the patient, and we had half an hour to get him to hospital or he would die.

To return down the river was out of the question: for one thing I couldn't bring myself to do it, for another we were short of fuel and finally, according to the doctor, the patient would die before we got to Sibu. I was going to have to climb out on instruments and fly direct to Sibu at a safe height above the surrounding hills - about 3000 feet.

It was a viciously bumpy ride in black, turbulent cloud, navigation no more than dead-reckoning, i.e. intelligent guesswork, and my main problem was how to be sure I was close enough to Sibu to let down safely. To make matters worse the engine started surging and I had to take out the governor and revert to manual throttle control. The doctor kept up a running commentary on his patient, a 17-year-old casualty of a longhouse feud, with one hand almost severed at the wrist by a parang.

We did have the *Violet Picture* radio-homing device, which Brian monitored constantly, but this relied on clear and frequent transmissions from Sibu ATC, whose transmissions at this time were infrequent and broken up and so not much use to us at all. When our 'navigation' told us we should be in the vicinity of Sibu, I forced myself to reduce power and descend in the cloud, knowing that if I had got my sums wrong the first we would know about it was when we hit high ground. The descent took a very long time. As the altimeter slowly unwound I was glad that the doctor and patient in the back didn't know what was going on. I was reflecting on the fine line between heroics and stupidity when I saw the lights of Sibu ahead in the gloom.

An ambulance rushed the Iban to hospital, where the excellent Chinese surgeon Wong Sungkei mended him as good as new, which of course made it all worthwhile. But I still can't decide if I was a hero or a fool. Either way, a young man's life was saved by a crazily-inaccurate Gurkha weather report, a slightly mad Royal Navy helicopter crew and a brilliant Chinese surgeon - all in the best tradition of Sarawak's amiable multi-racial society.

Part 3

Indonesian Confrontation April 1964 to April 1965

845 Squadron and HMS *Bulwark* 1964-65

Lieutenant Michael Reece Royal Marines – Pilot 845 Squadron (Wessex 1)

The story of 845 Naval Air Commando Squadron in the second commission of HMS *Bulwark* as a Commando Carrier really started at RNAS Culdrose in January 1964, with the formation of 706 'Bulwark' Flight. From that intensive and wintry beginning the Squadron aircraft have flown over the sands of North Africa and the jungles and waters of the Far East, encompassing every possible helicopter task.

The Squadron activities proved more diverse and the achievements greater than any of the 200 officers and ratings assembling at Culdrose could possibly have imagined. They encountered both triumph and tragedy in a commission of unprecedented hard work where, from the very beginning, never was the full complement of aircraft, aircrew and maintenance personnel assembled together as one squadron. Nevertheless the Squadron accrued the fantastic total of 10,000 flying hours in fourteen months of operations from HMS *Bulwark* and ashore in Borneo. It had its ups and downs, but the award to the Commanding Officer, Lieutenant Commander G.J. Sherman, of the Order of the Star of Sarawak, his later appointment as a Member of the Order of the British Empire in the New Year's Honours List and, finally, the award of the Boyd Trophy for 1964 to the Squadron, reflected the impact that 845 Squadron made in the Far East and, particularly, in Borneo operations.

In March 1964, the heat and sand of North Africa quickly warmed the chilled marrow in the bones caused not only by a vicious and freezing departure from Plymouth, but the battlefields of 'B' site, Predannack and the Salisbury Plain. In a few months 706B Flight worked hard to create a skilled team that would not flounder when thrown into the deep end of Borneo. It is hard to remember now how little helicopter, let alone Wessex, experience the Flight had when it formed at Culdrose.

Exercise 'Sandfly' in North Africa proved a valuable initiation into the Commando Ship assault role, working with 43 Commando, Royal Marines, but few would care to repeat those chaotic days on the Flight Deck. Deep in the comparative safety of the desert, our missiles made a three-ton lorry regret its parking lot, whilst machine-gun firing was enthusiastically pursued amongst the sand dunes.

HMS *Albion* was waiting gleefully to greet us in Aden and, judging by the comments on the aged aircraft which were transferred to *Bulwark*, our predecessors in 845 were very happy to be going home. In Aden we officially threw off the mantle of 706B Flight to become the new 845 Squadron, before going on to Singapore with our six new, camouflaged Wessex 1s, trying to ignore the four veterans scarred with much improper advice and graffiti from the old Squadron. Lt Cdr Tank Sherman, our new Commanding Officer, greeted his replacement Squadron on our arrival in Singapore and explained our future deployment. Half the squadron would be deployed in Sarawak, where there had developed a semi-permanent commitment in the Third Division, the other half remaining on board. The Squadron would change round every three months. And so a few days later, off the coast of Sarawak, the squadron split.

Thus, in April 1964, the Borneo half of the Squadron, eight Wessex and a Hiller, was deployed in three detachments at Sibu, Nanga Gaat and Simanggang to support counter-insurgency operations throughout the entire 2nd and 3rd Divisions of Sarawak. Everyone landed, each with his own idea of the conditions ashore - Sibu on stilts in a swamp, Nanga Gaat remote and carved from the jungle, and Simanggang, 'Never heard of it!' The Third Division of Sarawak has been aptly described as a giant, jungle-covered prune! It is a vast area, similar in size to Wales, mostly mountainous and almost entirely covered in jungle. It is very hot and wet, with early-morning low cloud and afternoon thunderstorms as constant problems.

Sibu, the capital of the Third Division, was a large town of mainly Chinese population, sitting on the Rajang River, which is the main water artery of the Division. The Squadron was cramped into bungalows near the airport, some three miles from Sibu town. Few will forget the overcrowding in the bungalows, or the Dining Hall and Galley thrown up near to the Control Tower by prison labour. Sibu remained the Squadron's main base ashore, coping with its flying tasks and supporting any detachments deployed 'up-country'.

Simanggang, capital town of Sarawak's 2nd Division, had a small airstrip on which the detachment was based while accommodated with firstly the 2nd/10th and then the 2nd/2nd Gurkha Rifles, whom we were supporting. The Second Division at that time had a very active border with Indonesia, and the Gurkhas were kept busy containing a number of incursions, supported by the Squadron. The number of aircraft varied from 3 down to 1, but strength remained at 10 ratings. Mail, stores and films were supplied from Sibu on an opportunity basis. The detachment gained some fame for designing and perfecting the 'Triple-Hack-Jub-Cinemascope' adaption kit, which married a Naval

Cinemascope lens to an Army film projector by a device of hacksaw blades and Jubilee clips! On one routine changeover of aircraft, the entire detachment left Simanggang at 0700 to have breakfast in Sibu at 0800, returning after breakfast with a replacement Wessex. After an Operation called 'Sabre Tooth' (described earlier in this book) had ended, the situation quietened down. The Simanggang detachment was withdrawn in June 1964 and replaced by RAF aircraft. Thereafter, Nanga Gaat remained the Squadron's permanent Forward Operating Base deep in the Eastern half of the Third Division.

Nanga Gaat lies a hundred miles to the East of Sibu, at the junction of the Baleh and Gaat rivers. 845 Squadron had first moved into "The Gaat" in November 1963, and constructed landing-pads and accommodation behind the bungalow belonging, with the land, to the Temonggong Jugah, The Paramount Chief of the Ibans. By April 1964, the Gaat was already a legend in Sarawak, unique for its way of life, the close association with the Ibans, the relaxed dress, the Anchor Inn, the premiere of *From Russia with Love*, and the unparalleled hospitality. Throughout the year many improvements were made. Notably, a substantial 240-volt generator was flown in and installed by HMS *Bulwark's* electrical department. There was soon more electricity available than could be absorbed by the small village that had grown up, consisting of the Jugah's family, Gurkhas, Surveyors, Malays, Border Scouts, coolies and 845 itself.

Deep in the eastern half of the Third Division, the Gaat became the very centre of the 'Hearts and Minds' campaign. The relations with local Ibans developed to the extent of embarrassing friendliness cultivated by longhouse visits, the Coolie party employed at the Gaat, medical services provided by the resident SBA, and the knowledge that any serious medical cases would always be flown to hospital at Kapit or Sibu.

The colour and character of Nanga Gaat, and the nights at the Anchor Inn, will be remembered by all that served and stayed there. But it must not be forgotten that it was from this jungle site that the majority of the Squadron's operational sorties were launched. The tasks increased throughout our stay until over 300 hours per month were being flown by the three Wessex and one (ex- 846 Squadron) Whirlwind based there. The jungle-covered mountainous terrain was almost entirely uninhabited except for the isolated military patrols, whose very presence depended on 845 Squadron. Trees, which soared to a height of 200 feet or more, made the landing-site clearings hazardous after transit flights where the three-to-six-thousand-foot mountain ranges, poor weather and inaccurate maps presented a continuous challenge.

The Nanga Gaat detachment not only supported the major units working in the Third Division but also, in particular, developed special relationships with the SAS, the Guards Independent Parachute Company, the Gurkha Independent Parachute Company and an Independent Company of the 2nd Battalion Parachute Regiment, whose 4-man patrols, alone in the jungle for two months at a time, we admired so much. Transit distances to the border sites from the Gaat were frequently 60-70 miles. From Sibu, aircraft supported all military activity in the Western half of the Third Division. It was not uncommon on troop lift or resupply sorties for the aircraft to be flying for 4 or 5 hours non-stop away from Sibu. Carrying CASEVAC cases from all over the Division to Sibu hospital was also a regular feature of the Squadron tasks, by both day and night. These mercy missions were too numerous to record in detail, but probably the most celebrated case during my time there was in August, when Kumbang, a 15-year-old Iban boy, was flown out of Entabai at night after a harpoon had pierced and passed through his head. After treatment, Kumbang was back in his longhouse apparently none the worse for his experience. Subsequently, the harpoon was presented to the first pilot of the aircraft, Lieutenant M.S.'Cosh' Kennard, who was later awarded a Queen's Commendation for the operation.

The majority of CASEVACs appeared to be women having difficulty in labour. No child was actually born in our aircraft but there were some close shaves, so much so that at Sibu some aircrewmen took a short course in midwifery. In the middle of May 1964 a cholera epidemic broke out in the Third Division and strict precautions were enforced at both Sibu and Nanga Gaat. Squadron helicopters were in daily use in this distressing CASEVAC role. With many of the victims coming from isolated longhouses, their swift delivery to hospital saved many lives. It has truly been said that the emergency in Borneo would never have been won unless the 'Hearts and Minds' of the people were also won over. In every aspect of the Squadron's life ashore, every opportunity was taken to improve relations with the local people. These were exemplified by the sick-bay and longhouse visits at the Gaat, children's Christmas parties, good conduct and example in Sibu and CASEVAC missions. The importance of these medical services cannot be overestimated, and Squadron aircraft were greeted with wild enthusiasm in previously dissident and remote areas. One life saved could alter the political complexion of a whole Kampong.

The maintenance record for the detachment ashore became a byword throughout the Far East. In July 1964, for example, there was not one day with less than 7 out of the 8 helicopters serviceable, and an overall serviceability of 95% was obtained with a flying rate in excess of 60 hours per aircraft. The consistently high serviceability was by no means because the aircraft never went unserviceable, quite the contrary, but was achieved by prolonged hard work on the part of the maintenance teams coupled with high priority stores backing. Every major component change was performed ashore at some time and small maintenance teams were dotted over the Third Division salvaging aircraft, changing engines, etc., often working under difficult and unpleasant conditions. Again, in the year since our arrival in HMS *Bulwark*, much happened worthy of record, but the following incidents stood out. The Hiller was recovered to Sibu slung under a Wessex on no less than three occasions, once from the headwaters of the Baleh - some 200 miles from Sibu. Two Wessex were salvaged to Sibu, one from Long Jawi, the other from Belaga, both distances approximately 150 miles. From Belaga it was the first time a Wessex had been salvaged entirely by Wessex, including the stripped-down fuselage. Many difficult engine-changes were carried out during our time, but changing 'O''s engine in five hours on a shingle bank in the Baleh River was a record, as was also the oleo change on 'M' in eight minutes with the aircraft in the hover.

Naturally, as one would expect in the Commando role flying over the Borneo jungle, we had our aircraft incidents. Nevertheless, we were stunned that after such a successful run in 1964, we should suffer a series of major accidents in February, March and April 1965, resulting in the loss of 5 aircraft, 3 pilots, 2 aircrewmen and 11 soldiers. However, in spite of these disasters the entire Squadron reacted with magnificent resilience, and any temporary effect on morale was quickly dissipated by continual tasking and ever-present hard work.

Although no positive enemy contacts were made in the Third Division of Sarawak during our stay, our helicopters enabled one battalion and the special companies in the SAS role to keep control over 25,000 square miles against the triple threat of border crossing, sea incursion and internal subversion. The continuous helicopter and troop activity, coupled with the difficult terrain, undoubtedly discouraged our Indonesian 'friend' Sukarno from our parish. Reflecting the importance and reputation of the Sarawak detachment, inevitably we played host to countless visitors and took as routine visits which would normally throw a Naval Air Station into chaos for weeks. At the top of an illustrious list were Prince Philip, Duke of Edinburgh, and Earl Jellicoe, then Minister of Defence.

The larger part of the Squadron remained based in *Bulwark*, except for periods in Singapore, where HMS Simbang/ RNAS Sembawang became its second home, and for certain detachments reacting to Indonesian incursions into Malaya. Aircraft were rotated with the Borneo aircraft to enable the larger servicing operations and planned component changes to take place on board or at Simbang. Therefore, the Squadron will look back on its ship time and remember the flat-out maintenance periods preparing for maximum aircraft efforts while endeavouring to provide rest and recuperation (R and R) for those returning from Borneo. Memories of the Flight Deck scenes will have mellowed with the years but few will forget the loop, the broadcast and the 'choppers' going up and down the lift like yo-yos. During *Bulwark's* first visit to Borneo in this commission, our new camouflaged Wessex 1s were exchanged for the old, yellow jobs which needed much attention back at Simbang before Exercise 'Ligtas' - the first major exercise with the Americans in the Philippines. The ship made several visits to Hong Kong and use was made of the Hong Kong Aircraft Company at Kai Tak for major modifications and repainting of the aircraft, enabling some light relief and limited leave to be given in the exotic port.

During August, all nine aircraft on board were prepared and kept serviceable for Exercise 'Horse's Neck' off Malaya's East Coast. Two aircraft were borrowed from 814 Squadron to back up 845 in the event of any unserviceability. However, with the exception of the inevitable minor snags, the Squadron operated intensively for the week in which 235 hours were flown and all nine aircraft remained on deck throughout. In the event, the second day of the 'Horse's Neck' demonstration was cancelled and four Squadron aircraft were maintained airborne continuously throughout the day for signs of the first incursion into Malaya in the Pontian area. A few weeks later, large numbers of Indonesian Paratroops landed in the Labis area of Malaya and four Wessex and a Hiller were landed to support the lst Battalion New Zealand Regiment and the 1st/10th Gurkha Rifles in the subsequent operations. Operation 'Lilac' lasted 16 days before the detachment was relieved by 814 Squadron. 270 hours were flown and the prompt reaction and deployment of the troops given by our aircraft were major factors in the success of the operation.

The Squadron on board had had many commitments. Between the periodic exercises involving maximum aircraft effort, there were heavy maintenance periods complicated by essential pilot continuation training, which could not be done in Borneo. Of all exercises and demonstrations tackled, the most ambitious were undoubtedly Exercises 'Ligtas' and 'March Hare'. In the latter exercise an assault, support and withdrawal of a unit, 40 Commando, was conducted from the Commando ship at night. This evolution was hitherto virtually theoretical and to make it a practical reality necessitated many hours of night-flying training, thus imposing a strain on both aircrew and groundcrew alike.

Sukarno chose to complicate the picture again in March by raiding the East Coast of Johore. A detachment of four aircraft was landed to take part in Operation 'Oaktree,' based at Seletar, flying in support of the 2nd Battalion, Singapore Infantry Regiment, the 4th and 8th Battalions of The Royal Malay Regiment, The Federation Artillery and the Malayan Police Field Force. As a result of the operation all but one of the original incursion of sixty people were eliminated.

At the beginning of April 1965, *Bulwark* commenced a main docking period and all the embarked Squadron migrated to Simbang for two months. This enabled both watches to have a fortnight's local leave in Malaya or Singapore, while many chose to take lower-deck leave, idly observing the industry of their fellows from the veranda of 'B' block. The heavy maintenance programme forever associated with Simbang was temporarily knocked askew when two *Wessex* and a Hiller were shipped to Sibu soon after our arrival to replace two aircraft so tragically lost in a crash at Nanga Gaat.

During the docking period the serviceable aircraft were, as always, flown to the maximum, providing continuation training for the pilots recently emerged from Borneo, and two aircraft were detached to Gemas airstrip for an exercise. A course for new local aircrewmen was also arranged. During the commission a significant number of our maintenance ratings served as local aircrewmen to supplement our complement of only four qualified crewmen. They worked extremely hard with only a few pence per diem as recompense. Without their untiring and skilled support guiding aircraft into otherwise impossible clearings, controlling the passengers, humping stores, caring for the CASEVACs and looking after their aircraft, the pilots would have been virtually impotent and the Squadron unable to fulfil half its tasks efficiently. This busy period saw the welcome arrival of 848 Squadron, which arrived in HMS *Albion* at the end of April 1965. Their sophisticated, two-engined Wessex Mk 5 aircraft appeared ideal for the job in Borneo and we wished them the best of luck in their commission, though we imagined that Sarawak still had a few problems tucked up its sleeve. We also hoped that as the Mark 5 pounded up and down the Rajang, Baleh, Balui, Katibas, etc., they would appreciate the pathfinding and endeavour by 845 Squadron that had gone before them.

Although primarily a Squadron formed to operate with Royal Marine Commandos on amphibious operations, it had been our good fortune to operate and work with the following units during our tour in Malaysia and elsewhere:

40 Commando Royal Marines

42 Commando Royal Marines

43 Commando Royal Marines

29 Commando Regiment, Royal Artillery

1/2nd Gurkha Rifles

2/2nd Gurkha Rifles

1 /6th Gurkha Rifles

1/7th Gurkha Rifles

1/10th Gurkha Rifles

2/10th Gurkha Rifles

1st Greenjackets

1st Battalion, Royal New Zealand Regiment

2nd Battalion, Singapore Infantry Regiment

2nd Battalion, Scots Guards

1st Battalion, Royal Ulster Rifles

3rd Battalion, Royal Malay Regiment

4th Battalion, Royal Malay Regiment

6th Battalion, Royal Malay Regiment

8th Battalion, Royal Malay Regiment

Federation Artillery

Special Air Service

Guards Independent Parachute Company

Gurkha Parachute Company

2nd Battalion Parachute Regiment

84 Squadron, Royal Engineers

Malayan and Sarawak Police Field Force

By the end of May 1965, 845 Squadron aircraft, both ashore and from the ship, had flown 10,000 hours since *Bulwark* left Plymouth. This figure was probably a record for a British Helicopter Squadron at that time, and represented a maintenance and flying effort for which all members could be justly proud, though the cost had been high. Ashore, our Wessex, Whirlwind and Hiller aircraft in the first 12 months flew 6,064 hours, including 54 night sorties, and lifted 32,629 passengers, 3,224,285 lb of stores and 903 CASEVACs. Impressive as these statistics are, those who had drunk their Tiger beer in Sibu, Simanggang or Nanga Gaat will realise they painted only part of the picture in Sarawak. The months were marked with a series of celebrations or milestones. These included: an Air Day at Sibu to celebrate the 50th Anniversary of the Fleet Air Arm; champagne on the Sibu runway to celebrate the 1,000 flying hours of 'L' (after that, many more aircraft were urged over this hurdle); Christmas 1964 was celebrated to the benefit of the children and old folks of Sibu (and the Squadron, of course) and even tuak was consumed to mark the 10,000 hours flown since the previous Squadron first landed in Borneo from *Albion*. In September, 1964 the Squadron flew 1,000 hours, again thought to be a record for a British Helicopter Squadron.

And, finally, the Squadron was awarded the coveted Boyd Trophy, awarded annually for the finest contribution to Naval Aviation. The citation of the Flag Officer Naval Air Command, Vice Admiral Sir Richard Smeeton, was a fitting summary of a remarkable commission in 845 Squadron. It said:

'By their operations and exercises both ashore and afloat, 845 Squadron set a standard of efficiency in Borneo unsurpassed by any other Squadron deployed there and made a considerable contribution to the defence of Malaysia. They earned the praise of all. Their flying was of the highest order and the enthusiasm and professional ability of the maintenance ratings enabled the Squadron to achieve an outstandingly high serviceability rate and the distinction of meeting every demand made upon it.'

Reminiscences of Operations in the Simanggang Area - 1964

By Lieutenant Peter Gregson 845 Squadron (Pilot Wessex 1)

For much of April through to June 1964 I was based in Simanggang, about an hour's flying time south of Sibu, close to the Indonesian border. Usually the task was flying local operations in the Jambu area in support of the resident battalion, in this case the 2nd/7th Gurkhas. It was a single-aircraft (Wessex Mk1) detachment with occasional increases to two when the need arose, or an aircraft could be spared from the main base at Sibu.

The small RN Detachment, consisting of one or two officers and about 10 men, was housed in Army accommodation in the small town of Simanggang. We lived in purpose-built atap huts with electricity and cold, running water, and used the Army's messing facilities. The airfield from where we operated was located about half a mile outside the town. It could only operate small aircraft, with its short runway surrounded by secondary jungle, and this made for an interesting spectator sport of watching the resident Army Air Corps Auster, known affectionately as TWA (Teeny Weeny Airways) stagger into the air with its rate of climb of around 100 ft per minute, and just clear the end of the runway. Air Traffic Control was provided by a lone RAF Pilot Officer, who incidentally had been a former midshipman at Dartmouth. His duties were hardly taxing, with the limited number of RN and Army movements and just the occasional visit from an RAF Single or Twin Pioneer based in Kuching. It was important to maintain professional standards at least for safety reasons, but on one occasion, when the Commander (Air) was visiting from *Albion*, these slipped. An aircraft was away on operations, but had failed to file an 'Airmove Departure' message; and, being unable to contact him by radio, it was impossible to check his whereabouts. This caused some fluttering in the dovecots when he returned – and not surprisingly so!

Simanggang was the capital of the Second Division of Sarawak and a reasonably civilised place from which to operate. The terrain was easier to navigate and landing sites more clearly marked than in other parts of Sarawak, and it had better radio communications than some other places the Squadron was used to. For example there was no need to airdrop food or the 44-gallon drums of AVTUR as there was an adequate, and generally secure, graded road to Kuching where our supplies came from, even if the journey took the best part of a day. By air it was only 55 minutes.

The flying was both rewarding and intensive, and during my nine weeks there I accumulated over 120 event-free flying hours. Although there was little time for recreation, I did manage one visit to a longhouse, drink a little arak and meet some Ibans, who were most agreeable and welcoming; and their loyalty to the Crown appeared unquestioning, with pictures of the royal family adorning the walls of the longhouse. These were indeed the halcyon days, with a great deal of latitude given to conduct flying operations as one saw fit. The primary task was to provide support for Army operations in any way we could. This loose directive gave a great deal of freedom, with a splendid opportunity to use initiative, but there was a down-side, namely that excessive enthusiasm did once lead to an accident with tragic results; but more of that later. Morale in the Detachment was excellent, and there was an intense sense of mission to do everything possible to assist the Gurkhas, with whom we built up an excellent working relationship.

The flying task in providing this support was relatively straightforward and consisted largely of logistic transfers of men and materiel to tactical landing sites. Occasionally, there were prisoners to be brought back for interrogation and, on one occasion, three unidentified heads, neatly parcelled-up in atap, were transported back for investigation. The odd body of a dead Indonesian also required airlifting out, which was always memorable for the characteristic extremely sickly smell akin to strong body odour that all corpses had in that climate.

The flexibility of operating helicopters was, of course, of huge benefit to the Gurkhas as it saved an immense amount of time lugging equipment and ammunition through the jungle, and it added to morale by providing speedy evacuation of any wounded personnel. There was also a tactical dimension in providing the ability to move troops quickly around the theatre to counter any incursion.

It has to be admitted that all this intensive flying was limited to daytime only, which coincided with the Gurkhas' requirements; but routine instrument and night flying practice were suspended as engine hours were reserved for operational flying, which could have made life a little difficult in a night-time emergency, but fortunately the occasion never arose at Simanggang whilst I was there.

Around this time there was growing concern that our aircraft were defenceless against any enemy aircraft or ground attack, and it was decided to fit two ancient and unsuitable fixed, forward-firing .303 machine-guns. Duly, these weapons were fitted and gun functioning trials carried out, with sighting arrangements that were primitive at best, and involved placing a chinagraph cross on the windscreen. We were issued with no Rules of Engagement and assumed we could have a pot-shot at anything that looked like something Indonesian. However, this was never put to the test as it quickly became apparent that these weapons would be utterly useless, and only added unnecessary weight to the aircraft. They were soon removed, never to be seen again during my time there. Similarly, in the tactical situation obtaining in the Simanggang area of operations, it was felt unnecessary to issue personal weapons for aircrew self-defence, which would have been the Sterling sub-machine-gun. This may or may not have been a sensible decision but, in the event, they were never needed and might have been more trouble than they were worth.

By the time the Simanggang Detachment had been established a new Commanding Officer had joined the Squadron fresh from UK but who, nevertheless, was an old hand at the Commando game. One of the things he said to all pilots shortly after arrival was that he required all aircraft to have a 'vertical performance' before approaching a landing site. This was because climatic conditions in Borneo, where temperatures averaged around 30° C with high humidity, caused a steep deterioration in engine performance (you could get the revs but not the torque). If this order was obeyed to the letter, it would have meant a significant reduction in payload, and therefore would have affected our support to the Gurkhas. Following the age-old principle that orders were for the obedience of fools and the guidance of wise men, this instruction was liberally interpreted in the Simanggang area. If a pilot didn't have the required 'vertical performance', he had to be very accurate in his full-power approach to the landing site before picking up the ground cushion. The landing sites were usually fairly tight, and the opportunity to 'go round again' if the pilot got it wrong was lost early in the descent. He was then committed to the approach come what may.

Although inherently dangerous, this procedure worked well except on one occasion a pilot did misjudge his approach to landing, with tragic consequences. This occurred on a routine flight towards the end of the period, when a helicopter carrying the second in command of the 2nd/7th Gurkhas crashed into the side of a landing site perched on a hill and rolled down it. It finally came to rest when a tree stump plunged through the open cabin door, pinioning the second in command's arm to the side wall of the aircraft, making it impossible for him to move. Very fortunately, it so happened that one of the passengers was the battalion Medical Officer, but who was travelling without any medical equipment. However, he did have an army clasp-knife, with which he was able to carry out an amputation. He was later awarded the George Medal.

I have a personal tailpiece to this unfortunate story, involving a dream. The Gurkha daily routine started early with miscellaneous duties, and it was not until around 1000 that a full breakfast was served, and the day's operations got under way. This suited the Detachment very well, as it was impossible to fly before mid-morning as the usual fog had not yet burned off. On this particular day the fateful flight departed late morning with the 2 i/c embarked, leaving me behind with little to do. At around normal lunch-time I repaired to the Officers' Mess, where I had the usual light meal consisting of a 'cheese toasty' with a glass of beer, and then went to sleep in a chair. I then had an extraordinary dream of 'seeing' a helicopter hitting the side of a hill and rolling down the side. The dream ended abruptly with me waking up to the sound of the telephone and being told of the accident. Later that day I flew the 2 i/c to Kuching where, on being stretchered out of the aircraft, he waved to me with his uninjured arm. He was then taken off to hospital before being sent to Singapore for major surgery. An amazingly brave man.

It was about this time that word was reaching us of a row brewing in the MOD between the RAF and the Navy over Flight Safety. It was becoming clear that the RN accident rate appeared to be higher than the RAF's, with the cause being a source of much heated debate. Setting aside the fact that the RN flew primarily over the sea, and that in Borneo the RN was flying more hours than the RAF, it was becoming clear that the two Services were ideologically opposed to each other. On the one hand, the RAF did everything 'by the book', and woe betide anyone who stepped out of line. The RN on the other had a much more relaxed, but positive 'can do' approach where, depending on the circumstances, aircrew could be supported by higher authority if things went wrong – taking into consideration the operational situation, weather conditions, etc. This philosophy had a lot to commend it, and the job got done much quicker and better, although I have to admit that, on some occasions, the RAF could have a point.

This inter-Service bickering about safety was brought sharply into focus when the RAF replaced the RN at Simanggang. A most uncrab-like Crab and his Whirlwind Mk10 were selected to take over and he was surprised to see how far the RN departed from official guidelines. He was uncrab-like because he fully understood where we were coming from, but said sadly that, if he operated in a similar manner and something went wrong, he would be for the high jump. He particularly mentioned our interpretation of the rules about recommended glide-path angles, and the landing areas that were not quite level with all tree stumps removed within a certain distance. All this must have come as quite a shock to the waiting Gurkhas, who did all the construction work, and I must admit I had a tinge of sympathy for him!

In early June 1964, responsibility for operational flying in the Simanggang area was handed over to the RAF and all RN personnel returned to the main base at Sibu, where we resumed operations in the Third Division.

Junglie Hiller

By Lieutenant Paul Barton RN - Pilot 845 Squadron (Hiller 12E)

A Role is Born. It is unlikely that many people now are aware of the brief moment in Fleet Air Arm history (less than two years) when the Hiller 12E helicopter was numbered amongst its front-line strength. An interesting enough tale in its own right, its main significance lies in the fact that it was the first link in the chain of evolution that led to the Royal Marines 3 Commando Brigade Air Wing.

Rumour had it that the idea was born in early 1963, when the then Flag Officer Naval Flying Training (Rear Admiral Percy Gick) and the head of the 6-year-old Army Air Corps (Brigadier Napier Crookenden) were discussing matters of mutual interest over a sociable glass. The suggestion was made that the Army's expertise in the use of light helicopters in the reconnaissance, Forward Air Control, observation, etc., roles might have something to offer to Navy Commando squadrons. Army response was, as always, enthusiastic and helpful, so the show got on the road. 705 Squadron had fairly recently re-equipped with the Hiller 12E from the old under-powered, four-wheeled 12B model for basic helicopter flying training and, since its performance was much akin to the Army's Bell 47 G-3B, it seemed the ideal machine for the purpose.

So it was that a 705 instructor (Lt Peter Deller) found himself taking a Hiller to Middle Wallop for the role conversion and Operational Flying Training, prior to converting the two designated pilots (myself and Sub Lt Mike 'Mini' Thompson), and in turn taking us through the Middle Wallop OFT. Once there, we really learnt the arts of map-reading at ultra-low level - measured in inches rather than feet! - concealment, confined-area operation, tactics, covert observation, etc., during the late summer and autumn of 1963. A marvellous time, spectacularly enhanced by a vigorous social life in the heart of Christine Keeler country!

In January 1964 Mike Thompson and I took our mighty steeds to join 706B Flight (Lt Cdr Brian Sarginson), an embryo Wessex 1 Commando squadron working up at RNAS Culdrose in Cornwall to embark in HMS *Bulwark*. It was then to proceed to the Far East to beef up 845 Squadron (Lt Cdr Tank Sherman), already ashore in support of military operations mounted in response to Indonesia's Confrontation in Borneo.

Our Hillers aroused a degree of amusement at first, which was largely replaced by respect when we showed the Junglies how we could use them. The 12E was a robust little dual-control three-seater in which the solo or student pilot sat in the centre surrounded by an array of about a dozen switches and dials, with the instructor, when carried, in the left-hand seat. This arrangement we rapidly reversed for single-pilot operation for two reasons. Unsupervised passengers tended to strap themselves in round the concealed left-hand collective lever and, with no windscreen wipers, forward vision was hopeless through the centre of the bubble canopy in heavy rain, a phenomenon we were to encounter in spades - or more accurately buckets - in Borneo. It was powered by a gutsy, unblown 305 HP Lycoming six-cylinder piston engine, initiated by an utterly reliable electric starter, that propelled the helicopter through the sky at a mind-blowing maximum speed (Vmax) of 83 knots (although 75-80 with a 70-knot cruise were more realistic planning figures). Engine/rotor RPM were manually controlled by a twist-grip throttle on the collective lever. Fuel capacity was 38 Imperial gallons (46 US) of AVGAS, good for about two and a half hours airborne under normal conditions.

The flying controls were unpowered, cyclic control being achieved aerodynamically by large pitch changes on two short-radius, wide-chord paddles mounted at ninety degrees to the two high-inertia main rotor blades. What there was of the machine, apart from cockpit bubble, engine and rotors, was painted in the current sandy commando colour, and the whole thing worked like a dream. The high-inertia rotor made engine-off landings a particular delight and, although illegal without an instructor also on board, I practised them solo *ad nauseam*, since future survival might well depend on a high level of skill in that area. If so minded, one could set take-off Rotor RPM on the ground, close the throttle, lift to the hover, spot turn through 90° and land again under full control. Incidentally the Bell 47, with an even higher-inertia rotor, was reputed to be able to achieve 270°, but I never saw it proved. Ultimately, I developed the ability to close the throttle within any part of the flight envelope and still land safely – but I never told anyone, since it was theoretically impossible and, as I've said, illegal!

Our early tasks while working up to Operational Readiness were covert reconnaissance, Forward Air Control and assault lead/guide. The last was a bit tricky in that we were notably slower than the Wessex, but we got round that by launching early to be in the critical position when the big boys arrived, and by using our concealment skills to take short cuts. It was a neat trick, low-level map-reading both for oneself and someone else in another bit of sky, but we got reasonably adept at it. The Operational Readiness Inspection itself was conducted at Predannack satellite airfield on the Lizard peninsula and went very well, with one notable exception - the re-arrangement by myself of some 270 yards of GPO telephone wire that I had failed to see in my enthusiasm. Apart from a slightly scratched bubble and a bent pitch-change rod, the Hiller was undamaged as, aside from ringing ears following a robust verbal de-brief from Admiral Gick himself, was I! However, the incident did have a beneficial side-effect - that of achieving an abrupt and long overdue termination of communications between myself and a not-so-young lady who dwelt at the Lizard!

A fortnight later, in March '64, 706B embarked in HMS *Bulwark* and headed for the Far East, via an exercise in Libya (not such a popular venue these days!) to warrant our sand-coloured paint jobs, finally arriving off Sarawak at the beginning of April. The plan now was for the enhanced 845 Squadron (18 Wessex 1 and 2 Hillers, plus reserves) to split evenly. One half was to remain in *Bulwark* for exercises and to sustain the financial viability of the various messes and clubs of the Singapore shore establishments HMS Simbang and Terror, the other was to remain ashore in Sarawak. Personnel would change round approximately every three months. And so it worked out, with me having the privilege of introducing the Hiller to Borneo on 6 April. The action did not take long to unfold!

Two days after arrival I was tasked to fly to Sarekei, a small, pleasant town on the coastal plain some 40 miles away, to collect a prisoner to bring back for questioning. Lt Geoff Thompson, the 845 Operations Officer and an old friend, accompanied me, and the wisdom of our unconventional seating arrangement rapidly became clear. Warned that the prisoner might be less than happy with plans for his immediate future, we placed him in the right-hand seat away from all controls with Geoff, complete with 'gat', as the buffer-zone in the middle, and off we set. With no doors on, the view our passenger had of the world around and beneath him, particularly in steep turns to the right, was superb and appeared to hold his undivided attention throughout the flight!

However, that proved to be a mere divertissement compared with what was to follow two days later. In order to set the scene, it would be helpful to describe the terrain and aeronautical environment of our patch.

The Third Division. For the duration of the Hiller's front-line existence, 845's primary role was to provide military helicopter support in the Third Division of Sarawak, with a detachment at Simmangang in the Second Division. The Third Division, although not particularly active in the military sense, was a very large area that offered more than enough challenge and excitement without unfriendly bullets flying around. In very rough terms it was a territory measuring some 300 miles east to west from the coast to the Indonesian border, by about 100 miles wide. The flat, largely waterlogged coastal plain gradually gave way, via partially-cultivated or secondary jungle-covered foothills, to the primary jungle-covered mountains of the hinterland, in which there were two small towns, Kapit and Belaga, and tiny areas of longhouse habitation and cultivation established adjacent to the rivers.

Rivers in fact provided the only means of inland transport - other than aircraft - the chief of which was the Rajang, a massive waterway which had its source near the border with Indonesian Borneo and which then flowed a circuitous route the entire length of the Third Division. On its banks lay most of the notable townships of the region, the biggest being Sibu, some 30 miles from the coast, with its properly established airport at which 845 had its main base. Sibu was an attractive, quite large, thriving and very friendly town inhabited by Europeans (mostly British), Chinese, plus Ibans and Dyaks - the native races of Borneo - plus the Army garrison. The RN was made incredibly welcome by all, who could never do enough to make our lives as enjoyable as possible.

The main forward base was at Nanga Gaat, an idyllic spot some 110 miles further inland, well into the mountainous region, and was a small miracle of military and nautical improvisation. Built on the confluence of the river Gaat (hence the name) with the Baleh, which further downstream fed the Rajang, it had five individual helicopter landing pads, mostly cut into the side of a small hill, and a number of bamboo and atap buildings. These were erected on stilts and connected by a series of elevated walkways, the purpose being to allow some air circulation and to give protection against the larger nocturnal creepy-crawlies.

The first to be constructed, and the most important, was the Anchor Inn, a splendidly-equipped hostelry with public and lounge bars, for junior rates and officers/senior rates respectively, which could provide almost unlimited quantities of cold Tiger beer. The other buildings were of an equally high standard, comprising a number of dormitories (including a very comfortable guest house!), galley and communal dining hall, toilets and showers, maintenance offices and a radio shack (call sign 'GRAPNEL').

Major supplies arrived from Kapit, the nearest town about 40 miles down-river, by longboats, hollowed-out tree-trunks powered by 40+ HP outboard motors that went like the clappers, and were landed by means of a cunning, home-made jackstay rig. Local labour was recruited from the ever-friendly Ibans, surely one of the most delightful races on earth - to their friends, at least - who in turn constantly invited us for convivial nocturnal gatherings in their longhouses. But that's another story!

There were two notable refuelling townships on the banks of the Rajang between Sibu and Nanga Gaat: Song at around the mid-point, and Kapit further inland. Song had two landing areas, one a small, elevated single-Wessex pad in the middle of the town close to the river's edge, the other a large padang (playing field) behind the town attached to the RC Mission. Kapit, likewise, had two landing areas: a rudimentary landing strip where the fuel was stored, and a large padang in the town on the water's edge overlooked by the cottage hospital - very convenient for the numerous MEDEVACs and CASEVACs 845 was called upon to carry out.

As an aside, on one occasion, fairly early in the morning, a Wessex landed on the padang with a medical casualty for the hospital. Such events always attracted a large and very interested audience, and this one was no exception. As it happened the pilot, one Lt Neil Burns-Thompson, one of our two Iban-speaking local liaison officers, had elected to land with the cabin door, and hence himself in the right-hand seat, facing the hospital. It also happened that Neil had decidedly overdone the tuak the previous evening during a longhouse visit. His stomach was therefore in a state of considerable rebellion, but which he had managed to keep in check until landing. However, once on the ground, it all became too much, and he threw up violently down the side of the Wessex, a performance that went down very big indeed with his audience and which earned him a standing ovation!

The inhospitable inland terrain consisted of a seemingly endless, random arrangement of hills and mountains - resembling a giant, dried prune - that gradually rose to meet the fairly-clearly-defined border ridge at around 5000 feet. The whole lot was topped with primary jungle whose almost unbroken canopy lay between 220 and 250 feet above ground level. An engine failure over that sort of country in our single-engined helicopters was not a welcome prospect; hence we tried to follow river routes whenever practical.

There was, however, one notable exception to the giant-prune topography. Kapit, being on the banks of the Rajang and on the more-or-less direct route from Nanga Gaat to Sibu, was a very frequent port of call. Belaga, on the other hand, was not, being out on a limb and very much further up the Rajang. Nonetheless, it was the civic centre of the Third Division highlands, had its own Twin Pioneer-capable airstrip, and was therefore a key operational port of call.

The route between Belaga and Nanga Gaat was, therefore, flown fairly regularly. However, as I explained earlier, for safety reasons we more or less followed the rivers, the Rajang down towards Kapit (apart from a monster double-hairpin at about half-way), then left up the Baleh to the Gaat, and vice versa. This added some 20 miles to the journey, but was a necessary good-sense complication. We therefore knew nothing of the nature of the territory directly between the two – until, that is, on one occasion when I left Belaga in the Hiller with insufficient time before nightfall to go the river route. I therefore went direct, leaving the Hose mountain range on my left - not that I really noticed.

I soon found myself flying over some of the most forbidding territory on earth. Elevated at some 3000 ft or so, it was a dead-flat plateau, maybe 10 or more miles across in the direction I was going, totally water-logged, with growth stunted to maybe 20 or 30ft, much less dense than elsewhere and with a ghastly, dead appearance. It was a seriously alarming landscape, which at the time immediately brought to mind Sir Arthur Conan Doyle's *Lost World* and conjured up visions of the most frightening creatures dwelling within. Should anything go wrong now, I knew, it would be 'curtains'. Happily, I crossed the territory safely, albeit at low level because, while I didn't like what I was seeing, I still wanted to see more, until I reached the end of the plateau and was, in effect, catapulted some 2000ft into the air as the plateau dropped away almost vertically. That was a seriously exhilarating (i.e. heart-thumping) flight experience, but one which I doubt anyone else flying single-engine helicopters saw - certainly not in my time in Borneo, anyway.

The weather was hot and wet, with overnight mist invariably shrouding the higher ground inland and rendering flying before 1000 and after 1800 almost impossible, a much appreciated phenomenon! There was never any wind, except for that generated by local thunderstorm activity, and it poured with rain almost every afternoon.

Navigation was something else! The only maps available in the early days were truly amazing. They consisted of large sheets of white paper covered in meaningless spider-like squiggles that became increasingly dense as the ground rose higher, until they reached an area to which noone had been before. There they abandoned the hopeless task of representing the terrain and were replaced by the legend 'Here Be Dragons'! The major rivers and mountains were indicated, as was the border ridge; however, the central massif, the Hose Mountains, together with the upper reaches of the Rajang and its associated tributaries, were misplaced by some 10 miles!

Despite the lack of topographical information, we did have two things going for us - the lack of wind, and nil magnetic variation. Once having located any particular point in terms of bearing and distance from another known point, it became a simple matter of compass heading and stopwatch to find it again, and it worked every time. All the up-country landing sites and some of the forward fuel dumps had been laboriously hacked out of the jungle by our troops and, with the limitation imposed by the Wessex 1's 60-foot winch-wire, those were virtually the only places they could go to by air. Still, there were plenty of them.

The military presence in the Third Division was provided by a number of regiments in rotation, a few British, but mostly Gurkhas and the Royal Malay Regiment. In addition, the SAS and Guards Paras provided deep penetration patrols, and the indigenous Police Field Force (PFF) of Iban trackers and scouts undertook guide and intelligence-gathering duties. The latter operated under the command of the redoubtable expat Major Bill Crennell, a splendid old Borneo hand who lived in downtown Sibu and who became a good friend. It was with the latter two covert forces that the Hiller became most involved.

Fig 35. Hiller gone native!

In at the Deep End! On 10 April 1964, 4 days after arrival in Borneo, while the Hiller and I were still acclimatising to the lowland environment around Sibu, we received the message that a four-man SAS patrol was in trouble near the eastern border, and urgently needed rescue from terrain in which the Wessex was helpless. Without further ado, I set off up the Rajang for Nanga Gaat, the first of many such journeys, re-fuelled, picked up Lt Rod Robertson and proceeded, mouth agape at the passing scene beneath, to Long Jawi, a military Forward Operating Base some 55 miles further into the mountains. There we took on more fuel and were briefed on the task. Rod was one of 845's most experienced jungle pilots who really knew his way around the wild uplands. He was also, incidentally, the other Iban-speaking liaison officer, and the closest friend I ever had.

Having learnt that an RAF Valetta transport aircraft was in the vicinity of the patrol and had established some form of communication with it, we set forth, in the company of a Wessex, to locate the missing men. It transpired that they had made contact with an Indonesian patrol and, contrary to normal covert practice, had had to shoot their way out. In the process of evading the enemy they had lost some of their vital supplies, were totally exhausted, unsure whether enemy contact had been completely broken, and were on the border. They badly wanted out. In at the deep end, me and my 12E, that was for sure!

Our first foray succeeded in identifying the rough location of the action, some 30-odd miles beyond Long Jawi, and allowed a plan to be formulated to evacuate the rescuees should I subsequently be able to reach them, their precise position still being unknown to us. The ground was horrendous - steep, cluttered, primary jungle slopes up to 5000 feet with, to me, no positively identifiable features apart from the border ridge. However, the plan seemed workable, so we returned to Long Jawi for more fuel and a second attempt at rescue.

On return to the scene, Rod and I elected to modify the search instructions issuing from the Valetta and apply our own thoughts to the problem, combining skills gained from his jungle and my Middle Wallop experiences - and almost immediately we were rewarded with success. The virtually carefree handling characteristics of the Hiller, once I had mastered the trick of aural RPM control, and the excellent visibility from the bubble cockpit, allowed us both to concentrate on the ground. We finally spotted our quarry at the bottom of an extremely deep, dark hole in the jungle, into which I would have to descend. Confined area landing practice on Salisbury Plain or at St Erth in Cornwall had hardly prepared one for this sort of thing! Anyway, having ensured that I could find the spot again, we called in the Wessex to the nearest landing site (a mile or so away, and just over the border ridge!), and transferred Rod to act as shepherd and shotgun. I then set about the hairiest bit of flying I have ever undertaken, before or since.

The SAS patrol was at the foot of a very steep valley, in which they had managed to fell one or two trees to make a minuscule landing site and a Hiller-size hole in the jungle canopy. The complete lack of wind allowed free selection of approach path, but even the best needed an almost vertical descent of nearly 1000 feet, with the last 300 feet being absolutely vertical. For the uninitiated, prolonged vertical descents in helicopters are very bad news, due to the phenomenon known as 'vortex ring' or 'power settling'. Airflow that has been propelled down through the rotor disc of a hovering helicopter naturally tends to spread out horizontally and dissipate. However, once a descent is initiated, this horizontal spread assumes, relative to the helicopter, a vertical component up round the outside of the downflow to form a potential vertical circulation pattern.

Unless the aircraft is descended very slowly and carefully, it can develop this potential circulation to complete the vortex loop. This sets up an endless-belt type of situation, in which the same air passes down through the disc, up round the outside and back down through the disc again, *ad infinitum*. The only sure way of recovering from the ensuing uncontrollable and high rate of descent is to resume forward flight and get into 'clean' air as quickly as possible. I was only too uncomfortably aware that this was not an option open to me, hence the descent was treated with a circumspection bordering on terror!

Once under the canopy it was an uncanny feeling, descending very slowly a further 200 feet or so into the heart of the jungle with the rotor tips feet from the surrounding tree-trunks. I was not absolutely sure that there were no ill-disposed persons about, or completely confident that I would be able to lift the patrol out without running out of power or hitting something. Actually, from my experience of the machine so far, I was reasonably confident about the power. Indeed, we subsequently found that up to about 5000 feet and 20°C it was just about capable of lifting its maximum all-up weight. Unfortunately, detailed performance graphs, or indeed any performance graphs at all, did not exist for our 12Es!

Having eventually landed safely in the patrol's midst, I discovered that they still had a hefty amount of kit. It became apparent that a minimum of three lifts up to the ridge site some 2500 feet above was going to be needed - twice with one man plus half the total kit, and once with the other two men. A rather daunting prospect, that amount of time at full power with nowhere survivable to go should the engine miss a beat or the noise attract unwelcome attention, but there was nothing else for it.

I lifted off with the first load and staggered vertically up and up and up, with those tree trunks still feet from the rotor tips, and a bare but nonetheless positive rate of ascent with the throttle hard on its stops. That engine was magnificent! Finally clear of the canopy, speed could be crept up to 20-30 knots to improve the rate of climb until I could get into forward flight proper for the short transit up to the ridge site. There I dropped my payload to embark in the Wessex, and went back for the next lot. In all, the three lifts took the best part of an hour and went without a hitch. However, relief at pulling out of the clearing for the last time, transferring the last load, re-embarking Rod for navigational purposes and setting off for Long Jawi was rather tempered by concern for my fuel situation. There was absolutely nowhere to land *en route*, and all that full-power work had not exactly helped the Lycoming's consumption figures. We finally made it after a heart-thumping, backside-twitching transit, to land on with the fuel gauge at zero after 2 hours and 5 minutes airborne. I had flown back at high level to conserve fuel and to be within autorotative range of Long Jawi as soon as possible, and had proved to my satisfaction that the stated quantity of unusable fuel (2½ pints) was a figure that had been properly researched!

Back at Long Jawi the RAF, who had been co-ordinating the overall rescue effort, wanted the patrol to stay overnight in the base's rudimentary facilities to be debriefed. However, we had other ideas. The light blue was severely outnumbered, the SAS was now in Navy hands - and we had the helicopters! Hospitality was next on the agenda, so we all refuelled again and legged it back to Nanga Gaat before nightfall for my - and the soldiers' - first introduction to the Anchor Inn and its legendary facilities. We ate and drank our fill in convivial and highly appreciative company under distinctly memorable circumstances, until I finally collapsed into bed in a state of advanced euphoria. A 'Mission Impossible' had been achieved, my beloved Hiller had won its spurs, and I had learnt an awful lot about jungle flying in the course of 6¼ hours airborne on my fifth day in Borneo! At that point I had a total of about 750 flying hours, of which some 130 were in the 12E.

Settling In. Having established with considerable panache that the 12E had a definite role to play in Borneo, while at the same time rendering any further 'theatre familiarisation' somewhat superfluous, employment quickly settled into a routine. Many missions involved the movement of one or two people - usually military or local government officers - around their parish, and the economical Hiller was clearly the ideal choice. Apart from the sheer flexibility of being able to stop and start almost anywhere with enough space to accommodate its rotor disc, its passengers travelled in much greater comfort than in the back of a Wessex and, of course, had an incomparably better view of the passing terrain. As a 'nice set of rotors' it caught on a treat and was much in demand as a means of seeing Borneo, whether from a high-level, panoramic viewpoint or flat-hatting down the Rajang carving up longboats!

The main drawback suffered by the aircraft was its lack of ability to communicate with the outside world. Its entire avionics suite consisted of the notorious 12-pre-set channel UHF PTR 170 radio, a gadget of dubious value even in the UK and which, more than 5 miles from Sibu, was about as much use as the fitted ashtrays with the cabin doors removed! However, air to air it worked well enough to pass 'Ops Normal' calls to the odd passing Wessex, should one happen to be airborne in the vicinity. The facts that 'ops' were anything but 'normal', and that almost no one had the remotest idea where they were taking place anyway, were treated as minor details not to lose sleep over. In the event, this lack of communications caused no direct problems, luckily enough, just a little worry from time to time.

On one occasion, after 8.05 hours airborne from Nanga Gaat, ranging deep into the wild hinterland mapping the Danum River (see 'The Dapper Mappers') without having spoken by radio to a soul, darkness descended before I could get home. Night flying, except in the direst emergency, was strictly for the bats since, in that part of the world, it could only be carried out at low level along rivers, and placed total reliance on the prolonged satisfactory function of the landing light. Prudence (amongst other things) therefore dictated that I remained overnight at Kapit. There, via a somewhat whimsical telephone link to Sibu and an extremely capricious HF link to the Gaat, I was ultimately able to let the latter know where I was before my unexplained absence completely soured the Detachment Commander's nightly intake of Tiger!

One of the most gratifying features of the Hiller was its stunning - for its day - performance hot and high. One remote but fairly frequently visited and remarkably open landing site was located about 50 miles from the nearest refuelling point at about 3000 ft. It lay in a bowl surrounded by much higher ground and maintained a steady 30+°C throughout the times we could reach it. Under those particular conditions of distance, temperature and altitude, the Wessex 1 was only capable of landing with one fully-equipped passenger. My 12E, on the other hand, was quite happy at its normal maximum All Up Weight, so could carry twice as many! The resulting 'heavy lift' mileage gained by the Hiller crew regularly lightened our spirits throughout the entire deployment! Similar circumstances of lifting capacity prevailed near the top of the 8000 ft Hose mountains, only about 30 miles from the Gaat, but at that height even my big-hearted little helicopter was running a bit short of puff.

As appreciation of the Hiller's versatility spread, its lack of stores-carrying capacity became felt. It did have quite a good 'boot' in the forward end of the tail cone just aft of the engine, but it was not really safely accessible unsupervised with the rotors turning. In any case it was always fairly well topped-up with tool kit, running spares, survival kit and any overnight gear I thought may come in useful - sarong, flip-flops, case of Tiger, that sort of thing. We therefore, under Iban guidance, constructed bamboo panniers lashed to the cross-members of the skid undercarriage assembly. After a few reasonably cautious flight trials they were pronounced fit for action; they served admirably for carrying modestly-sized, boxed stores thereafter.

It was on occasion necessary to betake oneself to the big city, Kuching in the First Division, for the purpose of liaison with military HQ and other, less formal, agencies. This involved a run each way of some 140 miles and thus necessitated a re-fuel at the RAF-run airfield before returning. Until I got wise to the procedure, I parked as ordered at the end of a queue of petrol-driven aircraft awaiting refreshment. These comprised Valettas, Hastings, Bristol Freighters and the like, all with large tanks to sustain their big, thirsty Hercules-variant engines. After waiting an hour or so, it was apparent that the one bowser was not going to reach the Hiller in time for me to conduct any worthwhile business in town. I therefore politely asked the operator if he could squeeze me in between the heavies: 'It won't take a moment; I only want about 30 gallons'. I will never forget his dead-pan response: 'Is that straight or mixture, sir?' I got my fuel, and a friend and, by judicious subsequent parking, suffered no further delays!

Most refuelling was, of course, self-help at the numerous fuel dumps established throughout the jungle. At first, being the only AVGAS-burning customer in the Third Division, this was distributed in little, 5-gallon disposable tins for the 12E's supposed exclusive use. Trouble was, not only did they tend to 'weep' in the high temperature and humidity, allowing the contents to become water-contaminated, they were also a bit too disposable while full. Thus the parameters of 'exclusive' customership had a habit of widening to embrace a goodly percentage of longboat operators in the vicinity, who thereafter enjoyed a spectacular, if short-lived, performance advantage over their rivals! With the re-introduction of the venerable piston-engined (ex 846 NACS) Whirlwind 7 to the Sarawak scene in December 1964 to take the load off the Wessex for lighter tasks, proper gasoline supplies were widely established. That is not to say that remnants of 44-gallon drums were not negotiable - they were, but to more mutual advantage than hitherto!

Much of the Hiller's day-to-day employment involved the movement of personnel around the Third Division's central region based on Bankit. This community was located about 20 miles south of Song, thus refuelling stops at the latter became a regular feature of life. The fuel was located at the padang attached to the Roman Catholic Mission just behind the town. This establishment consisted mainly of a large, open building fitted out with benches and tables. It served as chapel, schoolroom and general meeting-place, and was run by a splendid and convivial Dutch father. On my first visit I naturally called to pay my respects, and to introduce myself and my new-fangled flying machine to his ken. Thereupon a new and rewarding friendship immediately blossomed. Having shown me round his patch - which didn't take long - hospitality was next on the agenda and I was introduced to his pride and joy, the central feature of the Mission.

Situated at a well-chosen spot in the public area but close to his living quarters, from where he could conveniently monitor all goings-on in the vicinity, was an enormous, AVTUR(aviation kerosene)- powered 'fridge, the contents of which were revealed to me as consisting entirely of Tiger beer! Without further ado he helped us to refreshment and we sat down to discuss matters of moment.

It transpired that he had no difficulty in reconciling his religious beliefs with the military activities around him - after all our objectives, the welfare of the people of Sarawak, were very much the same. However, the image of snorting Wessex, disgorging fearsome, rifle-clutching troops, tended on occasion to bear a little heavily with him. My Hiller, on the other hand, presented anything but a warlike mien and was therefore much easier to recognise as being on the side of the angels. We were able to develop these enjoyable and philosophical trains of thought during many subsequent stops which, over the coming months, proved most welcome after the hot and energy-sapping work involved in hand-refuelling even something as small as the 12E.

Social Diversions. Working with the Police Field Force in their semi-covert monitoring of movements in the vicinity of the border involved regular visits to those longhouse communities living nearby. By their very location, they naturally had good intelligence about any unusual activity in their neighbourhood; however, this inevitably placed them in the front line in the event of an armed Indonesian incursion. It was, therefore, not only essential to see that they were motivated to stay on side and report anything suspicious, it was also vital to ensure their proper and visible protection against the threat of enemy action. It was a field in which the Hiller proved to be the perfect additional tool.

The central community of the area, Bankit, was a small village comprising a school and associated padang laid out in a natural bowl, surrounded by longhouse-like dwellings built on stilts at various levels on the hilly ground immediately nearby. It was the ideal garrison spot for the Gurkha military presence, rapid deployment to any adjacent trouble spot being readily facilitated by 845 Squadron's Wessex from their base at Sibu, some 40 minutes' flying time away.

Mobility was the name of the game to ensure the widely-felt presence of a small number of troops over a relatively large area, and this was in part achieved through regular visits by the local military commanders on the ground to every isolated longhouse community in the region. Since it generally only involved the movement of a couple of people at a time, the 12E was the obvious choice of vehicle. Not only was it manifestly more economical and less disruptive than the big troop-carriers, the view it offered provided the soldiers with the ideal means of familiarising themselves, in as much detail as they wished, with the overall layout of their territory. It was also, of course, just the thing for helping Bill Crennell to keep tabs on his PFF trackers and any intelligence they might have gleaned, hence his frequent use of the service and our developing friendship.

Superimposed on this well-organised military presence was the need to maintain a visible and effective 'hearts and minds' campaign, not only to bolster civilian morale and underpin the unity of purpose of us all but also, in the longer term, to safeguard regional political stability. In practical terms from 845's viewpoint, this mainly meant providing a regular 'flying doctor' service to outlying longhouse dwellings and, in the event of serious or urgent cases, providing medical and casualty evacuation (MEDEVAC/CASEVAC) to the nearest hospital. Not only did these facilities prove extremely popular, they offered a less obvious military benefit.

Although this area was relatively well-populated compared with the wild territory further inland, people were still very thinly spread. Moreover, the ground itself, while less forbidding than that found beyond Nanga Gaat, was nonetheless totally inimical to the operation of helicopters without human assistance. Apart from the Bankit padang and the major townships, there was simply nowhere to land, and winching was not a practical proposition. It was therefore necessary to establish numerous landing sites, both in strategic locations adjacent to the border and at each pocket of human habitation.

Construction of the former was fairly straightforward. A team of soldiers armed with explosives and cutting equipment was dropped at an already-constructed site as near as possible to the next one required. They were then invited to march to the appropriate spot, blow a suitably-sized hole in the jungle canopy and use the resulting logs to construct a robust and stable platform. Once established, the process was repeated for the next site, and so on.

However, sites adjacent to longhouses needed a rather different technology. This required lopping the top off the nearest convenient hill, levelling and stabilising the resulting plateau, and building a flight of steps to the top. Due to the enthusiasm with which our helicopter facilities were greeted, the Ibans and Dyaks needed no prodding to undertake the necessary construction in order to secure their availability for themselves. Good, well-maintained landing platforms soon became valuable community status symbols in their own right.

So much so that one day, Bill Crennell turned up at our operations room with an odd, but urgent, request. It seemed that the residents of one of the remoter longhouses in the region, having got wind of the value of possessing a dedicated landing site had, on their own initiative, gone ahead and built one. However, having completed the task, no helicopters came, from which they could only conclude that it was not big enough. So they set to and removed another layer from the hill, thereby substantially increasing the landing area, but again no helicopters arrived. Deciding that it must still be too small, they set about repeating their endeavours, at which point Bill got to hear of the situation. His urgent request to us was to go and pay them a visit before they unnecessarily flattened any more of the surrounding jungle.

Readily accepting the importance of the mission, we decided that proper recognition of the stalwart efforts of these good people warranted something with a little more impact than could be provided by the Hiller. A Wessex was clearly indicated. Moreover, since proper participation in the commissioning ceremony was manifestly going to involve the consumption of more than just a token sip of tuak, it was going to need two pilots - one exclusively for social duties, the other to ensure a safe return to Sibu on completion. Ian Thomson, with whom I was to share a singular adventure later in this deployment, drew the short straw and off we set. On arrival in the vicinity of the longhouse, the reason for Bill's concern became plainly evident. The landing site was beautifully constructed - and huge!

Anyway, having circled to attract attention, we duly landed and shut down, to be warmly greeted by every man, woman and child in the place. As predicted, the formalities were liberally lubricated and happily I was able to play a full part, without the constraints normally associated with having to fly back on completion of such festivities. Ian good-naturedly remained philosophical about his role in the proceedings!

It was not the only social event of note in the area. The Gurkha garrison in Bankit decided one day to hold a party for the dual benefit of themselves and the local inhabitants. Now these wonderful troops tend not to do things by halves. So, when they wanted a visiting guest of honour to arrive in some style to get things under way, the 12E provided the ideal means for me to fulfil this starring role to their complete satisfaction. The appropriate arrangements having been made, I duly arrived as dusk was falling, treated the assembled multitude to a few unnecessarily flamboyant manoeuvres and associated clattering of rotor blades, before landing and shutting down in the padang. I was then escorted into the school hall, invited to sit on the floor surrounded by grinning Gurkhas, and the thrash, chiefly comprising a number of bizarre and highly amusing 'entertainments', got into its swing.

Refreshments took the form of Tiger beer - which I knew I could handle in any sensible quantity that I could drink, and Gurkha rum (of identical lethality to Navy rum) - which I knew I most certainly could not! However, it was no good trying to refuse the latter libation on the weak grounds of being responsible for the safety of one of Her Majesty's pricier assets. The hosts' exclusive aim under such circumstances is the total paralysis of their guest, preferably accompanied by him throwing up in as public and comprehensive a fashion as possible. In any case, hadn't they now assumed full responsibility for guarding my helicopter, so wasn't I now a free spirit? Fortunately, I knew enough of what to expect to enable me to parry with some dexterity their best efforts at rendering me insensible, enough at least for them to recognise that they had a challenge on their hands. The ensuing battle of wits lent a delightful piquancy to the evening's activities!

At the end of the night we considered the whole thing to be an honourable draw. On the one hand, I still have a vivid memory of emerging into the darkness of the padang to be confronted by an apparently unguarded Hiller. However, on taking a step closer to investigate, it suddenly and silently sprouted the salutary addition of a glinting kukri surmounted by an enormous set of grinning teeth! On the other, I also recall a weary climb up hundreds of steps to the stilted 'guest room' allocated to me, an obstacle that I could never have overcome without assistance. Anyway, I slept like a baby and duly arrived back at Sibu the next morning in full fighting trim and with the happiest of memories!

The Dapper Mappers. The ludicrous quality of the maps initially available to the military forces in Sarawak was fortunately recognised and considerable resources were brought to bear to improve the situation. Firstly, a complete aerial 3-D photographic survey was made of the region using DC3s, although the persistent cloud covering large parts of the area for much of the day made provision of 100% coverage a rather prolonged and frustrating business. Nonetheless, the early results of this activity were made available to us, and represented a quantum improvement over anything that we had before. However, without being dovetailed into a matching and comprehensive ground survey and triangulation programme, their accuracy, particularly with respect to height, had to remain suspect. This was where the Royal Engineers Topographers, the Topos - or 'Dapper Mappers' as we termed them - entered the picture and our lives.

They arrived pale from the UK, looking generally pretty un-military in newly-issued and not notably well-fitting jungle-green uniforms. However, the latter characteristic may have been due more to the distinctly individualistic shape and size of their wearers, rather than to any sartorial shortcomings on the part of their manufacturer! Despite that, we very soon discovered that any judgement of their skills based purely on physical appearances was seriously wide of the mark. They rapidly impressed us as being as dedicated and professional a team as one could hope to meet, whose calm, indeed awe-inspiring, courage in the face of the unknown was an example to us all. It was their task to get to and survey every key point in the wild, inland country that was the Third Division. It was our task to get them there, support them and get them safely back again.

By and large, this involved taking them as near as possible to the point they wished to survey and dropping them off to march to their chosen site. Once there, it was obviously in their best interests not to have to walk back again, hence they too needed to master the rudiments of landing-site construction, both to allow us to re-supply them and, once their task was complete, to bring them home again. However, since they only needed to deploy in very small numbers to any one location to achieve their primary mission, they were obviously short on the kind of physical resources needed to clear proper, helicopter-size holes in the jungle. On occasions when the necessary manpower could not be provided by the resident combatant military and they had to fend for themselves, the resulting need to extricate them from some pretty marginal landing sites tended to challenge our jungle-flying skills to the utmost!

A significant proportion of the critical area between the Rajang and the border south of Song and Bankit was dominated by a spectacular and almost perpendicular pinnacle of jungle-covered rock close to the river, the top of which constituted an invaluable surveying point. However, there was a snag. The top of this pinnacle was a very small and exposed area, with absolutely no means of human access or escape other than by helicopter. It also, due to its height, spent a considerable amount of time in cloud. Nonetheless, given patience and fortitude, the wealth of survey data potentially obtainable from such a vantage point rendered a spell at its summit a high priority in the Dapper Mappers' programme.

As we had anticipated, getting them up there in the first place was not particularly difficult, it being one of the few places where the 65-ft winch-cables of our Wessex could be used effectively. We merely had to wait until there was a reasonable chance that the top would remain clear of cloud for long enough to winch them down, then suck it and see. However, as we had also anticipated, getting them back off the site was another matter altogether!

After a number of failed bids it became clear that, in the interests of their safety and general well-being, we were going to have to employ a pretty unconventional technique to effect their recovery. It really was a horrible spot on which to be marooned: totally isolated, totally inaccessible, totally shelterless and tiny. This was not Hiller territory - its blind-flying instrument outfit was far too rudimentary to allow deliberate entry into cloud with the need for any form of precision flying. However, the ability to maintain a stable hover in space with the minimum of external visual references was one of the great strengths of the Wessex. It fell to Ian Thomson to put this quality to good use.

He brought his helicopter to a stabilised hover as close as possible against the vertical pinnacle below the cloud base. The lack of any wind again helped, in that it allowed him to choose the optimum hover heading for visual reference, and which would later be the key to a safe escape manoeuvre. With this heading held automatically, he was able to concentrate purely on fine-tuning his hover to remain within visual range of the pinnacle as he applied power and ascended slowly up its face.

Meanwhile, the unhappy Dapper Mappers at the top, being unaware of what exactly we had in mind for them, became considerably mystified by the clattering din which began to emanate from immediately beneath their feet and which got perceptibly noisier by the minute. Peering agape into the impenetrable gloom below, they were eventually rewarded by the spectacle of a set of thrashing main rotor-blades, followed by a tail rotor and, finally, the complete Wessex itself. It emerged from the encircling gloom like a slow-motion but violently energetic demon king and presented itself in their immediate midst!

By dint of manoeuvring to bring the main cabin door close up to the top of the pinnacle, Ian was able to find sufficient outside cues to hold a brief and somewhat tenuous hover. Maintaining three-dimensional equilibrium by sole reference to a patch of jungle located roughly in the vicinity of your right ankle is not a procedure calculated to prolong active life. The situation therefore demanded prompt action on the part of the mappers if they were to embark safely before the stability of the hover deteriorated to the point that Ian needed to be elsewhere in a hurry.

He need not have worried; the Topos had summed up the situation at a glance. As he brought the machine to a halt, they literally and unceremoniously flung their equipment and themselves into the back with such gusto that there was no need to even try and actually establish a hover. He was able to snatch full power for a moment, whilst simultaneously nosing forward to clear the pinnacle, before easing off to let the Wessex drop through the cloud, away from the only obstruction within miles, to the clear air below. Safely accomplished, he was able to bring his highly-relieved passengers back to Sibu for subsequent well-earned plaudits. Although, as I've said, it was a manoeuvre that could not have been accomplished in the Hiller, the technique was not lost on me since I could see that some aspects of it might come in handy in the future. And so, indeed, it proved.

Some time later, I found myself supporting the Topos in the wild, mountainous country beyond the Hose range mapping the Danum River, a task which, incidentally, involved some serious, long-range work. Operating from Nanga Gaat, the first phase was to fly to Long Gong, a rudimentary forward base some 35 miles beyond Long Jawi, itself about 55 miles inland from the Gaat. There I embarked 2 Topos and flew three mapping sorties lasting a total of 5 hours and 40 mins, before dropping them off, picking up my supporting maintainer and heading for home. By this stage it was getting late, the light was fading and there were no other helicopters within at least 70 miles of the place. I therefore elected to pick a slightly safer but longer route home, which meant that I could get only as far as Kapit in daylight. At this point, after a further 70 mins airborne, the light failed completely, forcing the overnight stay mentioned earlier.

One aspect of the mapping task itself involved taking the Dapper Mappers to various points chosen by themselves to confirm spot-height figures derived from analysis of the three-dimensional photographic survey. It being impossible to land anywhere but at the handful of prepared sites in this region, most of which in any case were at river/habitation level, it was necessary to carry out this checking process without disembarking. Hence, a steady hover at tree-top height was required while the Dapper Mappers did their thing. Furthermore, since any peaks selected were intermittently but frequently covered in cloud, a considerable degree of flexibility was required in choice of exact location for the spot-height checks in any given area.

Criteria for their selection, therefore, boiled down to three basic parameters: geographical suitability, freedom from cloud cover and the probability that that condition would remain long enough for the task to be carried out. The lack of any ability to report position via radio and the totally unforgiving nature of the terrain meant that complete reliance had to be placed on faultless function of both my Hiller and me - in short, it was an activity that demanded, and got, my fullest attention! Particularly one day when I got the selection equation slightly wrong!

Maintaining a sufficiently steady hover amongst the treetops for the Topos to be able to use their instruments effectively naturally required a great deal of concentration, at the expense of keeping as good a weather-eye out as I would have wished. On this occasion, I had selected a peak that I thought would remain clear of cloud for long enough to get the job done. To my consternation, it suddenly became borne in upon me that, while gazing steadfastly at my immediate surroundings, the cloud had crept up - or in this case, down - unnoticed and was about to envelop us. As I said, the Hiller was not really equipped for an instrument departure into clear air and, in any case, by this stage I had no means of telling where I might find any without hitting something solid first.

It was at this point that Ian's exploit sprang to mind. With the excellent visibility conferred by the 12E's bubble canopy, it should be possible to repeat his trick, but in reverse. So, having invited the Topo in the right-hand seat to keep a good look out behind and below, while I did the same on my side, I gingerly set about backing down the mountain. However, it was not quite as straightforward – or backward – as it might sound. The terrain, although steep, was not a steady downslope, but was strewn with minor valleys and gullies which, from time to time, reversed the local gradient. To protect the tail rotor, this meant that each time we met one I had to stop, turn through 180°, ascend the short rise to the top, turn round again and continue the descent - all without losing spatial orientation or clear sight of the treetops. Happily there was not too far to go so we fairly quickly, and with much relief, found our way back to the clear air again. Nonetheless, it had been a demanding little exercise which, although it taught me a lot, I had no wish to repeat. From then on I made good and sure that I did not have to.

Flying in support of the mappers continued throughout my time in Borneo with the 12E, and it remained a demanding and challenging role. However, it did produce two significant benefits, the first and more obvious being the gradual introduction of really first-class maps. These were naturally of huge operational benefit, particularly when familiarising new arrivals with this awesome, alien country, and their very existence constituted a permanent and tangible token of our vital role in their production.

The second, less immediate but ultimately more rewarding, benefit for the pilots involved was the acquisition of pure, fundamental, aircraft-handling skills that are simply not known or required today. There was a constant need for inch-perfect positioning while at the very limit of the helicopter's performance abilities, which themselves very much depended on the precision with which manual control of engine and rotor RPM was maintained. One slip could be fatal. We were thus compelled to develop levels of concentration, dexterity and understanding of the dynamics involved that imbued a deep and abiding sense of oneness between man and machine. Those of us who were there will never forget it, and for that we owe the mappers a great debt.

Problems. Our Hillers gave us splendid service throughout their front-line careers. They were not, however, completely trouble-free, although mechanically the machines proved 100% reliable. The problems that did arise ranged from the ludicrous to, ultimately, the tragic, and were due either to the extreme heat and humidity affecting the helicopters or to human shortcomings affecting the performance of the pilots.

To start with the comical. Following some routine maintenance on the *Bulwark*-based helicopter, the need arose for a ground run but the qualified pilot, Mini, was not available. No problem, though. All the newly-qualified Wessex pilots joining the Squadron had fairly recently completed their basic helicopter training on the 12E so, with a quick reminder from the Pilot's Notes on how to start the thing, any one of them should have been able to manage it. As it happened, one Mac Macpherson was given the job. There was, however, a subtle little trap to catch the unwary, into which Mac fell headlong!

As I explained earlier, when the Hiller was flown solo in the training role, the pilot occupied the centre seat, the rudder pedals for which were located either side of the centre pedestal console. The instructor, when carried, was the only one to use the left seat and its associated flying controls. When sitting on his own in the left-hand seat, however, the pilot was faced with three rudder pedals equally displaced in an even row in front of him, his own left and right pedals and the left pedal of the centre-seat controls. Mac, having seen us fly the aircraft from the left seat, naturally assumed that this was the operational way to do it and elected to occupy the same seat himself. He had not ground-run or flown the aircraft from this position before.

With rotors turning from right to left, as seen from the pilot's view, torque reaction will try to turn the aircraft's nose the opposite way, i.e. to the right about the main-rotor-mast axis. As power is increased on the ground to accelerate the rotors to their normal operating RPM, a small amount of left pedal is needed to counter this effect. Because conditions were flat calm, with no deck movement whatsoever, there had apparently been no need to lash the Hiller for this ground-run, although the adhesion between skids and flight deck surface was not brilliant at the best of times. In consequence, anticipating the need for an anti-torque input as he wound up the rotors, Mac duly fed in what he believed to be an appropriate amount of left pedal. Due no doubt to lack of recent familiarity, he put in a little too much.

The Hiller, accordingly, began to skid round to the left. Unfortunately Mac, when selecting a pedal for his right foot to occupy from the two available to him, had opted for the wrong one. He had chosen the one on his far right, the centre-seat left pedal, ignoring the one in the middle. He therefore had both feet on left pedals. In applying what he thought to be corrective right pedal, he had in fact added more left rudder, which naturally considerably exacerbated the problem. Indeed, the more he added, the worse it got! This resulted in the Hiller conducting a series of potentially lethal pirouettes on *Bulwark's* flight deck, amongst ground crew scattering for their lives, until Mac got his head round the problem. He then managed to close the throttle before the whole lot could hit anything solid or fall over the side to drop 50ft into the sea.

Not unnaturally, he came in for a great deal of ribbing for this debacle, which lasted until he pulled an absolute masterstroke at a subsequent RAF briefing. Although nothing to do with the Hiller story, it's worth telling anyway. The Wessex 1 was not blessed with the most reliable of powerplants and every so often aircraft not actually engaged in operational work would be grounded pending investigation into the loss of yet another due to engine failure. One such grounding occurred just as a large number of Malaysian government VIPs and Press were due to embark by helicopter in HMS *Bulwark* to witness a 'Shop Window' display of nautical power.

The seaborne element of 845 was cleared for one flight only to disembark to the RN Air Station at Sembawang in Singapore, and the taxi job was given to the RAF and their Whirlwind 10s based at nearby Seletar. The Navy was asked to provide a pilot to brief the Air Force on carrier operations, and again it was Mac who drew the short straw. He duly presented himself at the Seletar briefing room, to be confronted by the daunting spectacle of a host of RAF aircrew, ranging from assorted Group Captains and Wing Commanders at the front to the *hoi polloi* at the back. Initially nervous in the extreme, Mac's thespian proclivities soon came to the fore as he warmed to his task.

After a suitable introductory preamble, he explained that the way to join a commando carrier in a helicopter, having established radio contact with 'Flyco', was to approach from the port quarter. The aim then was to establish a stable hover, over the sea, alongside your designated, numbered spot marked on the flight deck, under the control of a marshaller. At this point, he told us later, inspiration struck, rendering him totally incapable of preventing what followed. 'Under his guidance, you then,' he vouchsafed, 'if you'll forgive the expression, gentlemen, crab in sideways!' Apart from some muffled splutterings from the back of the auditorium, it did not go down well! However, he eventually managed to escape in one piece to relate the tale of his temerity to an extremely appreciative Squadron audience, and the stigma of his Hiller episode was expunged for evermore!

The wisdom of following rivers whenever possible was brought home to me in a big way during my second spell in Borneo. On 2 October '64, just 4 days after the protracted Danum River mapping saga, I was carrying two passengers on a routine mission to Nanga Gaat at about 1000ft. Suddenly, having left Kapit behind, the airframe gave a series of twitches in the yawing plane. Never having experienced this problem before, it was a few moments before I recognised what the symptoms meant - that the engine was misfiring intermittently. Having twigged, I immediately transmitted a 'Mayday', more in the hope that someone might hear than with any confidence of a positive response, and looked around for a site on which to carry out an emergency landing. I also thanked my lucky stars that I hadn't been flat-hatting up the Baleh trying to impress some visiting fireman!

From time to time in Borneo the total quantity of rain falling over the course of a few days reduced sufficiently for river levels to drop appreciably, which tended to leave areas of exposed shingle bed on the inside of almost every significant bend. That, happily, was the case on this occasion so, without wasting any time and while my engine was still delivering some power, I landed on the nearest shingle spit and hoped that my distress call had been heard. Actually, I wasn't too worried; the route was commonly flown so someone would pass before too long. Indeed, if the worst came to the worst, we could always hitch a ride in a passing longboat. It wasn't therefore our own welfare that was my chief concern, but that of my little rotary-wing pride and joy - these shingle banks were chiefly notable for the rapidity with which they disappeared after the next heavy rainfall. An early salvage operation would be a good move!

I cannot now recall what triggered the rescue operation, a reaction to the 'Mayday' or the chance passing of a Wessex. Whichever it was, the operation did not take long. Having prudently left room for one to land alongside my stricken charge, the salvage operation was completed successfully before the waters rose again. Actually, it was not a bad spot from which to sling the Hiller under a Wessex, well under 1000ft above sea level and relatively cool so close to the river. All we had to do was drain off the fuel and take off the two main rotor-blades before it could be lifted down-river to the Kapit airstrip for further investigation.

We actually had two of the three Hillers ashore at that stage, and four days later I was flying the other from Sibu to Song, with my specialist CPO maintainer Soapy Watson along for the ride. Suddenly, approaching the vicinity of Song, close to but not actually over the Rajang and at about 700ft, more or less the same thing happened. This time, however, the failure was far more positive and final. A couple of coughs accompanied by violent yaws, and the engine ran down to a spluttering idle. Another hasty 'Mayday' yell into the radio, then it was time to put to good use all that engine-off landing practice I'd gone in for back at Culdrose!

The ground below had been cleared of jungle for cultivation purposes, but was still pretty unfriendly. The clearing process - burning - had left the area seriously cluttered with the blackened, pointed remains of numerous tree-trunks sticking out of the ground between three and five feet high and only a few yards apart. Landing on one of those could wreck the Hiller and seriously damage the health of its occupants! Soapy told me afterwards that at this point he had clamped his eyes firmly shut and kept them that way throughout the rest of the proceedings!

The Hiller in autorotation under those conditions of weight and temperature came down quite fast, so there wasn't much time to pick a suitable spot for landing. However, having selected one large enough to accommodate the whole fuselage, if not necessarily the rotor disc, I was reasonably confident that I had adequate skill to put it down without damage. And so it transpired.

In a neat manoeuvre, for which I later received the accolade of a Green Endorsement signed by the Commander Far East Fleet, I managed to use all the high rotor inertia to touch down quite gently exactly where I had wanted. Moreover, I was able to achieve the zero groundspeed necessary to avoid running into any of the vicious-looking spikes. With the 12E completely undamaged, Soapy opened his eyes and acknowledged his relief by telling me that I must have done a pretty good job – high praise indeed from a seasoned maintainer! At that point I found that the engine was still capable of a very rough tick-over, so I kept it running just long enough to establish on the radio that the Squadron was aware of our predicament and was doing something about it. And indeed it was. In no time, Lt Jeremy Knapp appeared in his Wessex 1 and we were all safely back at Sibu, trying to figure out why our normally very reliable little helicopters had suddenly let us down in such a big way. The answer, when we got there, was fairly straightforward.

In an innovative and popular engineering development, almost all Fleet Air Arm maintenance work had recently moved away from the old 'Maincheck' principle. This was a wasteful practice in which specified areas of the aircraft were stripped and all components within thoroughly checked, whether they needed it or not. Introduction of the new system of 'Flexible Servicing Operations' acknowledged the wisdom of the 'if it ain't broke, don't fix it' philosophy by determining, for every single component or sub-assembly of an aircraft, the frequency with which it needed individually to be maintained. This could range from simple inspection, through lubrication, testing and, ultimately, replacement. It could be either on a calendar or hours-flown basis, with the frequency determined by a combination of manufacturer advice and in-service experience. In the absence of substantiated data from either source, it was clearly necessary to invoke an element of judgement or guesswork in determining the appropriate maintenance intervals.

With respect to the electrical harnesses for our Hillers' ignition systems, we found that, with no previous experience of the 12E in the Borneo environment, we had got this judgement wrong. Under the severe heat and extreme humidity, and with no hangarage available, the insulation was deteriorating faster than had been anticipated. The cure was obvious enough: improve and increase the frequency of protective maintenance, and reduce the installed life of the complete harness assembly. With these measures in place, there were no further engine reliability problems whatsoever. I did, however, consider that I had been extraordinarily fortunate that the two failures in four days had occurred during the very small percentage of airborne time in which I could land without damage. Indeed, for the majority of the time it was unlikely that such failures would have been survivable at all, and certainly not during most of the very recent Danum River work.

Away from Borneo. Although it had been intended that the turn-round intervals between ship and Sarawak would be three-monthly, this did not always work out in practice. As a result, I found myself reluctantly back on board just 6 weeks after introducing the 12E to Borneo. However I had learnt much, had a lot of fun and it was now Mini's turn. The *Bulwark* time was spent either on board conducting amphibious exercises or providing additional support to the Sarawak detachments, or disembarked to Singapore for maintenance, continuation training and R & R at RNAS Sembawang. This was a delightful grass airfield establishment run by the Royal Marines and located at Nee Soon. Life there had an idyllic quality. We worked 'tropical routine', which meant starting (fairly) early in the morning and finishing at around noon, leaving every afternoon free to pursue the ample range of social or sporting activities available. To be honest, though, this generally meant a tankful of lunchtime Tiger, followed by an afternoon spent disporting oneself at the Terror Officers' Club swimming pool, ogling and chatting up the abundance of nubile talent present!

Once back on board, an early task was participation with the Americans in a major SEATO exercise entitled 'LIGTAS', held on Mindoro in the Philippines. This enabled me to polish up some of the skills learnt at Middle Wallop, but which had since grown somewhat rusty through lack of use. These included low-level, covert reconnaissance, and Forward Air Control for US Phantoms, RN Sea Vixens and an RAF Canberra – exciting stuff! It also by chance provided the opportunity to further enhance my Hiller's street cred with my compatriots and the SAS.

The Squadron was at the time detached ashore at San Jose airfield in direct support of the military. Whilst there, we learnt of an SAS patrol that had got lost in a valley in the nearby mountainous exercise area. Several airborne forays by other helicopters to the vicinity of the patrol's reported position had drawn a blank so, with my recent Borneo experience very much in mind, I asked to have a go. Having picked up a military colleague, we first covered the reported area from the much better visual vantage-point offered by my 12E, but also drew a blank. We then took a closer look at the lie of the land, as would have been seen from ground level, and came to the conclusion that the adjacent terrain closely resembled that of another mountainous area a few miles away. We agreed that it was possible that the patrol had made an understandable map-reading error, and headed off to our new search area.

I have to say that the search co-ordinating authority, no doubt mistaking the unwarlike appearance of my Hiller for military incompetence, was sceptical in the extreme but, feigning radio problems – not difficult with the PTR 170, as I've said – we went anyway. We started by identifying, then searching, an area from which the surrounding countryside would have closely resembled that which would have been seen from their reported position - and almost immediately were rewarded with success! Making contact to ascertain the patrol's welfare, we established that with confirmation of their actual position, the immediate crisis was satisfactorily resolved. We then returned to the airfield feeling really rather pleased with ourselves. And rightly so - the previously-sceptical authorities had been impressed, and my wonderful little helicopter had gained yet more kudos and fans!

Apart from such operational high-points, one of the chief roles of the Hiller while disembarked was VIP carriage. As in Borneo, its outstanding view, comfort and versatility soon came to be much appreciated and demand for the use of the 'nice set of rotors' continued to spread. As a result, I had the pleasure of carrying a number of august personages about their business. However, from a professional viewpoint it was unremarkable work, so does not warrant any further expansion.

Undoubtedly the acme of my embarked time came the following year when participating in Operation 'SHOWPIECE', a sort of non-tactical amphibious exercise aimed at demonstrating to our political friends the hardware and skills involved. It took place at Pulau Lankawi, a picture-postcard group of islands off the northwest coast of Malaya, not far from the legendary Thai holiday island of Phuket. There was negligible war-like input to this exercise so, when one Sunday morning at anchor we learnt that Ursula Andress was filming on location in the vicinity, the Squadron was galvanised into action! This took the form of a concerted rush of Wessex into the air for 'test flights' various to try to track her down with a view to inviting her on board for cocktails. Come lunchtime, however, the last had landed back on board without success.

De-briefing this shameful failure in the bar over the usual gin and tonics, we concluded that it was simply not acceptable. With my reputation as a smart-arsed finder of SAS patrols lost in deep, primary jungle firmly established, it was agreed that the task should prove a mere bagatelle to me and my 12E, and that I should accordingly get going to restore the Squadron's reputation without delay. Pausing only long enough to empty my glass and to co-opt Ian Thomson as co-pilot/observer, I flashed up the helicopter and we were away. Being the only aircraft airborne, Flyco was manned by the Squadron Duty Officer.

Success was not long in coming! After about 10 minutes or so, we came across a number of dark, coffin-shaped objects floating in the sea a little distance offshore from one of the nearby islands. The beach itself was straight out of the brochures, a gleaming, golden strand backed by palm trees, under the broken canopy of which appeared evidence of human activity. On closer examination, the floating objects were found indeed to be coffins, each occupied by a member of the film crew sunbathing during their lunch break! So that was why the Wessex hadn't spotted them, they were busy under the palm canopy trying not to attract attention, in the hope that the noisy nuisances would soon go away! However, it seemed that the situation was now different. To test the theory, I treated them to a fairly sporty torque turn, which flowed smoothly into an approach to a modest gap in the palm canopy, through which I proposed to descend to join the party.

On closer inspection, it proved to be extremely modest, and without the lunchtime libation under the belt I would probably have never attempted it! However, after the success of my SAS rescue mission from far worse terrain very early in the deployment, this should be a comparative doddle, so in we went. The first part went fine, with the downdraft blowing the encroaching palm fronds aside to leave a perfectly adequate clearance for the rotor disc – well, a few feet to spare, anyway. Unfortunately, I had neglected to account for the altered characteristics of the downwash effect once the disc was below the canopy. Instead of blowing, it was now sucking, and the fronds duly closed in over the top in response!

Alarming and visually dramatic as this development appeared, it wasn't in fact particularly critical as long as I kept the tail rotor clear of interference. The Hiller's main-rotor tips, unlike the hollow, light-alloy fairings of other helicopters, were made of solid steel. Moreover, their construction incorporated a small, blade-like protuberance at the very end; in short, they constituted a robust and highly effective strimmer, which made short work of a few palm leaves! The tree-trunks themselves, though, posed an altogether more serious threat and were a great deal too close for comfort. Notwithstanding, if this spectacular arrival was to achieve anything useful and not fizzle out like a damp squib, there was nothing else for it but to continue the nerve-wracking descent.

After a masterful con from Ian, and to the film crew's manifest admiration, I eventually managed to touch down safely, whereupon we were immediately offered liberal liquid refreshment. After the longhouse visit with Ian in his Wessex to christen the hill-top landing site near Bankit, in which he had had to remain abstemious, the boot was now on the other foot, and it was my turn to abstain – well, sort of! So with the Hiller shut down, we joined the crew on the beach to await Miss Andress' pleasure – she and the leading man (Jean-Paul Belmondo - they were making *That Man from Hong Kong*) had been occupying two of the coffins. As she strode ashore, in a scene straight out of *Dr No*, we were forcibly struck by the realisation that we were in the presence of one of the most gorgeous creatures on the planet!

Mouths agape like schoolboys on their first visit to a strip-joint, we duly handed over our invitation. I must say, Ursula was gracious in the extreme, and tickled pink at the lengths to which we'd gone to deliver it! Unfortunately, though, it seemed most unlikely that she would be able to take up the offer, since the film crew's digs while on location were about 20 miles from *Bulwark's* anchorage, which put them substantially beyond the reach of any sensible boat-trip. Ah well, it had been a nice idea, and at least Ian and I got some serious quality time in her company, a cosy tête-à-tête that was brought to an abrupt halt by the noisy arrival overhead of a Wessex. Flashing up the 12E's radio to enquire the reason, we soon found out!

It seemed that the duty officer in Flyco, with nothing better to do, had been watching our progress through binoculars as we searched the islands for our quarry. Having therefore duly witnessed my sporty torque-turn, and having last seen the Hiller pointing vertically towards the ground, he was somewhat alarmed when it failed to re-appear. Moreover, in our total focus on the job in hand, and being unaccustomed to anyone knowing where I was anyway, I had unfortunately neglected to advise the ship of progress and of our plans for the immediate future.

Having no option, therefore, but to anticipate the worst, he had caused the Wessex to be scrambled to come and look for us. Having quickly found us at our last sighted position the crew, rudely snatched from its Sunday afternoon reverie, was singularly unimpressed by the spectacle of the pair of us chatting up this vision of beauty, cheerily waving beer cans in their general direction. Not only were they stone-cold sober and had obviously missed the party, the complete absence of a suitable landing site nearby made it impossible for them to cut their losses and join us.

It was now becoming clear that circumstances had developed to the point that prudence, as well as assurance of my continued independence of action, demanded our presence back on board without much further delay. In any case, the film crew had a busy schedule to keep, which wasn't being much progressed by all this un-scripted helicopter activity taking place in its midst. It was, we reluctantly concluded, time to go, but it was not a prospect that I was particularly relishing, given the need to extricate the Hiller from the quite extraordinarily small site into which I had shoehorned it! However, by exercising great care, and strimming a few more palm fronds as we emerged through the canopy, we were safely out. One more pass and a cheery wave, then back to the ship. Subsequent examination of the rotor tips revealed no visible evidence of the unconventional use to which they had been put – like I've said, it was a robust little machine!

Ultimately, the mission had failed in its primary purpose of securing the presence of the goddess on board. However, it was generally agreed that the Squadron had given the project its best shot, and had at least made convivial contact in an appropriately dramatic fashion in keeping with the best traditions of the Fleet Air Arm! Ian and I, as the only real beneficiaries of the whole episode, were more than happy with that conclusion!

Tragedy. Despite having escaped unharmed from our engine ignition problems, the Hiller was involved towards the end of its time in Borneo in one tragic event that cost the life of a very able and experienced pilot. Lt John Morgan had joined 845 in mid '64 as the Qualified Helicopter Instructor (QHI) whose job, amongst other duties, was to maintain control over flying standards in our diverse theatre. He also, incidentally, locally converted Mini and me to the Wessex 1 to expand our versatility and value to the Squadron. Apart from his manifest abilities, he was one of the most charming and thoughtful men one could hope to meet.

Mini subsequently became involved in a very serious Wessex crash on 4 March 1965, which resulted in him being invalided off the squadron. John, having previously instructed on the Hiller, then assumed main responsibility for the other aircraft, intending to rotate opposite me between the ship and Sarawak. At this point, he was ashore and I was embarked. I therefore did not have the opportunity to exchange 12E reminiscences and experiences with him, although I will never know to what extent, if any, that omission might have affected subsequent events.

Just over a month later, on the fatal day, 9 April 1965, the task had involved Topo deployments to Batu at 6600ft, near the top of the 8000ft Hose Mountains. Although the Hiller was running well short of power at that altitude it could still, with the exercise of considerable care, carry passengers into or out of the landing sites. I have no personal knowledge of the exact circumstances surrounding the event itself but somehow, while engaged in this activity, John had had the misfortune to strike and damage the two-bladed tail-rotor. He had then elected to land, shut down and attempt some form of temporary repair, no doubt motivated by the extreme difficulty of recovering the helicopter by any means readily available to Squadron resources.

It was reported that in a bid to reduce out-of-balance vibration for a recovery flight, this involved the trimming of material from the blades until they appeared to match each other. Each blade of the Hiller tail-rotor was constructed of a thin steel rod main spar, round which was wrapped the hollow, light-alloy material of the blade surface itself. There was no internal honeycomb filler, as is common with larger tail-rotor blades, thus structural integrity of the component relied entirely on its being physically intact in all respects. The paring work undertaken by John could never, therefore, have hoped to restore tail-rotor integrity to anything approaching a safe flight condition.

Nonetheless, having completed it he resolved to fly the Hiller out. Following a short test hover, in which a considerable degree of vibration was reportedly apparent, he departed the landing site. Some two minutes later the inevitable happened. After a 'Mayday' call announcing tail-rotor problems, the remains of the tail rotor seems to have disintegrated, leaving the 12E over mountainous, primary jungle with no anti-torque or directional control whatsoever. A number of helicopters, notably the Wessex, have large fin or sail areas well aft of the main-rotor mast, thus under similar circumstances a combination of moderate power and out-of-balance keel effect will allow control to be maintained for the transit to an acceptable landing area. The Hiller, sadly, completely lacked this attribute, with the inevitable consequence that it crashed, out of control and fatally, through the unforgiving jungle canopy below into a river bed.

I was at this stage flying the Hiller and Wessex, and also the Whirlwind 7s we'd acquired, on a wide variety of tasks in and around Singapore. Indeed, my last flight before reacting to John's tragic death was by chance a Wessex instrument-flying training sortie for Mac's benefit. When the news broke, we immediately prepared the spare Hiller, which I test flew before embarking it on 15 April in the LST *Maxwell Brander* for passage to Sibu, disembarking three days later.

I flew up to Nanga Gaat for several short, mostly VIP, visits soon after that, but it wasn't until a month later that I was able to get up there for long enough to become involved in Topo tasking in the Hose area. However, on 21 May I was able to discover what had probably happened to severely damage John's tail rotor. The vegetation at that point was fearsome, comprising extremely dense, robust and inter-twining liana-like growths extending to ten feet or more above ground level. Given the tools that we could transport to that altitude, it was practically impossible to clear the ground to build a conventional landing site. The construction method used, therefore, was to force four large stakes into this growth down to ground level to provide the supports for each landing-gear platform. It was unnecessary to drive them into the ground; gripped like limpets by the liana, and connected to each other by a framework attaching the tops, they formed a completely rigid foundation. Surmounting this structure, and supported partially by the liana itself, the platforms, each comprising a number of logs cut and lashed together, were attached. They were built in a group of three, one for each Wessex mainwheel and one for the tailwheel, and undoubtedly represented the fruits of some very hard work indeed, as well as considerable ingenuity.

Having arrived at the site with one Topo, I selected the largest of the three platforms, which was just wide enough to accommodate the track of the Hiller's skid undercarriage – but only just. By placing the left skid on the very edge, my Topo passenger advised me that the right skid could also be accommodated - but again, only just. Having settled, but keeping a lot of power on to avoid slipping off and risk catching a skid underneath the platform (that would have been curtains), I disembarked my passenger. Gaining confidence that I had achieved a stable situation, and to gain some adhesion for the skids to counter the risk of sliding off the platform, I reduced power slightly, although maintaining full flight RPM, to await my return passenger. Suddenly, the Hiller rocked backwards as the extreme rear of the platform pivoted down from the horizontal. Snatching a handful of power, I immediately lifted off, praying that I had not also damaged the tail rotor in the harsh manoeuvre.

After a few minutes of flying around in a state of intense alarm, I concluded that I must have caught the rock-back in time, and that all was well. One of the great advantages of fully-manual controls is that there is no hydraulic damping to mask any untoward developments, so if I had damaged the tail rotor in any way at all, I would undoubtedly have felt the resultant buzz or vibration through my feet on the rudder pedals. It must have been close, though! Gingerly returning to collect my passenger (trusting soul - but that was the Topos all over, we had learnt to have complete faith in each other), I touched down with extreme circumspection, and this time further forward on the log platform. At least I now knew that the structure was wide enough.

Examining the composition of the platform to try to figure out what had happened, the answer became clear. The horizontal log structure overlapped its supporting framework by a significant amount, the size and shape of the latter being determined by the availability of gaps in the liana growth into which the supporting stakes could be forced. The logs comprising the platform itself were orientated across the platforms. These structural features, which were not visually apparent without careful examination, were of no relevance to the Wessex, which aimed to put each wheel in the fully supported centre of its associated pad.

They were, however, for the Hiller, in which the weight of the machine is taken very much towards the rear of the skids. Having landed well aft on the platform to give myself the best visual references for the precision handling required, it was evident that I had placed the centre of gravity behind the rearmost solid support. As I eased off the power the aft, unsupported part of the structure suddenly folded downwards, tipping the 12E violently nose-up. I was undoubtedly fortunate to have caught the situation before it deteriorated to a tail-rotor strike. This was probably due to the extra degree of caution I was exercising in the light of John's accident, even though until that frightening and violent rock-back I had no idea what might have actually occurred. After it, I was fairly sure I knew.

The End. There were no more really remarkable adventures for my now very trusty Hiller and me, just more of the same seriously exciting, day-by-day flying, until our time in Borneo came to a close. However, there was in the end one notable exception, which had little to do with aviation accomplishment, more social, and that was 845 Squadron's final departure from Nanga Gaat on 15 June 1965. As a squadron, we had been relieved in Borneo by 848 Squadron from HMS *Albion*, with their infinitely more powerful Wessex Mk 5 s, plus two small Wasp helicopters to take over the Hillers' role.

We had formed a very strong and emotional bond with the local Ibans, even me, who was not by any means a regular resident. But they all knew and had great respect for my wee helicopter and, by association, me. The site at The Gaat included a series of tunnels, built in case the confrontation turned really nasty, in which case they might have been needed for bolt-holes. That, of course, never happened, but the tunnels remained and, I think, were largely unknown to the final 845 site residents. But not to the Ibans who had built them!

Anyway, we had arranged to fly our superseded helicopters from the base at about midday, leaving adequate time for whatever farewell celebrations might emerge. Prudent move, that, because they were, to say the least, unexpected! The Anchor Inn, with stocks checked and handover complete (with adequate reserves left for this occasion) was declared 'Free Bar' from mid-morning onwards and all, particularly our Iban friends, went for it.

We all recognised that we had to take our helicopters some 110 miles down-river to Sibu that afternoon, but for once we relaxed the normal rules, not stupidly, but just a little. I cannot speak for the rest, but I found myself in one of these tunnels, where I tarried awhile with a truly delightful young Iban lass and a can of Tiger. They are not renowned as head-hunters for nothing - only kidding, but it wasn't far short!

After our final and very fond farewells, we ultimately left, more or less on time. I cannot remember what the rest of the lantern-jawed aircrew looked like, but I was an absolute disgrace. A heady mixture of mud, Tiger and ....? had seen to that. The Wessex took just over an hour to cover the distance to Sibu. I took rather longer, so I had to establish, *en route*, a new landing site in the military helicopter lexicon, the 'PZ'. Fortunately, I had got far enough towards Sibu to know the ground and where I could land safely. A great relief!

And some experience! We finally left Borneo for good from Sibu a week later, on 22 June.

The rest, sadly from the Hiller story viewpoint, was an anti-climax (an appropriate phrase!). Obviously we didn't just spirit ourselves from Borneo back to the UK, but little of any note to my wee helicopters' front-line story took place during that long journey, which took us back to Singapore, on to Western Australia (Perth/Fremantle), and thence home.

There was, however, one more fairly major military activity *en route* – in Aden, which was seriously nasty at that time. But even that was not particularly remarkable, from the Hiller aspect at least, just more of the same; a superb set of rotors for very light transport, Forward Air Control (by now a somewhat rusty skill, although recovering the polish was fun) and reconnaissance. It was routinely exciting, with the added adrenaline of a new and very hostile environment and, of course, a dramatically different terrain, but it did not result in any incident worth recording.

Not for the Hillers, that is. But it did for our poor old Wessex 1s! Their Rolls Royce (née Napier) Gazelle engines were pretty tired by the time we got there, they having been intended only to operate at sea level in a maritime environment. Well, Borneo had put paid to that, but at least there the air had been clean and moist. Not so in Aden! It was notable for very fine sand which cleaned the compressors an absolute treat, and then very rapidly eroded them to a useless, paper-thin quality. Thereafter, the poor old Wessex was not going anywhere under its own steam. By the time we twigged what had happened, we had about 10 helicopters downed in Aden. But we had a saviour at hand – in an unlikely guise, a Crab!

We had embarked for theatre guidance a locally-based Wessex 2 (RAF version of our 5) with its properly-protected twin-Gnome powerplant. Also, we had one Wessex 1 on board that was seriously unserviceable, apart from its engine. Solution – remove engine, undersling it ashore to the first downed Wessex 1, change it in the field, and fly the helicopter back (while the Mark 2 returned the duff engine). Now, changing that engine, even in the controlled environment of *Bulwark's* hangar, was, as I recall, a lengthy operation calling for much care and supervision. Not only that, it required a post-change tie-down run to prove the installation, hardly a practical proposition under the circumstances!

However, the first recovery was successful, so the plan continued, until all the Wessex 1s had been retrieved. Our maintainers, a magnificent crew in whom we had the greatest faith anyway, rapidly got faster at the double engine-change (one out, one in), to the point that it rivalled the fabled RN Field Gun competition (which Fleet Air Arm maintainers regularly won anyway!). And, obviously, we were very grateful to the highly-professional and accommodating RAF crew.

But that, as I said, has nothing to do with the Hiller story. They performed faultlessly to the last, but in which activity, sadly, I was not allowed to participate. My final flight, back from Aden on 21 August 1965, was the last time I ever flew the 12E. Despite my protests, it was decreed that others should take my baby back to Culdrose on disembarkation.

I was sent on with *Bulwark* to disembark with the rest of the ship's company for post-deployment leave. I really hated that. My Hiller and I had become such good friends, who seemed to understand each other so well. She had never let me down - on both occasions of her engine failure we were, amazingly, over survivable territory. If I was good enough for her, she would save me, at least, that's what I came to believe. I was, and she did! I loved her to bits!

A Green Endorsement and a Long Night CASEVAC

By Lieutenant Jeremy Knapp Royal Navy - Pilot 845 Squadron (Wessex 1)

706B Flight/845 arrived in HMS *Bulwark* off Sarawak in early April 1964 and at first I was sent to Simanggang, in the Second Division, and the forward operating base at Jambu. It was whilst I was at Simanggang that we received an urgent request for a troop movement up-country which necessitated the use of two RAF Belvederes, for their greater lifting capacity; unfortunately, the weather was not too good and the flight would require some instrument flying. The Belvederes, however, were at this time not cleared for IMC so one of the RAF pilots suggested that, if I were to fly on instruments and they flew in formation on either side of me, they would be flying VMC. This plan was agreed and all was well, but what would have happened had I had an engine failure, leaving them without a visual reference unless they too had autorotated whilst still in formation?

Three weeks later I was transferred to Sibu in the Third Division. A few days later on 27th April I was being shown around the area by Lieutenant Martin Banks, Royal Marines, during a helicopter delivery service (HDS) flight to Nanga Gaat and then on to Long Jawi. After 4 hours of tasking, Martin put me into the right-hand seat for the return flight to Nanga Gaat. We were a crew of three plus three passengers and on take-off I experienced a significant loss of power due to ingestion of foreign matter. This resulted in a heavy landing a little distance away from the landing site, breaking off the starboard undercarriage and setting off the engine fire-extinguisher which released a cloud of smoke. I initially thought that the grass had been set alight. Having increased my rotor revs to the maximum permitted, I regained sufficient control to manoeuvre the aircraft and I immediately lifted off and, on seeing a convenient tree-stump a short distance away, managed to perch the starboard side of the aircraft on this and ordered the passengers and crewman to leave the aircraft. Martin also got out so as to reduce the all-up weight by as much as possible. Martin and the others made their way back to the landing site, where they organised some Gurkhas, who were guarding the Long Jawi site, to build a suitable ramp to rest the starboard side of the aircraft on so that it could be shut down. Meanwhile, with the reduced load I was able to 'hop' the aircraft from one tree-stump to another and into a position where I could see the landing site and watch the progress of the ramp. During the 25 minutes that it took to build the ramp I frequently had to lift into a hover, with fluctuating power, to break the incipient ground resonance which was building up. Once the ramp was completed I was marshalled forwards and onto the ramp and, when it seemed that the aircraft was reasonably stable on its port wheel and the ramp, I was given the signal to shut down. In a flash all the personnel who had been on or near the landing site disappeared down the bank towards the stream which was in front of the landing site. This action did little to instil much confidence in the stability of the ramp that they had built for me! However, all was well and I achieved an uneventful shut-down and the aircraft suffered no further damage, at this stage.

Back in Sibu, where I wrote-up the incident and described the uncontrolled landing which resulted in 'a forward nudge breaking off my starboard oleo', I was firmly informed by the AEO that this 'nudge' was in excess of 4g, since the engine fire-extinguisher had been set off by the collision with the ground!

I said earlier that when I shut the aircraft down there was 'no further damage at this stage'. This is true; however, after the aircraft had been stripped of its rotor blades, engine and gearbox, the RAF was called in to lift the fuselage with a Belvedere. Unfortunately, soon after lifting-off with its underslung load, an uncontrollable swing developed and my aircraft was unceremoniously dumped in the jungle! The gearbox was next and when it was being lifted out of Nanga Gaat, where it had arrived safely, the pilot of this Wessex was overpitching with his underslung load and he was forced to deposit it in the river Rajang!

I guess it is not often that one is rewarded with a Green Endorsement for crashing an aircraft but, on this occasion, Vice Admiral Dryer, The Commander Far East Fleet, saw fit to do so.

My second tale concerns a night CASEVAC. On 27th November 1964 one of the surveyors (Topos), who had been out in the Ulu helping to bring the totally inadequate maps up to date, was brought into Nanga Gaat feeling very unwell. During the evening he deteriorated to a point when our Medic had serious concerns as to whether he would survive through the night without hospital treatment. He diagnosed that he was probably suffering from leptospirosis (an infectious bacterial disease caught from rodents, dogs, and other mammals transmissible to humans). Lieutenant Malcolm Kennard (known to his friends as 'Kosh' – I have no idea why) was the officer in charge at Nanga Gaat and he asked me if I would fly the 'Topo' down to Sibu with Lieutenant Neil Foster as my co-pilot. There were a few problems: there were severe thunderstorms in the area and we had no HF communication with the outside world (our normal method for communications over longer distances); the cloud around Nanga Gaat was sitting on the tree tops and, if this was the case at Sibu where there was no Ground Control Approach radar, there would be no way of getting back down through the cloud; a flight at low level along the river was the only possibility - it was already dark and no one had any knowledge as to how long the landing-light might last if it was on for a long period. There was one considerable plus in that Neil had trained as an observer before he gained his pilot's wings.

By the time everything was prepared and the aircraft topped up with fuel, we took off at 0100. The cloud base proved to be at around 100 feet, so Neil and I decided that we would attempt to stay 'out of the river' and below 75 feet, with an airspeed above 35 knots but below 60. This is where Neil's skills were invaluable as he watched the instruments like a hawk, all the time keeping up a continuous commentary and flow of information whilst I flew the aircraft visually, with the aid of the landing-lamp, trying to keep out of the trees which overhung the river. Most of the time it was raining and the windscreen wipers were in fairly constant use. The normal flight time from Nanga Gaat to Sibu was a little over an hour and the distance to Kapit, the first village downstream where there was a stock of fuel drums, was about 50 miles. It must have taken us rather more than an hour to reach Kapit, where we had to take on more fuel and where we were also able to get a message through to Sibu to tell them we were *en route* with an urgent CASEVAC. At least now they would be expecting us. After refuelling and a welcome rest from peering into the darkness, we set of again with the in-flight conditions remaining much the same. As we neared Sibu we ran into a heavy thunderstorm which made further progress down river impossible. For some 15 minutes I hovered with the landing-lamp swivelled round to the 2 o'clock position, as by this time my windscreen wiper was leaking hydraulic fluid which melted the rubber compound of my wiper blade, giving me a 'blackout' straight ahead! Fortunately we were now close enough to be in touch with the Sibu control tower and, as the storm had abated a little, I increased my height to the level of the tree-tops and called for the control tower to fire a 'Verey light' to help me locate the airfield. As a red glow was visible through the rain, I asked for a continuous stream to be fired whilst I 'crabbed' the aircraft in a 2 o'clock direction. We landed safely at 0500, four hours after leaving Nanga Gaat. My eyes were undoubtedly sore, but probably nothing compared to Neil's throat! After some rest, Neil and I flew back to Nanga Gaat. I am happy to recall that the 'Topo' made a full recovery. I feel that Neil was the real hero, I had the easy bit! In June 1965 I was informed that I had been awarded a Queen's Commendation for this flight.

An Interesting Night Flight

By Lieutenant Commander G.J. 'Tank' Sherman (Commanding Officer 845 Squadron, Wessex 1)

One day in early 1964 I had led a flight of four helicopters from Nanga Gaat to Long Jawi to spend the day rotating and resupplying various patrols in the forward area.

At the end of the day the four aircraft were ready to return to Nanga Gaat to arrive in daylight. However, there was a delay on my aircraft so I sent the other three on, confident of my ability to night-fly back if this proved necessary - which was the case.

So eventually I took off after dark for what I anticipated would be an uneventful return to our base at Nanga Gaat. Halfway there, at the point of no return, the engine oil-pressure gauge started to indicate a marked loss of pressure. I therefore diverted from the direct track to Nanga Gaat to close on the Baleh River, which could be seen in the starlight and which would offer a better chance of survival if the engine should fail.

The Baleh was known to be wider than the rotor diameter of a Wessex all the way from where I joined the river up to Nanga Gaat, so I flew down the river at best speed at about 10ft above the surface, hoping for the best and prepared for the worst while the steadily falling oil-pressure gauge continued dropping until it reached zero.

Suddenly the aircrewman called out that the engine was on fire! On the 'e' of 'fire I stood the aircraft on its tail for an immediate quick stop and noticed just ahead the water rippling in the starlight, indicating some shallow rapids near one bank, and put the aircraft straight down into the water and immediately stopped the engine while the aircrewman leapt out and extinguished the fire - caused by oil leaking on to the jet-pipes - with his CO_2 extinguisher. The water in the shallows proved less than a foot deep and did us no harm.

I had been in touch with Nanga Gaat by radio and they immediately sent a longboat with a maintenance team and enough oil for the engine, while we waited for them to appear.

About a couple of hours later the longboat appeared and topped up the engine oil and also ascertained that the leaking oil seal could not be replaced without using the engine running-out gear - the nearest of which was in Sibu. Also there were huge cumulus clouds and heavy rain close upstream and I knew just how quickly the river levels could rise.

The aircraft had to be moved. The trim separating the rear cabin from the engine compartment was removed so that the aircrewman would be able to mop up the oil leak as it occurred and prevent another fire. When all was ready I started the engine, broke the starting-cycle with throttle as soon at 6,000 rpm was achieved, engaged the rotor and got airborne within about 20 seconds of starting the engine and flew at max speed to Nanga Gaat and got there just as the oil pressure was reading zero again!

In due course the engine running-out gear was flown up from Sibu to Nanga Gaat, the rear oil seal replaced and the engine was then as good as new.

846 Squadron at Tawau 1964

By Electrical Mechanic David Fisher 846 Squadron

My memories of service with 846 Squadron begin when, as a 17-year-old, very naive young man I saw on the Squadron notice-board at Culdrose, Cornwall, a notice seeking volunteers to fly out to Borneo in order to relieve personnel serving on 846 who were to return to UK. The notice stated the volunteers would be required to fly out to Borneo, remain there for approximately six weeks, then join an aircraft carrier and sail back to UK.

Having never been abroad before, other than a school trip to Holland, I thought this sounded like an opportunity not to be missed, as it would mean I would see a part of the world that I had never seen before, with the added bonus of not being away from home for too long.

My request was duly submitted, but the following day I was called to see the Regulating Chief, who said words to the effect 'What the Hell do you think you are doing, Fisher, by volunteering to go to Borneo? Don't you know there is a war going on there?' Well, I had no idea, but in good old Naval tradition, found myself on a flight to Singapore a few weeks later.

I remember that my first impression upon landing in Singapore was the terrible smell and heat that I had never in my life experienced. We were taken to our temporary accommodation where, during the following week or so, we were issued with very strange kit which I never in my life believed I would be wearing as, after all, I was in the Navy! Jungle Greens and Snake Boots - whatever next?

My next printable recollection, bearing in mind I was an extremely fit 17-year-old in Singapore, was when we boarded an RAF Argosy and flew to Tawau in North Borneo, recently renamed as Sabah.

When we arrived we were shown our accommodation, which consisted of three to a two-man tent, a camp bed with mosquito net, and little else.

Within a day or so the next shock occurred when we were all issued with Sterling sub-machine-guns and ammunition. My only experience with firearms was during my basic training, which consisted of shooting at targets with a .303 rifle. What I was supposed to do with this vicious-looking weapon I, with several others, had no idea.

The six-week stay turned into nine months and many of my experiences will be etched in my mind forever. Some laughable, but others taught me to grow up very, very quickly.

I believe that I was the youngest person in the Squadron at the time but did, during my time in Singapore prior to arriving in Tawau, think slightly ahead and purchased a camera which went with me at all times during my stay. I enclose a sample of the photographs taken, which I hope some will find of interest.

Fig 36. 846 Squadron Dispersal at Tawau

Fig 37. The Young David Fisher

Disbanding of 846 Squadron and Continuing Support by 845 Squadron

Taken from contemporary *Evening News* article and publicity photos

'Servicing helicopters under a scorching Borneo sun, flying troops to advance positions near the Indonesian border, and regularly resupplying them with food and ammunition, tending to the needs of sick natives and their families, these and a hundred-and-one other tasks have been carried out, and are still being, by naval pilots and maintenance crews of 845 and 846 Squadrons, disembarked ashore in Sarawak and North Borneo.

'No. 846 Squadron, commanded by Lieutenant Commander John H S Jervis, RN, has recently disbanded after sterling service over and in the dense jungles of Borneo, but, when I left it some three weeks ago, it was still in commission, operating from the airfield of Tawau in the State of Sabah.

'Much to the relief of soldiers and marines serving under great stress in this tropical outpost, the Navy helicopters are still flying in their support.

No. 845, commanded by Lieutenant Commander 'Tank' Sherman, RN, continues to operate from Sibu, inland from Sarawak's South China Sea coast, and from that incredible 'make-believe' jungle air-base of Nangga Gaat.

'In this, the second instalment of the Borneo helicopter story, some of the personalities in both squadrons are featured…men who have won unstinted praise from their superiors, from the natives whom they have assisted, soldier, British, Gurkha, or from the natives whom they have helped in a variety of ways. "Our job," said Lieutenant Commander Brian Sarginson, R.N. (Senior Pilot of 845) "is to see that no Malaysian, operating in the jungle, is without food or ammo., and to make sure that when he is required elsewhere, he is 'lifted' there promptly and safely."

'To fulfil these tasks, 100 per cent, serviceability of the helicopters is the chief concern of all maintenance crews. Under sometimes primitive conditions, they work day and night and often it is necessary to work under the light of torches.'

Taking the salute

Farewell presentation

T A W A U –

846 Squadron
Depart

Last land-on

Colours lowered

Fig 38. 846 Disbanding Pictures

An Observer's Part in Borneo Confrontation June - August 1964

By Lieutenant Jim Milne – ASW Observer 814 Squadron Wessex 1 attached to 845 Squadron.

In June 1964 I was serving as a fairly junior Observer in 814 Squadron (Anti-Submarine Wessex HAS 1) on board HMS *Victorious*. The ship was due for a Maintenance Period in Singapore and 814 Squadron was to disembark to RNAS Sembawang. Over in Borneo 845 Squadron was looking for a stand-in for its Operations Officer, Lieutenant Peter Dullingham, at Sibu for six weeks. I volunteered and was given the job.

My journey from Changi to Kuching was courtesy of an RAF Hastings and was routine. My flight from Kuching to Sibu was by a Dakota of Borneo Airways. This second flight was enlivened by the variety of passengers. I distinctly remember a crate of chickens and a goat.

I was met at Sibu Airport by Peter Dullingham and given a five-minute handover, met the CO, Lieutenant Commander Tank Sherman, and was whisked off into Sibu Town to the hotel where most of the 845 Sibu Detachment were living.

The next six weeks were spent as the 845 Operations Officer operating between Sibu and Nanga Gaat, and they were a memorable six weeks. I have tried to recall the most memorable incidents, some of which are as clear in my mind now as they were 47 years ago.

Back to the Stone Age. On 7 July I was acting as an Aircrewman on a Resupply Flight out of Nanga Gaat with Lieutenants McPherson and Tim Donkin. The Resupply was to an SAS patrol somewhere in the Borneo jungle. Our passenger was an SAS officer, Major Pat Beresford (later to become Lord Beresford). Eventually we landed in a jungle clearing and the Major disappeared into the trees. I remember we sat on the ground, turning and burning, for what appeared to be an interminable time and I became aware of people, quite small people, appearing in the shadows and on the low branches of the trees. Not too many clothes on, I thought. They looked at us, we looked at them. After an age the Major reappeared, climbed back into the aircraft, sat at the rear of the cabin, got out his notebook and started writing. Time to go; straight up and the moment we got above the jungle canopy we hit wind-shear and the aircraft very unexpectedly veered sharply to port. I had been checking the aft clearances as we took off and was sitting in the door. I looked to the back of the cabin, where the effect of the sharp movement was being most felt. Major Beresford was still sitting there calmly writing in his notebook, as though the quite violent manoeuvre we had just been through was a normal occurrence. I later learnt that the small, naked people I had seen in the clearing were members of the Punan tribe.

Night Scramble. During the night of 12/13 July I was staying at Nanga Gaat. Sometime after midnight there was gunfire on the perimeter from the Royal Irish Rangers, who had the task of guarding Nanga Gaat at that time. I manned one of the Wessex on the Upper Site with Lieutenant John Nicholls. I well remember sitting up in the left-hand seat with my Sterling sub-machine-gun ready for action, in the pitch darkness. All of a sudden the aircraft rocked slightly; someone was climbing up the outside of the aircraft. A face appeared at my side – talk about a fright. Lucky for him the safety catch was on! It was a maintainer – all aircraft to take off immediately and fly to Sibu. My logbook shows takeoff was at 0315. Up through the cloud into the moonlight. There was no contact with Sibu, we were flying above the cloud and cover was continuous all the way to the coast. I did my best on dead reckoning, and an hour and a half later we arrived over what I hoped was Sibu Airport. The details are slightly hazy but I believe a Squadron member at Sibu had been awoken by the noise, had realised that aircraft were coming in and had driven a vehicle onto the runway and used the vehicle lights to illuminate the strip. Luckily the cloud had begun to thin and we were able to land safely. The reason for the initial gunfire is another story! Apparently the Royal Irish Rangers, who had only recently taken over the task of guarding Nanga Gaat, were spooked by the story/rumour that there had been a massacre of Japanese soldiers at Nanga Gaat and ghosts were occasionally seen, and had fired at movement outside the perimeter. At daybreak the 'movement' was found to have been a cow! Now deceased. The Squadron maintainers could not resist finding another cow and painting in large, white letters the word 'COW' on its side!

Airborne Birth. On 14 July the Sibu Ops Room received a call to pick up a woman who had been in labour for a number of days from Mukam, a small, Dyak village some 40 miles away, and take her to Sibu Hospital. I went along up front as an extra pair of eyes/navigator, the pilot being Lieutenant Neil Burns-Thompson. The outbound flight was uneventful; the lady was picked up and she was obviously in some pain. The inbound flight obviously had the desired effect and the lady delivered her baby just as we landed, or just after we landed - my memory is slightly hazy. What I do remember however, is that a cutting from *Flight* magazine a few months later contained the information that mother and baby were doing well and that the baby had been named 'Helicopter'.

Wet Mail. On 16 July there was a requirement to get mail up to Nanga Gaat from Sibu. No 845 aircraft were available but the Army Air Corps had an Auster based at Sibu, flown by one Sergeant Thackeray. He volunteered to fly the mail up to Nanga Gaat, and do some practice landings at the Kapit airstrip on the way back. Of course he could not land at Nanga Gaat, so it would have to be an Air Drop. I volunteered to go as his Despatcher. Simple - he would fly over the site at slow speed, I would open the door and despatch the mail bags. We arrived at Nanga Gaat; there were aircraft on the Upper and Lower Sites, so it was decided we would drop the mail-bags in the area between the accommodation and the River Rajang. Had a practice pass, seemed to be fine, came in for the drop, out went the mail bags, seemed to go OK, came round for a third pass, the drop zone party were holding up their mail-bags and waving madly – obviously glad to get their mail. Off we went to Kapit and, eventually, Sibu. On my return to the Ops Room at Sibu I had some rather rude messages waiting. Apparently we had managed to drop the mail straight into the Rajang. The 'waving madly' should have been interpreted as shaking fists!

Gulong Spali. 25th July was an exciting day! The Army needed to evacuate their listening post on Gulong Spali, a 3000ft mountain which, if I remember correctly, could be seen from Sibu Airport. Most of the kit and people had been evacuated already and Lieutenant Cosh Kennard and myself as Aircrewman took off at 1400 to complete the evacuation. On arrival at the site, which was on the edge of a 1000ft cliff, we discovered that maybe there was more than we had bargained for; instead of 4 there were 8 people plus their kit! A few calculations proved that we were going to be well overweight and this was a Wessex Mk 1, not the later, more powerful, Mk 5. Cosh reckoned that if we loaded everyone in with the aircraft close to the edge and we did a 'jump take-off', and used the 1000ft drop to gain speed, then we would be all right and it would save yet another trip back. Cosh was very convincing, very bold, and looked very old, so I was happy. Minutes later I regretted agreeing with him as, to me in the back, we 'fell' off the ledge and began the long descent (fall) towards the point at which we had enough airspeed to begin to level out and head towards Sibu. It was probably a matter of seconds but it seemed like minutes to me. My background was ASW, where power margins and AUWs were important, and 'falling like a stone' was not in our repertoire.

The Radar Expert. As the Operations Officer at Sibu I received a tasking message requesting 845 to provide an aircraft for a reconnaissance in the local area to look for a site to locate an Air Defence RAF radar site looking towards the Indonesian border. The Squadron Leader arrived, complete with umbrella and a map of the local area. His map had large areas of white, surrounded by high ground. His interpretation was that the white areas were flat plains and therefore the surrounding high ground would be perfect for his radar site. He was a little bit miffed to be told that the white areas were areas which had not yet been 'mapped' and that they were like the rest of Borneo, valleys and mountains, very much akin to 'a wrinkled prune'. He obviously thought we were pulling his leg and demanded to be flown as previously arranged on his reconnaissance. This duly took place; he made his excuses and returned to whence he came with a suitably doctored umbrella. I would like to have been present when he next opened it.

The RAF VIP. An RAF VIP arrived to fly up to Nanga Gaat. I believe this was in preparation for the RAF to take over Nanga Gaat. An RAF Whirlwind 10 had pre-positioned from Labuan, complete with VIP-licensed pilot. RAF VIP arrives. RAF VIP 'Flag Lieutenant' checks that RAF VIP Whirlwind pilot has necessary 'VIP Licence'. Horror, consternation, his 'VIP Licence' does not qualify him to fly the VIP. Flag Lieutenant arrives in the Ops Room and asks if 845 has an aircraft which could carry out the task – one RAF VIP to Nanga Gaat and return. So who did I task? 2 weeks previously, a Sub-Lieutenant straight out of training had arrived; he had completed his famil up to Nanga Gaat, the weather was good, the route to Nanga Gaat was quite straightforward – follow the Rajang. Sub-Lieutenant was briefed, neither the RAF VIP nor his Flags asked for the pilot's credentials, and away they went. Later on in the day the aircraft and passengers returned. Mission accomplished.

Despite what the reader might infer from the above, I am not anti-RAF. But they do sometimes get themselves hung up on rules and regulations!

The Flight Back. Having thoroughly enjoyed my time in Borneo with 845 Squadron, it was time to leave. Back to Kuching via Borneo Airways, no goats this time, to be collected in company with a mixed bunch of Army, RAF and RN personnel for a flight back to Changi in an RAF Argosy. The Argosy duly appeared, we all embarked and the aircraft was just preparing to leave the chocks when there was a thunderous banging on the rear personnel door next to where I was sitting. A shouted conversation between the Loadmaster and somebody outside resulted in the Argosy shutting down and all 30-plus passengers were invited to leave the aircraft. As we sat on the grass pondering on whether we would ever get back to Singapore, an animated conversation was taking place between one of the RAF passengers and a Flight Lieutenant whom we took to be one of the crew. Minutes later, the Flight Lieutenant started a journey around all of the passengers. Apparently the Argosy and crew had been carrying out other tasks before arriving in Kuching. It was scheduled to refuel at Kuching but the crew had 'forgotten' this important detail. Somehow the senior RAF officer passenger had elicited this information from the crew and ordered the aircraft captain, the young Flight Lieutenant, to come round and apologise personally to every passenger. Red faces were the order of the day. We did eventually arrive back at RAF Changi, safely, but a little later than expected.

In Conclusion. I enjoyed my time in Borneo and my experiences there led me eventually to employment as Operations Officer of 848 Squadron (Lieutenant Commander Peter Williams as CO), and Operations Officer 2 in HMS *Bulwark* (Capt Godfrey Place VC). Both appointments interesting, with bags of job satisfaction.

Borneo Memories 1964 to 65

By Lieutenant Ian Thomson Royal Navy - Pilot 845 Squadron (Wessex 1)

My first flight into Borneo was on 12 June 1964 and my last flight out on 22 June 1965. About half that time would have been spent ashore, mostly in Sibu, with the rest at Nanga Gaat.

It is a long time ago and I suspect my memory has become rather distorted with time. Exactly who did what and when and where becomes difficult to pinpoint - my apologies to those concerned if I have got it wrong.

Lots of little things come to mind rather than one dramatic incident, so in no particular order:-

Off-duty time spent in the Capitol Hotel in Sibu, where Sydney would organise anything. A plate of chilli prawns and a can of beer while having a bath after a hot day always went down well. One evening the Boss (Tank Sherman) decided to go to bed early so we asked Sydney to provide a couple of young girls in his room. About ten minutes later Tank reappeared with two ladies; he was not impressed.

Two helicopters returning to Sibu taxy into dispersal down the newly-painted white lines. Unfortunately the lines had been painted too close together. Blades touch, ground resonance, two upside-down helicopters, two very red-faced pilots, but no one hurt.

Fig 39. Wessex Collision at Sibu

One night I was duty boy at Sibu when a CASEVAC was requested. Cosh Kennard and Mac Macpherson set off on a filthy, wet night while I phoned the hospital to arrange an ambulance. An hour or so later the helicopter returned and a young lad walked out of the aircraft cabin unaided. We were all a bit annoyed because it was not the sort of night to go out for minor casualties. The door at the back of the ambulance was opened, but it was only when we realised both doors had to be opened for him to get in that we saw he had an arrow clean through his head, sticking out about a foot either side. This was the subject of various newspaper articles and was probably one of the better PR exercises.

I think it was Brian Sarginson who went out to pick up a couple of Gurkhas from a small clearing in the Whirlwind. He let down between the trees but could not land because of the tree-stumps at the bottom. Unfortunately there were about six troops waiting to come out and all of them jumped in the back. The poor old Whirlwind (which could normally only carry 2 troops and no aircrewman in Borneo) was left balancing on the tree-stumps at max power and no hope of climbing out. After some minutes, 3 or 4 of the Gurkhas jumped out to see what was wrong. With a lot less weight in the back the Whirlwind slowly climbed away, much to the relief of the pilot.

In a Wessex, from *Bulwark* to Sibu with a large generator as an underslung load and Commander 'S' sat in the left-hand seat. About halfway to Sibu the pilot (Mac?) felt a bump in an otherwise smooth flight and realised the load had probably detached. The conversation went as follows:

Pilot: - 'Excuse me, Sir, can you confirm I am not touching anything?'

Commander S: - 'That is correct.'

Pilot: - "Good, because your generator has just dropped into the jungle and it wasn't my fault!'

The 'Hearts and Minds' campaign meant that, on occasions, we gave lifts to locals if there was no other load. One of the Mappers came up to me in Kapit and said that a local trader had been particularly helpful and could I give him and his stores a lift back to Sibu? What he failed to tell me was that he was taking a load of Durian to Sibu market. It took two days to get rid of the smell.

Thinking about Mappers reminds me of when I was picking up a group of them off the top of a mountain in cloud. They had been stuck for some days and were very pleased to see me. I know that Paul Barton has written about this so I will say no more except that I will never do it again!

It was also Paul Barton who dumped his Hiller on a sand bank in the river with engine problems. It had to be retrieved before the river flooded so I went up with a Wessex and a crewman (Carney Blaine?) to bring it back as an underslung load. However, with a Hiller hanging underneath the Wessex couldn't carry much fuel, so refuelling stops had to be arranged on other river banks in the general direction of Sibu. The sequence of events was as follows: - I land by the Hiller, crewman gets out and marshals me over the Hiller, crewman runs in and hooks up Hiller, crewman runs out and waves to me so I lower the winch, crewman gets into strop, waves the winch wire about, so I winch him up, crewman gets into back and up we go - very slowly to next refuelling stop where we reverse the procedure. Shut down, refuel and start again. I think we did it three times and definitely needed a beer afterwards.

Same crewman, dropping Gurkhas at a border site; part of their rations included a tin of rum which they seldom took with them. Pulling up out of the site I asked the crewman if they had left us the rum. 'Glug' was all I heard- throat mikes are wonderful things!

Fishing at Nanga Gaat. The Gurkhas made superb use of those small *Nescafé* coffee tins. I remember going out into the middle of the river with them and a tin filled with explosive and a detonator. They dropped the tin in the water and then let the boat drift downstream, paying out the wire fixed to the detonator until we were at a safe distance - it seemed pretty close to me - they then connected up. The resulting explosion made us all very wet but it did produce a good supply of fish floating on the surface, which were soon collected for supper.

Working with the Guards Paras at Nanga Gaat. I was getting ready to fly a few of them up-country. I remember that numbers had to be reduced when they were with us because they weighed about twice the amount of the average Gurkha. On this occasion one of the Paras was Lord Patrick Beresford and, just before we all climbed in, I noticed him checking all his pockets very carefully. I made some comment about last-minute checks. 'Yes' he said, 'Just want to make sure I have my cheque-book with me.' I must have looked a bit surprised, so he grinned and said: 'Everyone has their price, my boy.'

Heli-skiing on the river. Somebody found a pair of water-skis. It seemed a great shame not to use them, but no suitable boat was available. So we obviously had to use one of the helicopters. I am pretty certain it was Tim Donkin who volunteered to ski and, since I had towed quite a few skiers in a boat before, I was in the helicopter. It worked surprisingly well. I hovered over the river, the crewman let out the winch-wire to Tim and away we went. I carried on down the river at what I felt was a good speed, but very quickly the crewman told me that Tim wanted to go faster. I can't remember the exact speed I got up to, but it was quite quick. I don't think it was tried again; perhaps the CO (Tank Sherman) got to hear about it and confiscated the skis.

Heroic Army Doctor. In 1964, Captain Patrick Crawford was the Regimental MO of the 1st/7th (Duke of Edinburgh's Own) Gurkha Rifles, in Sarawak.

On April 20th 1964, he flew in an 845 Wessex helicopter with Major Eric 'Birdie' Smith DSO, and six Gurkhas to visit a company which was operating near the Indonesian border. The helicopter landing platform was in a small clearing in dense jungle on the top of a ridge that dropped into a deep ravine.

The helicopter began descending from about 100ft and was short of the platform when the engine gave a cough and cut out. It dropped like a stone and there was a splintering crash as it slammed tail-first into the ground, hung for a second on its crumbling tail, and toppled over the edge of the ravine.

It somersaulted down the steep slope before its descent was arrested by a tree-stump which punched a hole in the cabin, crushing Major Smith's right arm and breaking his hip. Crawford, bruised and badly shaken, helped the Gurkhas to escape through the broken-off tail section and, ignoring a shouted warning that the aircraft could go up in flames at any moment, clambered through the wreckage to Smith, who was hanging by his shattered arm.

He got under Smith to support his weight and for almost an hour, in the stifling heat and semi-darkness of the fume-filled cabin, he worked on the man's injuries. He had no morphia or surgical instruments and was praying that Smith would faint from shock or loss of blood, but he remained conscious throughout.

First, Crawford applied a tourniquet and then, using a clasp-knife which had been hastily sharpened by one of the Gurkhas, he carried out an amputation of Smith's arm. He dressed the wound, held the man up until a stretcher party arrived, and then helped to improvise a hoist to lift him through the doorway, which was at a very awkward angle.

Crawford, who had refused to take a moment's rest or even a glass of water, was completely exhausted but he insisted on staying at Smith's side while the stretcher was carried up the hillside. He then flew with him in the relief helicopter to Simanggang and Kuching. In the operating theatres in both places he helped the doctors to perform tidying-up surgery. He was awarded the George Medal.

The Lads' Bar. The junior rates had been allowed to run their own bar in their bungalow, but things went astray and it had got into debt. Tank spoke to me one day and said that something needed to be done, because we were approaching the end of our time on shore and I was told to 'sort it'. I went and had a look round, changed their method of recording drinks and cigarettes taken, and put the two biggest blokes I could find in charge. There were also dire threats about money being deducted if it wasn't all in order in a fairly short space of time. It worked beautifully, all lost money was found, and all I had to do was order fresh supplies from the ship when needed.

The Squadron was nearing the end of its time in Sibu and we were getting visits from the RAF in Kuching talking about handovers. I am not sure how much later this happened, as I went back to the ship very soon after this. The RAF were quite anxious to help and said that if there was anything we needed they could bring it up on their next trip in the Twin Pioneer. My two Bar Men were about and suggested that a large carton of cigarettes and a few cases of beer would keep things running along nicely until they returned to *Bulwark*.

I went back to the ship for a few days and next time in Sibu asked the lads if all was well. 'No problem' they said. 'The stuff arrived from

Kuching and it's all been sorted out.' I flew back to the ship the next day (22 June 1965) and that was my last visit to Sibu.

That's the end of the story as far as Sibu and 845 were concerned, but....

About one year later I was on the SAR flight at Brawdy. I was shutting down at the end of a routine trip when one of the other crewmen (it could have been Den Woodhams) came out and said that two RAF policemen were waiting to speak to me. I spent 5 minutes longer than usual sorting out the machine and wondering what I had done. Once inside, I was taken into an office and asked if, when I had been in Sibu, etc., had I been in charge of a bar, and what did I know about cartons of cigarettes and cases of beer that had been delivered on a certain date and still not paid for? I said I knew nothing about it. (This was true because I was on the ship that day.) I was, of course, terribly sorry not to be of any help.

After about 20 minutes they left, not happy! It seemed strange to chase this up a year later; the costs of two police to Brawdy must have been greater than the 'lost' delivery, so I forgot all about it.

A few months later I left the Navy, worked in Uganda, Iran, Dubai and Aberdeen and then down to Redhill as an instructor at Bristow Helicopters' Training School.

Some 12-13 years after I had left the RN and bought a house in Handcross, just south of Gatwick, I often played squash with the village bobby who lived just up the road. One evening he knocked on the door and said he had to talk to me about a very serious matter. He said the RAF police had passed on information to the local police about a missing consignment of beer and cigarettes. I burst out laughing, which seemed to upset him. I told him I could not help and asked if he thought it was worth wasting police time chasing up something that had happened over 12 years ago in Borneo. He was actually quite upset and told me that it was in my best interests to tell all, etc. I suggested that we should go to the pub for a beer, but he refused and never spoke to me again.

It seems unbelievable that a little file was pushed from desk to desk for nearly 13 years and nobody had the common sense to bin it.

So far I have heard nothing more. But I am on alert for a visit from a Gendarme one day down here in France.

Borneo and 845 had their good times, but also their sad times, with some bad accidents. It is not a place I would want to return to. Very hot and sticky. Although, having said that, I did go back and work for Shell in Brunei, which is not far up the coast and, at the same time, Mike Thompson was working not many miles away in Miri. But it was a bit more civilized then.

A Light-hearted Advertisement for 845 (or How to Exist with a Sarong and a Spanner)

By Lieutenant 'Stu' Thompson Royal Navy Pilot 845 Squadron (Wessex 1)

For those of you itching for an 18-month unaccompanied commission with 845 Squadron on the strength of an article in 'Flight Deck', here are a few more facts to titillate your fancy and buttress your resolve.

Never fear, the luxuries of life are here in the jungle, with a new generating set at Nanga Gaat (the forward base) and new flats at Sibu (the backward base). Running water, electricity, films every night - what else do you want, women? Well there are some here too, and they have hardly heard of *Maidenform* and say 'never 'appen' and 'ello me old' all day long. In fact, with the new cookers and the running water at the Gaat we could qualify for Butlin status, but the conditions of entry are 70 hours per aircraft per month, 95% serviceability and a good tolerance for Tiger Beer. If you have all these things, apply to Lee and we are sure they will view your application with favour, especially if you have an aptitude for darts, a penchant for informal evening wear and a positive passion for monkeys coiled round your neck.

Although there has been no armed incursion or open internal threat in the Squadron parish for a few months, the time is well-occupied resupplying the jungle patrols, troop lifts, CASEVACs, and special flights for the Royal Corps of Swanners. (Yes, they really do exist).

The Hillers have been performing well until recently, when two dropped out of the luft within three days, fortunately without damage. However, they continue to delight the hearts of all Battalion

Commanders, who had read about Recce helicopter support for the Infantry at Staff College but have never seen it materialise. Temperature and height have, of course, affected the troop-carrying ability of the Squadron aircraft compared to colder climates, but the Wessex are performing magnificently in the conditions and are the subject of recognisable tattoos among the Iban tribesmen. CASEVACs are still an important part of the job, and babies will insist on trying to be born in mid-air. So much so that it is an advantage if the aircrewmen are qualified midwives, as well as being able to act as air-hostesses, quartermasters, pilot nurses and CCA controllers. Indeed, one delightful little girl has ended up with the name of 'Helicopter' and another with the charming handle of 'Emergency'. The doctors say it is something to do with the vibration.

The rainy season has arrived to foul up the electrics, so don't forget to bring an umbrella and a sackful of dessicant!

Hearts and Minds in the Jungle

From a 1964 *Evening News* Article

'From the rafters above us dangled a couple of human skulls, the dusty trophies of old Borneo feuds. A beautiful girl in a topless dress poured rice wine for the visitors in jungle green. In a corner squatted the elders of the long-house, the head-hunters themselves, Iban tribesmen with long hair and fantastic tattoos.

'They were deep in conference with a young Englishman wearing the necklace of many-coloured beads that is the Iban symbol of brotherhood. He was talking in the Iban language, and the head-hunters were listening with respect, though he was talking about nothing more exciting than building an Elsan for the long-house.

'Who was this young man? He might have been a colonial officer of the good old Sanders-of-the-River sort, but for his jungle green and the self-loading rifle that he always carries. In fact, writes Peter Duval Smith, he is a helicopter pilot in the Royal Navy called Neil Burns-Thompson, and his job in Borneo is to lift men and supplies to the Commonwealth forces guarding the jungle frontier between Malaysia and Indonesia.

'At least, that is half of his job: the other half is what he was doing in the longhouse at Long Jawi where he took me. "A useful bit of Hearts and Minds" was how he described his Elsan to me afterwards, and one of the biggest British contributions to the struggle in Borneo is this thing called the Hearts and Minds campaign.

'The hearts and minds in question are those of the tribes such as the Ibans and the Dyaks in whose inaccessible mountains the Indonesian confrontation is being staged. The frontier here is a colonial hangover, ill-defined and arbitrary, and the hill-tribes are straddled uncomfortably across it not feeling very much as if they belonged to either Indonesia or Malaysia.

'Traditionally their loyalties outside the tribe have been to Britain since the days of Rajah Brooke, and Malaysia seems a new-fangled idea that many feel has been foisted on them. Yet to defend the new federation without their help would be impossible.

'Borneo contains some of the most difficult country in the world, mountainous primary jungle with rushing rivers, and only the hill-people know the tracks and crossings that the Indonesian raiding parties use. More than that, with their contacts on the other side, they can give information that ensures a warm welcome for the invaders.

'This is why Hearts and Minds is so important, and why every British soldier on arrival in Borneo is given a little green booklet written with the help of the redoubtable Tom Harrisson, anthropologist and inventor of Mass Observation, and a great figure in Borneo, where he lives.

'He starts off in capital letters:

"THE WINNING OF THE HEARTS AND MINDS OF THE PEOPLES OF BORNEO IS OF GREAT IMPORTANCE," and goes on with a list of Do's and Don'ts.

There are not many Don'ts. "Don't shout at people: they hate it", "Don't take anything without paying for it", "Don't bathe in the nude."

'The Do's are the important thing. They are numerous and strictly practical. "Do help with making foot paths and bridges", "Do help in the killing of vermin", "Do learn to speak the local language", "Do deliver letters to and from remote areas." They go on in this tenor, summed up by the final injunction: "Do go out of your way to find out what the local problems are and try to solve them".

'This is the crux of the Hearts and Minds campaign: that the Commonwealth soldiery should not be a more or less friendly occupying force but an integral part of the country they are defending.

'It is a nice idea, but the question is, does it work? The British professional soldier these days is a pretty rough nut, and there is a do-gooding ring about Hearts and Minds he might be expected to shy away from. The answer is that the campaign is a runaway success, and looking after the locals is the favourite hobby of half the troops in Borneo.

'There was nothing special about the helicopter pilot sitting in council with his blood brothers, the head hunters. Sometimes indeed, the Hearts and Minds are overdone. I remember a young officer who explained shyly why his room was full of Huntley and Palmers' empty biscuit boxes. They were useful, he said, for the heads: just the right size for packing them off to the police in Kuching for identification.

'But, seriously, I met a medical orderly who worked 12 hours a day touring the longhouses: a corporal of the Jocks who was virtually mayor of a village of the primitive Punan tribesmen, who'd started a little school, and taught these people from the stone age to grow crops for the first time: a quartermaster who proudly pointed out the stack of tins of baby's milk he had managed to wheedle out of army stores: a young platoon commander of a frontier post who was the Tuan of villages on both sides of the border.

'Hearts and minds are being won, then, but that is not the end of the matter. Nothing is simple in this strange war that is not a war. Who are the hearts and minds being won by? Who commands the loyalties of the Borneo people? The answer is, of course, the British, just as they always did.

'It is an embarrassing answer, because Sukarno's loudest complaint is precisely that Malaysia is a neo-colonialist state. In the longhouses today coloured pictures of Tunku Abdul Rahman and the railway station at

Kuala Lumpur have taken, the place of the Queen and Westminster, but that is not enough to make Borneo people feel like Malaysians.

'The sad truth is that the Malays look down on them as savages, and they dislike the Malays. Most federation government servants in Borneo are Malays, and they are inclined to be high-handed. They do not get out enough into the mountain areas, and very little government money goes towards the mountain people. Considering how much depends on them in the present struggle, it is strange that Kuala Lumpur is not building clinics, schools, roads and airstrips on the largest possible scale.

'In the meantime, when a Navy helicopter clatters down-river past the longhouses, it's quite likely to have been seconded from military duty to carry a sick Iban or Dyak or Kelabit child to hospital on the coast. The hill-people know this, and as one tattooed old man said in my presence, "What will we do when the British go? We hope they never do go."'

My Confrontation in Malaya, Borneo and Singapore

By Lieutenant Jimmy James Royal Navy - Pilot 845 Squadron (Wessex 1)

Malaya - September 1964. It was reported that parachutists had flown into the Segamat/Labis, Malaya early in the month. On 6th I was tasked with Johnny Foster as my number 2 to collect General Joly from GHQ in Tanglin and take him to the area. He met the Malay Regiment people on the ground and we tried to return him to Singapore. The weather as we approached Johore deteriorated and we had to return to Kluang, whence the General proceeded by road. The weather cleared and we returned to Sembawang. I reported to The CO (Lt Cdr Tank Sherman) who was generous in agreeing that we had done the right thing despite our embarrassment that we had not completed the task. This was reinforced when the Squadron received a thank-you message from the General congratulating us on the efforts we had made.

The Squadron re-embarked on 7th September for exercises with HMS *Centaur* off the East Coast of Malaya. On 11th September we were tasked to search the area between Labis and the sea to try to find if there were any parachutes still showing in the trees. It must have been on about this day that General Joly decided that the Malay Regiment was not achieving the success he expected in their operations against the Indonesians, and so decided to put in 1/10th Gurkha Rifles and 1st Royal New Zealand Regiment supported by three aircraft from 845. In command of the detachment was John Morgan, with Martin Banks as the SP and Tim Donkin, Lindsay Macpherson and me as the pilots.

We were first based at Segamat and subsequently at Labis. It is sad to record that on the first night that the 1/10th went in, one of the British Officers, a company commander, was killed under suspicious circumstances following a possible surrender. We did not see a live Indonesian after that. We just pulled out bodies. The 1/10th would not let the Kiwis in close - they formed an outside ring!

After a few days we moved to the airstrip at Labis. Here we were in an oil-palm plantation. The rats liked the oil palm and the cobras liked the rats. One morning, doing a Before Flight Inspection (B/F) on an aircraft, a cobra was found curled up on the seat in the after cabin below the pilot's seat. The Kiwis referred to it as a 'helicobra'!

One morning we were tasked for a troop lift with all three aircraft from a Gurkha position. We arrived slightly early and had to hold in the area. At the de-brief that night the CO of the regiment, Lieutenant Colonel 'Bunny' Burnett, said to John Morgan – 'John, any fool can be late, any fool can be early, but it takes a good man to be on time!' (This is a lesson I have never forgotten in any part of my life!)

One evening the Kiwi Colonel invited us all to go to his briefing in the local police station. After the formal part the Colonel announced to his team that he had invited the 'Navy Boys' up for a beer. Crates appeared – to be followed by 'the little brown jug'. It is the only time that I have been thrown out of a police station by the police, who wanted us back in our camp!

On our return we continued with a few beers in the HQ Company Commander's tent. Lindsay Macpherson decided that the Kiwis should have nuclear protection and proceed to start an underground HQ for them. Next morning, as we passed the tent on our way to the aircraft, we heard the voice of Major Des Smith, in his broad New Zealand accent saying – 'I wish I could get hold of the bugger who dug a hole in the middle of my CP!' We tip-toed on!

Nanga Gaat – 1965. On 25th February, I was tasked to fly as Number 2 to Neil Burns-Thompson to pull out a Gurkha Para patrol that (against published policy) had carried out an operation 'over the border'. The pick-up was also to be 'over the border' at the headwaters of the Baleh and at a considerable height. On our arrival Neil had problems with his intercom and, since we were going to have to be in the tops of the trees, I was going to have to do the lift of nine Gurkhas with Neil 'riding shotgun'. Because of the height, our lift capability was to be much reduced and we positioned fuel drums and a pump by the river. At the landing site we put out the winch to its full extent but, despite being into the top of the trees, the strop did not reach the ground. My crewman, NA Harrison, hooked the climbing rope onto the winch and the Ghurkhas tied their packs to the rope, climbed up the rope and fitted themselves into the strop to be winched up. It took a couple of runs to achieve the task because of the height and the Wessex 1's limited power at that height. Neil's encouragement from time to time over the radio was most welcome!

Boyd Trophy. I have a copy in my Log Book of Naval Air Command Weekly Orders 12/2nd/6th5, which announced the award of the Boyd Trophy for 1964 to 845 Squadron.

April 1965 – Singapore. I was charged with the organisation of John Morgan's funeral in Singapore. I was most upset when, as we prepared for the service outside the church in the Naval Base, one of the Ship's Engineer Officers expressed his sorrow at what had happened. I replied that it was very sad because John had been such a good man and most experienced pilot. He said that it was not that – it was the accident at Nanga Gaat the night before when Rod Robertson and Johnny Hapgood had had their mid-air collision. This was the first I had heard of that. I returned to UK soon afterwards and took with me the jewellery that John had bought for his wife. I delivered it to her since she lived a hundred yards away from us in Helston, next door to Geoff Andrews. This was my saddest task in 845.

I held a party in Sembawang Mess the night before I left, followed by dinner at the Tanglin Club. The next morning, I arrived at the Britannia Charter aircraft that was to take me back to UK and sat next to the OC Troops – an elderly Major. On questioning him over his three and a half years in Singapore, I asked if he had had a party the night before. He reported he had had a quiet dinner at the Tanglin Club. I said 'Oh! We were at the Tanglin Club.' 'Oh!' he replied, 'You were the party with the hunting-horn, were you?' He did not speak to me all the way to Bombay! (Thanks to Neil B-T!)

My Longest Day

By Lieutenant Michael Reece Royal Marines - Pilot 845 Squadron (Wessex 1)

During my tour at Sibu and Nanga Gaat, many of the most demanding tasks 845 Squadron faced were the insertion, support, resupply and extraction of the four-man patrols based in Sibu but spread throughout the Third Division in the SAS role. Initially, an SAS Squadron provided these patrols but, as the duration of the conflict extended, specially-trained companies from other units replaced them. These were: a company formed from the 2nd Parachute Battalion, the Gurkha Parachute Company and the Guards Independent Parachute Company. I believe, without exception, we all admired the professionalism of these remarkable men who patrolled in such a vast area of primary jungle for one to two months at a time, isolated and entirely reliant on our support. However, some forty-five years later, without degrading at all the standards and accomplishments of the others, the company that stands out in my memory was the inimitable Guards Independent Parachute Company. Not only was their organisation and patrolling highly professional, but they had - STYLE.

Sadly, to my shame, I cannot now recall the name of their Company Commander, who was responsible for overall operational and administrative competence of the company. From the Sibu perspective he was excellent, particularly as he had to lead (control) such highly individualistic officers as Robin Dixon, who had won a gold medal as a member of the Olympic Bobsleigh team, Algy Clough of Clough Oil, who, I recall on one occasion at Long Jawi, carried a cheque-book in his hip pocket, and Lord Patrick Beresford.

As examples of 'style', it was not uncommon for us to deliver with the standard 'compo' resupply sorties a hamper ordered from *Fortnum & Masons* - STYLE! Also, I witnessed certain patrol commanders on return to Sibu from a one to two month patrol, hand all their 'grotty' kit and weapons over to an orderly, then take a shower at the airport before catching the next Borneo Airways flight enroute to Singapore, or even Hong Kong. They returned just in time to meet up with their guardsmen and lead them back into the jungle - STYLE!

My 'Longest Day' fell on 9th October 1964 when Major General Nelson, The General Officer Commanding the Household Division, decided it would be a good idea, before his imminent retirement, to visit as many guardsmen as he could serving around the globe. Not surprisingly, the Guards Independent Parachute Company presented a particular challenge. My task was to fly him in what was a well-co-ordinated operation to meet and speak, very briefly, to all the patrols scattered throughout the Third Division on that particular day. My abiding memory is landing on a reasonably large shingle bank in the midst of a fast-flowing river. Naturally, there was no question of shutting down, but nor was there any sight of the patrol. After what I suspect was a minute or two, but seemed an age at the time, I spotted the patrol wading up the river towards us. The water was over waist height and their rifles were raised above their heads. Only then did I permit the General to leave the aircraft and advance across the shingle bank. I then witnessed the magnificent spectacle of this soaking-wet, four-man patrol gradually emerge from the river, place their rifles at the shoulder and take up their dressing in a single rank. And then, as the General approached, the patrol commander took an immaculate parade-ground pace forward, saluted and presented his patrol for inspection - STYLE.

The whole task absorbed 8 hours 10 minutes of precious Wessex hours, of which the last hour was at night returning from Nanga Gaat and with the gallant General, not surprisingly, asleep. In slight mitigation to the General's main objective, wherever possible we did combine these separate patrol RVs with a resupply. Nevertheless, with hindsight, I think it was remiss of us not to send an invoice. Knowing the Guards at the time, I suspect they would have paid in style!

THE DAY - March 4th 1965

By Mike Thompson 845 Squadron (Pilot Wessex 1)

On 16th February 1965 I was directed to take a Wessex from the 845 Squadron main base at Sibu airport to Nanga Gaat, with the intention that I should be based at Nanga Gaat for a period to gain some intensive flying on the Wessex, having mainly been operating the Hiller 12E from the Sibu base prior to that. In the period from 16th February to 3rd March, I actually flew 27 hours 15 minutes on the Wessex.

On the morning of 4th March two Wessex Mk 1 helicopters were tasked to recover a 1st Royal Malay Regiment platoon-strength patrol from a landing site (LS) at a location on a river, Ulu Sungai Puro, about 25nm South of Nanga Gaat. Squadron procedures were, whenever possible, to always fly in company over primary jungle.

Myself, in Wessex side letter 'E' (Echo), (registration XP108), and Lieutenant Derek Scott, in Wessex 'H' (Hotel), took off from Nanga Gaat soon after the early jungle mists cleared at about 1030. My aircrewman was Petty Officer Radio Electrical Artificer (REA) 2c (A), Alan J. Williams, Service Number F956483.

We flew in loose formation to the pick-up landing site on a clearing near a river, capable of taking one helicopter at a time, picked up one load of troops each, flew them back to Nanga Gaat and then both returned to collect the remaining troops.

Derek Scott landed and picked up his load first and I followed immediately afterwards and picked up the final six soldiers. I climbed up to about 1500 feet above ground level and headed back towards Nanga Gaat, in visual (and radio) contact with Derek in 'Hotel' some distance in front of me.

In order to conserve fuel I decided to revert from automatic to manual throttle control - this being a procedure recommended in Squadron Standing Orders for pilots to practise regularly on routine flights. The procedure involved reducing power temporarily by lowering the collective lever, flicking a switch to disengage automatic throttle and reverting to manual, twist-grip, throttle on the collective lever.

As soon as I flicked the switch and began to raise the collective again things started to go very wrong. There was a deep rumbling noise from the engine, immediately recognizable as compressor 'surge', an obvious lack of power, resulting in having to lower the collective lever to maintain rotor revolutions (revs) and very visible (and worrying!) six-foot flames emitting from both pairs of jet-pipe exhausts on either side of the engine. The jet-pipes are located just below cockpit level and the flames coming out of the starboard side exhausts seemed very close to the open cockpit window!

As the rotor revs started to reduce rapidly due to lack of power it was immediately necessary to lower the collective completely, reduce airspeed and enter autorotation. This meant that we were descending at about 1200 to 1500 feet per minute, with no power – and with flames coming out on both sides.

The first action was to make a MAYDAY call, which was answered immediately by Derek in 'Hotel'.

'MAYDAY, MAYDAY, MAYDAY – Echo, Echo, Echo – engine failure over primary jungle - intending engine-off landing on jungle canopy.'

Three urgent decisions had to be made. Firstly, was it possible to shut the engine down and attempt a re-start? Quickly disregarded as a viable option due to the remaining time available before reaching the ground and the obviously impaired state of the engine, with the Turbine Outlet Temperature having gone 'off the clock'.

Secondly, should I shut down the engine or was there a chance that there would be some power remaining to assist in the now inevitable landing on the jungle canopy? (The jungle tree-cover was 100 percent complete and usually referred to as 'cauliflower jungle', with absolutely no clearings). No contest – the engine had to be shut down to avoid arriving on the ground in an uncontrolled landing with a very obvious ignition source.

Lastly, the topography was rough; sharply-ridged, jungle-covered hills with steep-sided slopes leading down to narrow stream beds, the water not being visible due to forest tree cover.

Should I attempt the engine-off landing on top of a ridge? Rejected as too sharp. On the slopes? Rejected as too steep. Or at the bottom of the valley? – selected as the 'best bet' choice.

Time is passing rapidly. The whole autorotation descent time from 1500 feet to ground level is about 60 seconds!

Check the airspeed (60 to 70 knots) and rotor revolutions; pick an intended landing spot at the bottom of a valley, brief the crewman (who I heard immediately organizing the cabin – weapons on the floor under the seats, standby to brace, demonstrate brace position, BRACE! BRACE! BRACE!)

Remember thinking that the situation was not good. This might be the end… but being too busy to worry about it!

Approaching the jungle canopy at the selected position at bottom of a steep valley; raise the nose to flare off forward speed; check rotor revs increasing in the flare; level the helicopter and raise collective to cushion the descent as we sink the final few feet onto the canopy. Canopy looks less dense than expected close up! But still a long way off the ground!

Brace myself as the aircraft descends into the canopy and the rotor blades contact the tree branches - noise, tremendous forces and total mayhem - then nothing further……..

The Rescue. Due to the low fuel situation, Derek Scott in 'Hotel' was unable to remain at the crash site but, having established the position, returned directly to Nanga Gaat, offloaded his passengers, refuelled and picked up Lieutenant Tim Donkin, Royal Marines, the Nanga Gaat Detachment Commander to return to the site to initiate the rescue.

Tim Donkin's account. I got Derek Scott to take me to look for you very quickly. I guess we were overhead 'Echo' in about 20 minutes after your forced landing. I went down below from the left-hand seat and got ready to be winched down by the crewman, NA Harrison. As I got to within about one foot of the stream in which 'Echo' had ended up, at the full extent of the 120-ft winch-line - and could see the flattened 'Echo' and yourself looking completely lifeless - the winch started taking me up! Not good.

Once back up in the left-hand seat, I asked Derek what was going on. He had had no option but to pull me back up, as Hotel's throttle had jammed at nearly full power. We flew to Kapit, where a small landing strip had recently been built. Derek didn't wish to do an engine-off, nor did I, sitting in the 'wrong' seat and having just seen 'Echo' at close quarters! I still feel guilty about doing what I did, namely a run-on landing but, at the time, I reckoned we could not afford to risk another potential aircraft write-off. The priority was to get help to 'Echo'.

From dangling on the (very!) end of the winch-wire looking at you and then being pulled up again, it was no more than, say, 20 min before Derek and I were on the strip at Kapit. On the way there I asked for the second Wessex, which was already on its way either to Nanga Gaat from Sibu or to 'Echo' from the Gaat, to divert and pick me up. They were at Kapit within about 5 or 10 min after we had 'landed' - and immediately took off again with me in the cabin *en route* back to Echo – another 15-20 min - so by the time I'd got down to you the second time, I guess probably about 1 hour had elapsed since the crash.

Roger Edmonds was flying the aircraft that picked me and Harrison up from Kapit and, after returning to the crash site, winched us both down to you and 'Echo'.

On reaching your aircraft it seemed that you were a goner - and there looked to be little chance of anyone else having survived either. As I climbed up onto the wreckage you opened a very black and blood-shot eye. Such indescribable relief that you were OK! We somehow got you out of the right-hand door (open as usual, luckily) and into a stretcher from Roger's aircraft, 'Bravo'. There being no apparent chance of extricating anyone else at this stage, Roger took you straight down to Sibu and thence to hospital.

What I never told you was that, once finally on the wreckage, Harrison and I were listening to the most horrible groaning coming from some of the Malay soldiers completely trapped in the wreckage. As we struggled to extricate the passengers, their groans became weaker and eventually fell silent. By the time we got their bodies out no-one was still alive.

We had called PO Williams by name, but I feel quite sure that he was almost certainly dead on impact as the main gearbox and engine had all seemingly folded in on his crewman's position/seat. We could not see his body at all.

We got 4 bodies out and up in stretchers to Michael Reece and Neil Burns-Thompson in another Wessex. By this time dusk was falling (you will remember how quickly that happens in the tropics) and

Michael, who was in the 'clearing' hovering on his landing light, was telling us (somehow!) that we had to choose between getting out ourselves now, or staying there overnight. No thank you to the latter!!

However, before leaving the crash site we managed to extricate the last two soldiers' bodies and placed them under a tree well up from the stream and 'Echo'. 'Echo' had lost its blades as it came down through the trees and had crashed onto a large rock in the middle of a tiny stream. The aircraft had more or less flattened itself onto its port side. This was so lucky for you, as you ended up almost out in the open, high starboard (and still strapped in).

We could not get to PO Williams as he was totally unreachable somewhere under the gearbox.

Michael and Neil finally got us out of the clearing and back to Nanga Gaat in the pitch black, as far as I recall. Early the next morning, after a torrential storm that night, Derek Scott, again, took me and a Leading Airman (LAM) aircrewman (can't remember his name, but might have been Blain?- Harrison having understandably declined to return!) back to 'Echo' to collect the two bodies previously removed from the crash site and placed well up the slope. There was much mist around and everything looked spookily different. Indeed we went to the right place, yet could see no trace of any aircraft at all. Quite unnerving, believe me!

After further searching we realised we were in the correct place and Derek's aircraft winched us down to the small stream bed. For that is what it had been, and had now returned to being. However, it soon became clear that during the night a roaring river of extreme ferocity must have washed down the valley and taken with it the whole aircraft, PO Williams' body included, and the two soldiers whom we had had to leave up the slope. From the jungle debris now hanging from the trees, we reckoned the river must have risen by at least 30 to 40 feet overnight. A flash flood of awesome power it must have been.

The only proof that 'Echo' had been there at all was various small yellow paint marks on the rock. We then went down-river, searching on either side, and eventually came across the two soldiers' bodies in separate locations. Of The helicopter 'Echo' there was no sign at all. Several days later, even weeks I think it may have been, the remains of 'Echo' were discovered miles downstream in the Rajang River.

Fig 40. 'E' wreckage, after being washed downstream

PO Alan Williams' body was never recovered. One can only imagine that whilst being washed down the river that night from where you had force-landed, the aircraft had gradually disintegrated, leaving poor Alan Williams' broken body to be freed into the swirling waters and away. As I'm sure you know, the wreckage was about the size of a compressed Gazelle engine and gearbox combined! This 'block' was taken back to UK, where Rolls-Royce engineers were able to identify that a small nut had worked loose and had been ingested via the engine air intake and thence through the inlet guide-vanes and on through the turbine blades, causing your engine to suffer catastrophic surge followed by engine failure. The cause of the crash was thus shown to have been entirely due to mechanical failure.

Afterwards – by Mike Thompson again. After the forced landing I remember nothing until a vague recollection of green leaves and branches circling before my eyes. I am informed that, having been placed on a rigid stretcher, whilst obviously still unconscious, to be winched up to the rescue helicopter, I apparently showed signs of regaining consciousness and attempting to sit up whilst half-way up to the helicopter. Luckily, due to my injuries and being strapped in, I was unable to move much.

My next memory is attempting to enquire, whilst on a stretcher in the helicopter in flight to Sibu, about the status of my crewman, Alan Williams, and the six Royal Malay Regiment soldiers who were on board during the crash landing. The reply was evasive but I remember not believing that anyone could have been seriously injured or killed whilst I was still alive and (relatively) undamaged.

I was flown to Sibu airport and transferred to Sibu hospital for specialist assessment and initial treatment. The doctor responsible for this was

Dr Wong Soon Kai, a highly-qualified and successful Sarawak citizen doctor.

X-rays confirmed that I had suffered a compound fracture of Lumbar 2 vertebrae but, luckily, had avoided spinal-cord damage. Quite painful, though! Treatment comprised prone bed-rest and extremely painful vitamin B complex injections into the thighs!

After about one week in Sibu hospital I was transferred, by air, via Kuching, to the British Military hospital in Singapore, where I spent another three weeks recovering before being released to convalesce in Singapore, based at HMS Simbang, RNAS Sembawang.

Whilst in BMH Singapore the tragic news was received on 9th April that Lieutenant John Morgan had been killed in an air accident whilst piloting a Hiller 12E in the Hose Mountains near Nanga Gaat and then, on 12th April, that a further two squadron pilots, Rod Robertson and 'Happy' Hapgood and one crewman, plus 5 soldiers, had died following a mid-air collision between two Wessex helicopters whilst approaching to land at Nanga Gaat.

The decision was made for me to remain in Singapore until deemed fit enough to fly again and then to 'get straight back onto the horse', and recommence Squadron flying. In my opinion this was the correct course of action and, with the confidence of youth, I assessed that, having had one engine failure over primary jungle, the risk of that happening again was remote! I commenced flying again on 27th May 1965 in Singapore.

Part 4

Indonesian Confrontation May 1965 to October 1966

848 Squadron Relieves 845 Squadron in Borneo in May 1965

By Lieutenant Commander Geoff Andrews, CO 848 Squadron – Wessex Mk 5

848 Squadron arrived in Borneo in HMS *Albion* on 22nd May 1965 equipped with the new Wessex Mk 5, and the transition from 845 to 848 Squadron responsibility commenced on 23rd May and was completed on 30th June 1965. During this time the detachments at both Sibu and Nanga Gaat were relieved, the Wessex Mk 1 re-embarked in HMS *Albion* and 848 Squadron assumed full responsibility for the provision of tactical and logistic helicopter support to Security Forces in the 3rd Division of Sarawak on 22nd June. Although hectic, the period proved invaluable and the actual method of hand-over devised by the Commanding Officer of 845 Squadron proved very satisfactory.

Experience had shown that maximum Commando Squadron flexibility could be achieved by operating in groups of four aircraft. In consequence, 848 Squadron was organised into five distinct sections as follows:

a.   HQ Flight (2 Wessex Mk 5).

Commanding Officer, newly-joined Officers (P), Air Engineering Officers, majority of Squadron senior rates and all non-technical Complement.

Lieutenant Commander (P) (Senior Pilot embarked) (Detachment Commander disembarked)

Lieutenant Commander (P) (Detachment Commander disembarked)

b.   A, B, C and D Flights, each with 4 Wessex Mk 5,

Lieutenant (P) in Command with 5-plus pilots and balanced First Line Servicing Team.

The above organisation was capable of disembarking four or multiples of four aircraft, as required, to support shore operations as self-contained units. In addition, HQ Flight personnel could be disembarked as necessary to supply Second Line Servicing and administrative support.

Further advantages were that:

HQ Flight could also give Theatre and Ship familiarisation to officers and men who join the Commando Ship in the Far East.

A Lieutenant Commander was always disembarked with one or more Flights and was designated 'Detachment Commander'.

Each Flight was commanded by an experienced Lieutenant.

The Flights could be rotated with the minimum of administrative disruption and each Flight was self-contained to the extent of having permanent Divisional Officers, Stores, Staff Officer, etc.

The Commanding Officer was able to position himself ashore or on board depending on the current situation regarding operations and exercises.

A quite unintentional but nevertheless significant side-effect of this organisation had become apparent. The increased responsibility conferred upon officers and ratings throughout the Squadron had a very beneficial effect. The friendly rivalry generated between Flights gave an edge to morale, initiative and standard of maintenance. In a Squadron consisting of 18 Wessex Mk 5 aircraft, 2 Whirlwind Mk.7 aircraft and a total complement of 250 officers and men, this sense of belonging to the 'Best' Flight was a very important factor, which was encouraged.

The administration of this organisation from the more mundane points such as pay, documentation and records, etc., provided some headaches, but the Squadron Staff Officer and Leading Writer proved admirable.

On the other hand, there were some shortcomings. Neither the Ship Depot Task List of Stores and Spares, nor the Squadron mobile support equipment, was capable of supporting the Squadron efficiently when it was required to operate in three, sometimes four locations at one and the same time. As an example, at one period the Squadron was dispersed as follows:

'A' Flight (4 aircraft) disembarked at Aden;

HQ & 'B' Flights (6 aircraft) embarked in HMS *Albion*;

'C' Flight (4 aircraft) disembarked at Sibu;

'D' Flight (4 aircraft) disembarked at Nangga Gaat.

The answer proposed was to increase *Albion's* Depot Task List considerably in order that Flights could be given a proportion of it whenever they disembarked for lengthy periods. The Naval Air Stores Organisation backed us magnificently, but the urgent despatch by air freight from all four corners of the World was an expensive alternative to the proposed solution.

Previously the 845 Squadron Borneo Detachments, consisting of 7 Wessex Mk 1, 2 Whirlwind Mk 7 and 1 Hiller aircraft, averaged 490 flying hours per month during the period January to June, 1965.

In order to compete with this average tasking rate it was considered essential to disembark two 4-aircraft Flights of 848 Squadron and to transfer the two Whirlwind Mk 7 aircraft to 848. The Wessex Mk 5 aircraft was at that time limited to a maximum of 40 flying hours per aircraft per month in the Borneo theatre. The theoretical shortfall in tasking hours available per month compared with 845 operations was, therefore, 170. The Whirlwind Mk 7 was restricted to flying on relatively safe routes for Flight Safety reasons, but it was confidently expected that Whirlwind Mk 7 utilisation plus the superior performance of the Wessex Mk 5 would compensate. The improved performance of the Wessex Mk 5 could not, however, always be fully utilised due to the prevailing requirement to also fly two aircraft on the majority of the tasks for purely Flight Safety reasons. Lack of reliable communications and the nature of the geography rendered this an essential Standard Operating Procedure. Nevertheless, all tasks were met as well as the numerous requests for MEDEVACs, etc.

The Squadron was unfortunate to suffer a spate of previously unexperienced engine problems immediately on assumption of responsibility in the operational theatre. However, as far as that particular defect was concerned, the cause was identified and remedial action to prevent recurrence put in hand.

The cost in man-hours in unscheduled maintenance was considerable, but the fact that this extra work was achieved by a small body of skilled technicians over a period of approximately three weeks spoke eloquently of the devotion to duty of the Fleet Air Arm maintenance ratings in general and of the Squadron personnel in particular. A large proportion of this work entailed robbing action to 'keep 'em flying' and could have been avoided had more components been available 'on the shelf'.

I felt that many of the minor unserviceabilities experienced during Wessex Mk 5 operations could have been avoided had the aircraft been designed to operate in temperatures ranging from minus 15° C to plus 40° C, and the aircraft flown for protracted periods in Far East theatre conditions before being committed to the deep end.

Nevertheless, despite these teething troubles, we had a very fine aircraft which we were proud of and which went on to provide good service for many years to come.

During August 1965, serviceability of the aircraft improved markedly following the incorporation of modifications to the Inlet Guide Vanes (IGV), Actuator Filters and Engine Air Intakes. The necessary reduction in flying intensity due to the re-organisation of re-supply to patrols was, of course, a major factor. However, Pressure Transmitters still formed a major proportion of our minor unserviceabilities.

An incident occurred during the month where an unserviceable Army Scout helicopter was inadvertently dropped from a low hover. In the past, human error has accounted for more than one such drop but in this case full investigation revealed that hook malfunction was the cause.

The duplicate Rotor Tachometer, sited on top of the 1st Pilot's instrument coaming, provided a hazard to restricted area landings. Its presence impeded an essential line of vision and, as a large proportion of the approaches made in the operating theatre are into jungle clearings, several pilots had complained that this instrument rendered an approach hazardous.

Early in August, COMBRITBOR proposed a plan to re-deploy the 848 Squadron detachments to Labuan and Bario in order to rationalise the disposition of heavy-lift helicopters in Borneo. This plan was approved and subsequently carried out.

September/October 1965

The transfer of 848 Squadron Sibu and Nanga Gaat detachments from the 3rd to the 4th Division of Sarawak went more smoothly than I had anticipated. Originally 110 Squadron RAF was to have been based at Kapit and this would have entailed withdrawing every item of Naval Stores from both Sibu and Nanga Gaat. After reconnaissance, the RAF authorities decided that facilities offered at Sibu and Nanga Gaat were better and 848 was, therefore, able to transfer many items of a more permanent nature direct to the RAF; this, of course, reduced the work entailed considerably. Nevertheless, there remained sufficient items of stores and equipment to provide an LST with a useful cargo.

An early reconnaissance of Bario indicated the necessity for extra accommodation, four new landing pads and extra generator capacity, and the Squadron was indebted to the Royal Engineers, commanded by Lieutenant Colonel Arnold of COMBRITBOR's staff, for providing these facilities at such short notice.

The Commanding Officer and administrative staff of RAF Labuan were most cooperative and both Squadron dispersal and accommodation offered good facilities for work and relaxation.

By the end of October, when a complete month of operations had been completed in Central Brigade area, a general pattern of tasks had emerged. Tasking of aircraft at Bario was usually confined to sorties in direct support of border positions, rotation and re-supply of troops. An additional task, very expensive in flying hours, was the roulement of Battalions, the 2nd/6th Gurkhas being replaced by the 1st Battalion, Gordon Highlanders in the Bario operational area. The aircraft at Labuan were basically held in reserve for Bario, but were also employed quite heavily in the rear areas deploying troops and stores to TAC HQs and sometimes helping out with larger troop movements in the Sepulot/Pensiangan area, which was primarily supported by Whirlwind Mk 10 aircraft of 230 Squadron RAF.

The Squadron had now settled in thoroughly at Labuan and Bario. The facilities and accommodation at Labuan were good and, although those at Bario were rather more primitive, they were offset by the climate - which was far cooler.

848 Squadron Takes Over at Nanga Gaat

By Lieutenant John Kelly Royal Navy - 848 Squadron (Wessex Mk 5)

'Delta' Flight Commander

848 Squadron 'Delta' Flight disembarked from *Albion* to Sibu on 22nd May 1965. The following day four pilots moved to Nanga Gaat to familiarise themselves with the operational area by flying with 845 Squadron pilots in their Wessex Mk 1s. On 31st May, two 848 Wessex Mk 5 aircraft were detached to Nanga Gaat permanently. By 15th June the detachment had built up to four aircraft and 845 Squadron then withdrew. At the end of June we commenced familiarising the first of 'Charlie' Flight pilots who were due to relieve us towards the end of July.

The Independent Company 2nd Battalion Parachute Regiment was in the process of withdrawing from the 3rd Division. On one occasion we flew armed sorties with three aircraft on two successive days to search for an overdue patrol. On the first day they were located by SARBE and on the second day winched out. One sortie extracted another patrol whose boat had capsized and been lost. The only other unusual incident was a search by two aircraft of the Belaga area where a parachute drop was suspected. The report was found to be false.

With the withdrawal of the Paratroops, 3rd Battalion Royal Malay Regiment (RMR) took over their responsibilities. The RMR patrols were some 20 to 30 men strong, necessitating three or even four aircraft tasks at times. The added payload of the Wessex Mk 5, however, offset the larger numbers. Also, the RMR seemed to be more static than the Paras and used well-established landing zones. Both features helped to reduce our flying hours.

Another unit, No. 1 Topographical Survey Troop Royal Engineers, completed its surveying tasks on Bukit, Demas, Punan and Bora, simultaneously. There then followed a most spectacular day when we lifted all three teams, each weighing 2,500 lbs. Their main effort then concentrated to the South and East of Nanga Gaat, where one site had been completed; a further two had to be engineered before the survey teams could be deployed.

A four-day Forward Air Control Exercise was carried out using a Whirlwind Mk.7, based either at Nanga Gaat or Long Jawi, to provide aerial observation and command for the Forward Air Controller. The Whirlwind proved invaluable, saving 20 Wessex hours, and the ARC 52 UHF radio avoided the necessity of fitting special crystals in a Wessex Mk 5 FTR 170 UHF set.

Where possible, our four Wessex Mk 5s and one Whirlwind Mk 7 were maintained at Nanga Gaat. All operational tasks were met but not without some skilful juggling of aircraft between there and Sibu. During the month the aircraft flew 290 hours. There were 19 days with all aircraft serviceable, 9 days with one serviceable and 2 days with two serviceable. This serviceability figure, at Nanga Gaat, was achieved largely due to the first-class maintenance effort of both the Sibu and Nanga Gaat detachments, despite the teething troubles of our new Wessex Mk 5s.

Two major improvements were introduced at Nanga Gaat. A new dining hall and galley was completed with overhead fans. A new generator was air-lifted from Kapit, installed and commissioned. However, a fractured fuel-line necessitated operating on three cylinders only, but this still produced ample power for our needs. One black note, however; the new generator caused interference with our Nanga Gaat COMCEN H/F frequencies, so much so that during the day, whilst aircraft were airborne, it had to be switched off and the original, smaller generator used in lieu to provide power for the refrigerator and the Sick Bay steriliser. The 'Anchor Inn' was completely re-decorated and a new bar installed. The Operations Room and Flying Clothing stowage were 'face-lifted' and one bridge between the Naval and RMR site, with adjoining steps, was rebuilt. The next step was to have tapped running water in the bar, the sink already being there.

Our introduction to the Ibans was gradual, largely because of the heavy maintenance task. However, all of us could converse to a limited extent with our local neighbours; Lieutenant Robert Faulks, our Iban Liaison Officer, and P.O.A.F. Osborne (the Buffer), in particular, became very expert. On 30th June the District Officer was flown from Kapit to Rumah Kumbong, which was 15 minutes' flying time from Nanga Gaat. This particular Long House was celebrating its own New Year. There were some 500 guests, of whom 15 were from Nanga Gaat. We were now all experts on sticking wild pigs.

A simple but very moving Service of Dedication was held and a memorial erected to commemorate those members of 845 Squadron and officers and men of the Security Services who had lost their lives whilst serving on operations in the Nanga Gaat area.

Flight Lieutenant McCrann RAF was appointed as tasking officer on a trial basis. His presence was most welcome and ensured continuity in operational matters throughout the day in the absence of the Detachment Commander. The planning of the following day's tasking could now be completed satisfactorily by 1800. We hoped that this appointment would be made permanent after the initial trial period and thus relieve the Flight Commander of an unnecessary burden on completion of each day's task.

Overall, we had a busy first month's flying at Nanga Gaat, during which a running battle was fought every day between aircraft serviceability problems and the operational task.

848 Squadron Detachment May and June 1965

From a Report by Lieutenant Ben Caesar - Pilot 848 Squadron (Wessex Mk.5)

In addition to 'Delta' Flight of 848 Squadron's disembarkation already described, the Commanding Officer of 848 Squadron (Lieutenant Commander Geoff Andrews) also came ashore, together with the Squadron Deputy Air Engineer Officer (Electrical Lieutenant G. A. Madgwick) and the Squadron Staff Officer (Lieutenant B. Madgwick). The Flight was backed by a small number of Senior Rates from HQ Flight to provide Second Line Servicing.

The first month at Sibu was spent working alongside 845 Squadron, gradually taking over the task at Nanga Gaat. Working and living conditions at both Nanga Gaat and Sibu were cramped, but 845 Squadron did their utmost to make life as comfortable as possible for us. By 15th June, 848 had taken over the Nanga Gaat, leaving only a small number of 848 personnel at Sibu.

845 Squadron departed for HMS *Bulwark* leaving only the Squadron Commanding Officer (Lieutenant Commander A. D. Levy) and one Wessex 1 for the Squadron hand-over ceremony. This ceremony was both simple and informal. It was attended by the Captains of both HM Ships *Albion* and *Bulwark*, the Resident of the Third Division and Air Vice-Marshal Foxley-Norris (the Air Officer Commanding 224 Group RAF) – who was visiting Sibu for the day. The last Wessex 1 was given a rousing send-off and 848 Squadron assumed operational responsibility for Helicopter Support in the Third Division.

'Charlie' Flight, under the command of Lieutenant Commander Peter Deller, disembarked to Sibu on 22nd June with a further 4 Wessex Mk 5 aircraft, 8 pilots and 35 ratings. 'Charlie' Flight arrived at a time when the Wessex Mk 5 engine troubles ashore were at their height. Two aircraft and two pilots were sent immediately to Nanga Gaat and, within the next week, all 'Delta' Flight aircraft were returned to Sibu for investigation.

It was an extremely busy six weeks for 848 Squadron at Sibu, made more difficult by the spate of Wessex Mk 5 maintenance problems. The main flying effort was concentrated at Nanga Gaat, leaving precious few flying hours at Sibu for the purpose of giving 'Charlie' Flight pilots area familiarisation.

However, the two 'Delta' Flight pilots left at Sibu after the rest had gone to Nanga Gaat were given area familiarisation by 845 pilots and were also re-familiarised on the two Whirlwind Mk 7 aircraft which were taken over from 845. These two aircraft proved to be invaluable for minor tasks that did not necessitate a Wessex Mk 5, and for periods when the Wessex aircraft were experiencing engine problems. The Whirlwinds were used for CASEVACs (11 of these were flown to Sibu hospital in May/June), area recces, smaller HDS lifts and pilot continuation training.

On the domestic side, we settled in very well and the long hours of work required in difficult conditions did not affect the morale of the Squadron personnel.

UP THE 'ULU'

By Andy Knapp - Aircrewman 820 Squadron (Wessex HAS Mk 1)

The Wessex Mk 1 stood in the early morning sunshine on the hardstanding in front of the Squadron crew rooms at RNAS Sembawang in Singapore. I was supervising the loading of 20 five-gallon jerrycans of fresh water and six boxes of armament which, by the shapes of the ammo boxes, looked like 'trip flares'. The boxes were about 18 inches in width and nearly 5 feet in length, olive green in colour, with the red band denoting 'live ammunition'. Our (anti-submarine) Wessex were being used in support of 845 Commando Squadron whilst we were on detached duty from HMS *Eagle*, and this particular morning I had been crewed up with Lt Tony Wigley to fly the requested stores out to the Royal Marine detachment on anti-infiltration patrol, somewhere on the Eastern part of the Malaysian Peninsula. Once the stores had been loaded I returned to the Briefing Room to get the map co-ordinates of the 'drop area'. This was to be a delivery to a 'drop zone' as opposed to delivery to a 'landing zone', where the helicopter actually landed. Both methods needed careful aircraft handling, especially the landing type because, as the helicopter descended below tree-top level, the intake of air through the blades tended to pull the upper branches through the blades, leading to dire consequences to both the aircraft and the crew. The pilot usually kept a pretty sharp lookout to the front and sides, but the rear of the helicopter was the crewman's responsibility, having particular regard to the tail rotor; helicopters don't fly very well without their tail rotors! To obtain a clear view of the back end of the aircraft entailed standing with one leg inside the rear door, and one leg on the starboard wheel, facing the rear of the helicopter, which made you virtually the 'eyes in the back of the pilot's head'.

This trip, however, was to be carried out by hovering over a small, cleared area in the jungle too small to achieve a landing. Once established in the hover the stores would be despatched by the crewman out of the door. Helicopters hover best when there is some wind; we knew we could count on 'nil' wind conditions and very high humidity, which would hamper the 'bite' that the rotor blades could achieve to maintain a prolonged hover, which in turn meant that more power would be required to carry out that particular manoeuvre! These were all problems that we were very familiar with, operating over the jungle.

After a quick coffee on the completion of the briefing, we manned the aircraft and prepared for a running take-off as we were quite heavy, with a full load of fuel and 100 gallons of fresh water and the ammunition. We were near the aircraft operating limits and, as per usual, there was no wind to assist, so by doing a running take-off like a normal aircraft, we would provide our own wind speed, and achieve the 'lift' we would need to get airborne. Conventional aircraft can achieve this by running down the runway and creating wind over the wings to obtain 'lift'. A helicopter can also carry out this method of take-off, using the rotor blades as a wing, which in fact they are, only a flexible type of wing.

We did quite a long run down the runway and clawed our way into the air; we must have been pulling quite a lot of power because we were 'smoking' quite a lot from the jet-pipes. Wessex Mk ls were renowned for being 'Smoky Joes'.

Once we had achieved some height we were soon over the backwater and above Johore Bahru, where we set course for our rendezvous. We kept low, in fact, just above tree-top level. Helicopters don't offer much protection for their crews and even small-arms fire can do an awful lot of damage to both aircraft and crew. The trees got taller and taller as we progressed until, once over the area we were operating in, they were up to 150 to 200 feet tall. Below was just a sea of green and no terrain was visible through the canopy of leaves. Once in the local area of our 'drop', we circled for a few minutes, to allow the people on the ground to set off a smoke marker. The orange smoke takes a few minutes to filter through the trees, but eventually we saw it and began to really scan the tree tops to try and establish where the actual 'gap' was located, so that we could do our 'drop'. Finally we found it, and I conned the pilot down to where the wheels were almost at tree-top level whilst keeping a good lookout behind to make sure we wouldn't snag anything in the tail rotor. Once we were relatively happy with the situation, the pilot concentrated on keeping a 'good' hover. This entails him keeping his eyes focused on an imaginary point on the horizon and, therefore, he cannot look down or to the left or right, so the crewman really does become his 'eyes'. Obviously he does 'wander' from time to time and it is up to the crewman to talk to him continuously to correct his positioning of the aircraft.

While talking the pilot into a hover, maintaining it and keeping a good lookout on the tail rotor, I still had to find time to despatch the stores, which was the whole point of us being there in the first place. The pilot told me he was 'pulling' quite a lot of power, as the humidity had reached about 80 per cent by that time of day and, with no wind to speak of, it was essential to get rid of the water first, as that was the heaviest part of our cargo. Without further ado I started heaving 5-gallon jerrycans out of the door, and soon began to sweat as much water as I was throwing out the door. The next thing was to get rid of the ammo. Due to the shape of the boxes I had to upend them and slide them out of the door, end first. They were soon gone and I gave the pilot the command of 'up, up, up', and we were soon making forward speed, and I sat myself in the doorway to take advantage of the airflow. We remained at tree-top level, just in case anyone took a pot-shot at us. We were offered flak-jackets, but I never knew anyone who took advantage of having them. For one thing, they were very cumbersome, and the other thing was that most incoming fire came from below so, unless you sat on the thing, it wasn't a lot of good!

We finally arrived back at Sembawang and, after signing the aircraft in, made our way to the accommodation area and got some lunch. Just another day in the life of a front-line squadron!

Two weeks later, and in the bar, I overheard a conversation between two Royal Marines, who were asking one of our Squadron groundcrew who was the crewman that had carried out the drop on that particular day? The groundcrewman said he didn't know but they could easily find out by referring to the aircraft log at the Squadron in the morning. That satisfied them and they left. I asked the groundcrewman, what was that all about? Apparently, upon hitting the ground the 5-gallon water jerrycans had burst, like oversized 'water bombs'; this in turn had saturated the ground so much that by the time the ammunition cases had reached the ground they dug into the earth right up to their wire handles, which were located in the ends of the boxes. That meant that the boxes, all 5 foot of them, were buried up to their handles, and had to be dug out, much to the annoyance of the Royal Marines, who were now out to extract vengeance on the hapless aircrewman who happened to have dropped them!

I must say, in my defence, that the MOD, in its wisdom, had changed the usual metal jerrycans for black plastic ones at about that time! Obviously the plastic ones were not up to the job!

That was not going to save me so, early the next morning, I went down to the Squadron and removed the aircraft logs for 'statistical' purposes. The Royal Marines did turn up, but unfortunately the logs were unavailable, and they had to leave without ever discovering who the aircrewman was that had carried out that sortie!

Jungle Engine-Change

By Lieutenant John Kelly and Sub-Lieutenant David Baston 848 Squadron (Pilots Wessex Mk 5)

By David. I was flying over the jungle with John Kelly when we both noticed that the temperatures and pressures (ts and ps) of the engine cockpit dials were not very healthy and suggested an imminent drama. Fortunately, a small landing site appeared right in front of us at the right moment and we hastily plonked ourselves down. We had a port engine and coupling gearbox failure! The landing site was one of those cleared by the locals and there was only room for one Wessex, so the replacement engine and gearbox had to be winched in and changed on site.

Fig 41. 'Papa''s port engine being examined

By John. The 'Holsett' coupling between the port engine and coupling gearbox had failed. This allowed the port engine to precess, or 'wobble', rather like a top slowing down, as John lowered the collective. This, in turn, allowed the turbine blades to strike the outer shroud of the engine. We did, however, land with both engines running, though David was pdq at shutting the port as soon as we were on the ground.

Both engines and the coupling gearbox had to be removed. A replacement coupling gearbox and port engine were flown up from Sibu, winched down and fitted on site; the original starboard engine was then refitted.

Fig 42. Wessex 'Romeo' arriving with spare engine and gearbox for Wessex 'Papa'

The incident occurred on 11th July 1965. We kept a 24-hour guard on 'Papa' until I flew her out 8 days later on the 19th.

848 Squadron Brunei Detachment August 1965

From a report by Lieutenant Geoff Atkin (F) 848 Squadron Pilot Wessex Mk 5 - Brunei Detachment Commander

In accordance with COMBRITBOR's instructions, two Wessex Mk 5s were detached from Sibu for deployment in the Central Brigade area.

On Wednesday 4th August the detachment, consisting of three officers, four senior ratings and four junior ratings, departed from Sibu at 1100 in 'G' and 'H' and arrived at Bario at 1400, having refuelled at Belaga *en route*. On arrival, the aircraft were unloaded and, after the rain had ceased, I took off in 'H' to recover a Scout helicopter belonging to the Army Air Corps. The aircraft was at 4,500 ft on a small mountain-top 105 mm Howitzer gun position. I hooked the Scout, but unfortunately the hook failed whilst still in a low hover and the Scout struck the ground, causing Cat 2 damage. I returned to Bario and the next day, after changing the hook of 'H' for those of 'G' (which had an unserviceable torquemeter) I lifted the Scout successfully and took it to Bario.

On completion of this task, our two aircraft then removed the Howitzer, ammunition and crew to Pamain. Due to a lack of gun slings, the gun had to be dismantled and taken as an internal load. Having completed this task, the aircraft were loaded with the detachment personnel and gear and then proceeded to Brunei airfield, arriving at 1745. No flying took place on Friday 6th August while the detachment settled in at Brunei.

Saturday and Sunday saw the aircraft employed in troop movements and logistics support to the 1/2 and 2nd/6th Gurkhas in the Semada/Bakelalan and Pamain areas. On completion of Sunday's flying, the detachment had completed 40 hours flying and carried 199 passengers and 39,475 lbs of freight in 62 sorties.

The detachment returned to Sibu on 12th August.

A subsequent Engineering Report on the investigation into 'H''s (Rollason Mk 1) hook whilst attempting to lift the Scout helicopter concluded that the failure was impossible to explain.

The load was hooked on in the clearing; the crewman hooking on checked the hook by pulling his weight on the strop, gave the 'Thumbs Up', and jumped clear.

As soon as the aircraft took the strain, the hook opened, releasing the load.

The aircraft flew clear and had a second run in. The geometric lock had to be released on the hook, although the hook itself was open.

On the second hook-on, the procedure was repeated. This time the load was lifted six feet clear of the ground when the hook opened. The geometric lock was again unbroken.

It should be impossible for the Freight Hook to function in a normal manner without the geometric lock being broken and remaining broken and, unless the hook was correctly engaged, it should have been impossible to take the weight of a heavy load. This is proof that the Freight Hook was correctly cocked.

The relevant Pilot's release switches were checked after both malfunctions of the Freight Hook, and were found to be in the 'Off' positions. Also, the Pilot's Foot Jettison Plunger was checked and found not to have been operated.

At Sibu, a full and functional check was carried out on the Hook in the Electrical Workshop and it was found to be completely serviceable. The Hook was despatched to RNSD Llangennech for further investigation and the hope that instructions would be issued for a manufacturer's investigation.

Personal Reminiscences of a Flight Commander

By Lieutenant John Kelly RN 848 Squadron Delta Flight Commander (Pilot Wessex Mk 5).

Prologue.

My first flight into Sarawak in 848 Squadron in July 1962 (before Confrontation) was very nearly my last.

We were flying a Malaysian Regiment ashore from *Bulwark* to relieve a New Zealand Battalion based in the 3rd Division close to the coast, not far from Sibu. 3 Malays in and 2 Maoris out, was all we could manage in our venerable Whirlwind Mk7s. I had to use all 44 inches of boost to clear the jungle canopy on take-off.

Imagine my surprise, therefore, having made the transition to forward flight with the second stick of Maoris, when I found I had only 37 inches available. Somehow I scraped through the tree-tops to make it back on board. A fatigue crack in the inlet manifold was found to be the cause. This taught me a valuable lesson: always check full power is available on leaving a jungle clearing, before committing yourself to forward flight.

Albion, with 845 Squadron and her Wessex 1s embarked, relieved us on our way home at Aden on 21st November. The Brunei Revolt then occurred on 8th December. This was followed by Indonesia's declaration of Confrontation with Malaysia on 20th January 1963. 845 Squadron moved rapidly into theatre. Their sterling exploits over the ensuing 24 months have already been covered in some detail in preceding articles.

Meantime 848 Squadron, having disbanded at RNAS Culdrose in March 1963, reformed in 4 flights, each with 4 Wessex Mk 5s in May 1964, before embarking in *Albion* on 12th March 1965 to return again to the Far East.

Nanga Gaat

We disembarked to Sibu on 23rd May, flying forward the next day to relieve the 845 Squadron detachment based 150 miles inland at Nanga Gaat, where the Gaat flows into the mighty Rajang, the longest river in Borneo. Tingaan, the headman of the nearest longhouse, greeted us in Iban on our arrival saying, loosely translated:

'We welcome the new white chiefs with their great metal birds powered by two outboard motors, that can carry more than the great metal birds, powered by only one.'

Fig 43. Nanga Gaat May 1965

This we set out to prove immediately, but only once, by taking off at maximum all-up weight, from one of the lower landing sites, some 1,000lbs heavier than our Wessex 1 counterparts.

Thereafter, we adhered strictly to the policy of flying each aircraft empty from the lower sites to one on the upper ridge, before taking off with a full payload, in order to gain translational lift while descending, in case an engine should fail. This proved eminently sensible. Remember that the Wessex Mk 5 Intensive Flying Trials had only finished a year previously, without any hot weather trials. This shortcoming soon made itself apparent as we began to experience a number of throttle actuator (TA) failures. These occurred, almost invariably, on lowering the collective to descend, which resulted in the involuntary shutting-down of one engine; not the happiest of experiences to contemplate when descending into a clearing at high all-up weight. We despatched the offending TAs to Sibu to be tested rigorously on the bench. Nothing untoward was found as each, in turn, was declared serviceable and duly returned for refitting to our aircraft. Eventually, sensing that a crisis of confidence might be arising within the Flight, I took a very lightly-laden Wessex Mk 5 solo to 3,000 ft above the shingle banks across the Rajang from Nanga Gaat and lowered the collective violently. After five attempts, one engine shut down. Returning to Nanga Gaat, I signalled *Albion* and Sibu stating that 'I considered the aircraft was unfit to fly operationally'.

Unsurprisingly, this had the desired effect. It immediately attracted a lot of senior attention, which then started to look beyond the function of the TA to the fuel itself. A fine, micronic filter situated early in the line from the fuel tank was found to be the culprit. The fuel ashore in 45-gallon drums proved to be dirtier than that on board. Dirt had partially blocked the filter, restricting the fuel flow which, when coupled with the TA reducing the fuel flow even further on lowering the collective, had caused the engines to flame out. Altering the position of the filter in the fuel line cured the problem.

Thanks to Martin Banks and his 845 Detachment, we quickly became familiar with sites and places that have long since passed into Junglie folklore; Long Jawi, the Balui Boat Station, Belaga, Poonan Busang, and the Hose Mountain Radio Relay Station at 6,000ft , to name but a few. We also flew the Malaysian and Parachute Regiments 100 miles further inland to patrol the border. Long and demanding though the days were, for both air and ground crews, most passed without incident, but three events are perhaps worth recalling.

First, many may remember that Tun Temoggong Jugah allowed his two prized water buffalo to roam freely at Nanga Gaat. Apparently, their curiosity seems not to have been aroused by the Wessex 1, but things changed with the arrival of the Wessex Mk 5 equipped with HF aerials mounted either side of the fuselage. They found these irresistible as scratching-posts. We were forced to erect a white guardrail around each landing pad to protect the aircraft from their amorous advances.

Enter then the Gurkha Engineers, who had kindly offered to be taken forward to improve our unmanned refuelling site on the Baleh River, where

45-gallon fuel drums had fallen at random around the overgrown clearing after each air drop. One week later we returned to find the drums stacked neatly alongside two immaculate landing pads, complete with white guardrails, and not a single water buffalo in sight.........

More seriously, on 11th July while airborne with David Baston some 10 minutes out of Nanga Gaat,

en route to Belaga for a roulement of the 3rd Battalion Royal Malaysian Regiment, we experienced a Holsett coupling failure connecting the rear of the port engine's free power turbine to the coupling gearbox. This necessitated an emergency landing in a convenient small clearing on a hillock above the Rumah Sibat longhouse. The details of this event have been described earlier in this book.

Thirdly, and perhaps arguably, our most lasting legacy to the people of Sarawak came from our involvement in the surveys by No1 Topographical Survey Troop Royal Engineers, who mapped much of the interior accurately for the first time. The 'Topos' needed a framework of triangulation (trig) points on which to hang aerial photographs in order to produce accurate maps. This could only be achieved by line-of-sight surveys from one mountain top to another, many of which were covered in 200ft-high primary jungle. Hovering in free air between 4,000 and 6,000 ft while lowering 'Topos' on a 100ft rope attached to the end of a 100ft winch-wire, through the jungle canopy, was demanding stuff. They were amazing. We would return a week later to find six men had cleared an entire mountain-top to surmount it with a brand-new landing pad. Slowly their lattice spread, from one mountain to the next, until the maps could be produced, from which we ourselves later benefitted.

But it was now time to leave this magical place. We were relieved by 'C' Flight on 28th July who, in turn, were relieved when No230 Squadron RAF, equipped with Whirlwind 10s, assumed command at Sibu and Nanga Gaat on 11th August.

Bario.

Fig 44. Bario – Sarawak, 5th Division – 848 Squadron

The heavier lift capability of the Wessex Mk 5 in 848 Squadron was then deployed to Bario, situated at 3,500 ft just 10 miles from the border in one direction, with the Kelabit Mountains rising to 6,000ft surrounding it in the other.

John Rawlins and I made an initial reconnaissance on 23rd September, before 'A' Flight deployed to Bario on the 25th. 'D' Flight followed later on 11th December.

It could not have been more different. Gone were the sea-level humid, riverine airs of Nanga Gaat. Instead, we enjoyed an altogether crisper climate, with blankets on our beds at night, based at an airstrip on the relatively flat plain between the border and the mountains. Sibu to

Nanga Gaat and Labuan to Bario were similarly distanced, at a little over an hour's flying time, but the latter required traversing a 6,000 ft mountain range instead of blithely following the Rajang. Troops were brought forward largely by RAF Twin Pioneer and AAC Beaver, instead of by boat and river. Patrol insertions, with the border in close proximity, were much shorter, though at higher altitude, typically 4,000ft or more.

Long-range SAS tasking with their locally recruited Kelabit Border Scouts, on Operation 'Claret' patrols over the border down in the 3rd Division, provided notable exceptions. Drop-tanks were needed for these 6-hour flights from Bario to Pa Tik in the Kelabit Mountains, thence to the Balui Boat Station in the 3rd Division via Long Banga and Long Jawi, before returning to Bario. The Border Scouts, armed with Armalite rifles, were dressed curiously in navy-blue boiler-suits. I was not to realise until much later that the latter were probably removed before going on patrol and only worn while airborne.

Fig 45. SAS CASEVAC – BRX Border Site - Sarawak, 5ᵗʰ Division - 848 Squadron

The 4,500ft border site at BRX, some 15 miles from Bario, also posed quite a challenge, particularly with a 105 mm gun underslung. There was only one way in and out of the clearing. Ben Caesar lost one engine on his approach with a 105mm underslung. Somehow, he managed to land the gun without damage, rotate through 180 degrees and return safely to Bario. The above photograph, of a CASEVAC from this site, provides some idea. The aircraft is pointing towards Sarawak; beyond the tail, over the trees,lies Indonesia. The 105mms were zeroed-in on an Indonesian airstrip just over the border. Resupplying the Gurkhas' Radio Relay Station on top of Gunong Murud at 7,500 ft also often found us pushing at the boundaries of the Wessex Mk 5 flight envelope.

Fig 46. Pa Main Border Site – Sarawak, 5th Division – 848 Squadron

Pa Main, however, was perhaps the most heavily-defended border site. It stood astride the lowest point on the border ridge, less than 10 miles from Bario, guarding the most likely line of attack. Dick Steil and I flew a night CASEVAC from here over the Kelabit Mountains to Brunei on 5th January 1966. Joining the Gordon Highlanders on an overnight foot patrol from Pa Main across the border was quite illuminating too.

'D' Flight was relieved by 'C' Flight on 19th February. We then returned in theatre for the last time in June, based at Labuan. 848 Squadron's final flypast took place at Labuan on 5th August. Meantime, 845 Squadron (re-equipped with Wessex Mk 5s) had flown out an advance party to take over at Labuan and Bario, using aircraft from 848 until their main party arrived in *Bulwark* in September. *Albion* sailed for home from Singapore on 11th August. Indonesia ratified the peace treaty 2 days later, on 13th August 1966. 845 Squadron finally withdrew from Borneo on 7th October 1966.

Epilogue

5 years later, having disbanded 847 Squadron at Sembawang during the withdrawal from East of Suez, my wife, Sue, and I accompanied Tank and Shirley Sherman on a visit to Nanga Gaat. Tingaan met us with his longboat at Kapit. Rajah Brooke's white-painted, wooden fort looked much the same, as did the fuselage of Roger Bryant's Wessex 1 on the bank of the Rajang near the old fuel-drop zone, and 845 Squadron's memorial still stood proudly at Nanga Gaat. The landing pads were overgrown, but we were still able to find spent cartridge-cases in the perimeter trench.

The welcome at Tingaan's Longhouse was just as it always had been. We offered their food to their gods before talking long into the night. Looking up at the stars, I thought how privileged we had all been to be able to help these kind, smiling people in their hour of need.

To Peter Stevens, Peter Faulks (sadly no longer with us), Peter Nicholson and John Hall, our aircrewmen Chris Grant and Ginger Abrahams, and our Buffer, Petty Officer Osborne and all in 'D' Flight whose names I can no longer remember, thank you all for your support.

But it is to our Commanding Officer, Geoff Andrews, and Senior Pilot, Peter Deller, that we owe the most. They encouraged our enthusiasm, while leading us safely through the shoals of our youthful exuberance on the adventure of a lifetime, and we should all be thankful for that.

The Wessex Mk 5 and its Inability to Start when Hot.

By Lieutenant David Baston RN 848 Squadron (Pilot Wessex Mk 5)

In the initial days of the deployment of the Wessex Mk 5, it was a brute to restart the engines when they were hot. This meant that, on landing in a clearing or at a camp, one could not shut down if there was a bit of a wait, as you might spend the rest of the day there. This meant that one had to sit in the cockpit, burning and turning, to drink the proffered Tiger beer. To reduce noise and fuel consumption it was normal to pull back the engine speed selects to reduce the rotor RPM to about 200, and that made a big difference to the noise.

You know what's coming next!

When the load was on board and one was all set for a jazzy and dramatic departure to impress the troops, you leapt into the air to be immediately surprised by the lack of power, the lack of rate of climb, the coning angle of the rotor blades and a general feeling of doom. Flying with one hand, knee under the collective, and pushing the speed select levers forward as quickly as one dared, whilst hopefully finding a bit of a downslope in the surrounding area to gain speed without hitting anything, certainly impressed the troops – especially those in the back!

It was a mistake you only made once, and you never told anyone about it. Would you have spoken out to your Senior Pilot (Peter Deller)? No – I thought not.

Borneo Recollections

By Lieutenant Colin Howgill Royal Marines: Pilot – 848 Squadron (Wessex Mk 5) 1965-66.

First Impressions - 1962

My first memories of Borneo, a few years before I found myself back there as a pilot with 848 NACS, are from my time as a subaltern rifle-troop commander in 40 Commando RM very shortly after the unit's return to the Far East from Malta in 1962. While the 'Confrontation with Indonesia' had not yet broken-out, the scene was being set with the publication of the Cobalt Commission report on the future of Borneo and Sarawak. 40 Commando was embarked in HMS *Bulwark* and deployed to Borneo to conduct 'hearts and minds' operations to help ensure that the indigenous Dyak people remained loyal, and sympathetic to the report's proposals.

Thus I was, early one morning off the coast of the 3rd Division of Sarawak, part of the deployment of 'A' Company, 40 Commando to Sibu by Whirlwind Mk 7 helicopters of 848 NACS. The deployment took hours as the ship/shore distance was tight for the aircraft if they were to have any effective payload, and most aircraft transited with just part of a rifle section and, in many cases, with just two passengers. Indeed, I recall the general mirth about the 'touch and go' decision on whether our formidable Company Quartermaster Sergeant, Colour Sergeant Mathews RM, would have to travel alone! In the end he made it with one of the smaller Marines, but that memory was to stand me in good stead a few years later when payload range was always a significant concern over the vast distances of Borneo jungle.

Our Sibu deployment was uneventful, with a soccer game against a local team as its highlight. We did a number of other shore deployments in Borneo around that time that involved doing foot patrols, carrying a good-sized individual load through jungle, coastal mangrove, grasslands and more open areas. This first-hand knowledge of Commando infantry operations in Borneo was a great starting point for helping me better appreciate my later role as part of the helicopter force supporting ground forces in the area.

Tawau and Pulau Sebatic area of Sabah, Borneo – 'B' Flight, 848 NACS – 1965

May 1965 heralded the return of HMS *Albion* in Singapore, with 848 NACS embarked with 24 Wessex Mk 5 helicopters (18 squadron aircraft and 6 Ship reserves). Within a day of arrival I was dispatched to Tawau, on the Indonesian border in Sarawak, to plan the helicopter operational change-over in that area between 1st Battalion, Gordon Highlanders and 42 Commando, RM. The change-over was uneventful, as was the pull-out of 42 Commando in December 1965, when 2nd/2nd Gurkha Rifles took over operations in that area.

During the planning of the Gordons' handover to 42 Commando, I had my first experience in hovercraft operations. Helicopter availability in that area was limited, and the hovercraft were ideal for logistic support by river for the forward companies. So it was that I travelled up-river from Tawau to a forward company base, where the advance party of the incoming company from 42 Commando was already deployed. Part of the cargo was a load of freshly-killed chickens to give the troops a little variety. For one it was its lucky day! They had been supposedly killed by wringing their necks, with the feathers plucked from the breast to make life easier on the 'front line'; but one had survived. The Marine cook who was helping prepare dinner noticed it, had not the heart to kill, and resuscitated it. 6 months later, when I was again present at the base for the pull-out of 42 Commando the hen, by then a company mascot, was better tanned, still largely featherless and, had it known, no doubt hoping the incoming Gurkhas would have such a soft animal streak.

The pull-out of 42 Commando from Tawau had one historic disaster. Like all good regiments before them, the unit had deployed to Sarawak with a fair proportion of its Officers' Mess Silver; such were the times! During the re-embarkation to HMS *Albion* the Mess Silver was, for whatever reason, packed in pannier containers as part of an underslung load for transfer to the ship. The sling hook-up was messed up and the load fell, resulting in serious damage to many historic pieces of Royal Marines' Regimental Silver and the end of the practice of forward operational deployment of the Silver. Many years later, as CO 42 Commando, the safety of the Mess Silver had a whole new meaning for me!

The routine changeover of infantry units in Borneo was, until the availability of the Wessex Mk 5 helicopters with their greater payload/range, an extremely time-consuming business. The new capability was quickly recognized, and so it was that we were deployed from *Albion* in late July '65 to execute the changeover in place between 10th Gurkha Rifles and Royal Malay Regiment. Nothing spectacular, but our ability to move troops and stores, both internally and under-slung, saved days and also made the changeover both operationally more effective and, for the outgoing troops in particular, very welcome.

Return to Sibu – B Flight 848 NACS – July 1965

August 3rd 1965 saw me, together with my fellow 'B' Flight pilots (Mike Smith as Flight Commander, plus Chalky White, Nigel Osborne and Pat McHaffey) back in Sibu, the capital of Sarawak's 3rd Division. Sibu lies some 70 miles directly inland from the Borneo coast on the banks of the Rajang River. Inland from Sibu 3rd Division is huge, not just the largest by far of Borneo's provinces but, as one moves further south, a wilderness of primary jungle with rivers as the principal longer-distance transportation used by the native Dyak tribespeople. Sibu was also a town of anomalies. While it was the remotest of

Borneo's divisional capitals, it also enjoyed a sort of political patronage that provided funds 'in respect of its comparative size' for strange projects that the politicians in Borneo's capital, Kuching, thought may help win the 'hearts and minds' of the town's occupants. Hence, some two miles out from the center of town, it boasted an Olympic swimming-pool complete with the high diving-boards. The only trouble was that the funds to run it on a consistent basis hadn't been provided, so it was hardly ever open and, when it was, the sole occupants were normally from 848 NACS.

At the time of our deployment, mapping of much of Borneo, and particularly of the Southern parts of 3rd Division, was non-existent. The coastal areas, including that portion of the major rivers that was navigable in RN Survey vessels, had been well charted in the 1930s; indeed my new father-in-law, (at that stage of just 3 weeks!), Lt Cdr Alfred Hughes RN, had commanded one of the survey vessels that had done much of the work, becoming in the process both a close friend to, and eventual executor of the will of, the Rajah Brooke, the last white colonial, dynastic ruler of Sarawak. For navigation inland, however, we were blessed by maps with large, totally blank areas. Fortunately, pilots from earlier Naval Helicopter deployments, and those of 845 NACS in particular, had added to those blank areas key terrain features that took some of the exploration guesswork out of navigating that still largely undiscovered jungle.

Soon after arriving our CO, Lt Cdr Geoff Andrews, took myself and Sub Lt Mike Woodford on our first operational sortie deep into the 3rd Division hinterland. This entailed landing at one of the hill-top landing sites that the military cleared for us. They were extremely confined and much care was needed to ensure a safe transition to and from the site. Our gallant leader showed us the way, losing three rotor-tips in a great demonstration that led us, having dropped our loads at the site, to follow a vibrating Boss back to base. The lesson, however, wasn't lost, as over the months we took extreme care to evaluate newly-cut sites before using them.

While support of the infantry was our priority task, 'hearts and minds' operations were also extremely important. Three instances are still fresh in my mind some 47 years later.

On 13th September 1965, following radio notification of the authorities by an Army patrol, I was tasked, along with PO Ward as my aircrewman, to CASEVAC an Iban lady whose child had 'hung up' during labour to an extent that it was potentially life-threatening for both her and the still-unborn child. Half-way back, flying at about 1000 feet and still some 30 minutes out from Sibu hospital, PO Ward called me from back, saying: 'Boss, do you remember that first aid training we did?' 'Yes; why?' I responded, only to be told that the trip seemed to be doing wonders for the patient, who was about to produce. As so often, our aircrewmen were the salvation of many of our missions and, in this instance, PO Ward was no exception. Thus I was able to call ahead to announce that we were arriving with an extra, very small passenger.

While I was Sibu-based we had three 848 Squadron wives in Sibu. Borneo was an unaccompanied location and so off-limits to wives. Nevertheless, C-in-C Far East Fleet 'COMFEF', Admiral Twiss, rationalized that as *Albion* was on an unaccompanied Far East deployment, our wives technically did not exist in station, and certainly no allowances were payable. Thus, he ruled that if Squadron wives could, having got there under their own steam, be present but officially 'non-existent' in Singapore, why not the same in Sibu? So it was that Diane Mackenzie and Chris Osborne with two children, who had both flown from UK to Singapore as RAF indulgence passengers, and my new wife, Pam Howgill, found themselves in Sibu sharing a house on stilts alongside the Rajang River. Local history said the house was floated down-river many years earlier and, when the monsoon rains came, it certainly felt as though it was still afloat! Taking 'hearts and minds' seriously, one Sunday we all visited a longhouse some miles up-river from Sibu. It gave the girls a chance to sample their 'Vintage Tuak' wine (about 3 days old) and have a reminder that Borneo wasn't that many years out of its gallant, head-hunting past. On one of the main ridge-poles of the longhouse was a vine basket of shrunken heads, with the top one still adorned by a non-shrunk pair of wire glasses-frames. Our curiosity brought a huge smile to the headman who explained to us in Malay, plus substantial sign language, the he had taken the head. During WWII a Japanese soldier had apparently got lost from his patrol and, without the British Raj to object, it just seemed the right thing to keep the head-shrinking skill set alive; and there he was!!

Fig 47. Wives' Longhouse at Sibu

While we were based in Sibu the Forces entertainment show visited, with Shirley Abicair as the lead singer. I was tasked to take her for a show at Nanga Gaat. What a great person and with a professional stoicism that was, for most, unimaginable. While waiting to do the show at Nanga Gaat, the base pet monkey peed all over her dress. As if the day was just part of her normal routine, and without any change of clothing, she performed beautifully. On the way back we had to take a sick Iban child with its mother to Kapit Fort. Unfortunately, the child was performing with gusto from both ends, so everyone riding in the back arrived back at Sibu both late and smelling none too good. The delay in going via Kapit, and some mixed weather, meant we arrived back at Sibu with only minutes before her evening show and, rather than disappoint those waiting while she changed, she went right on stage with another fabulous performance; what a trouper!

On another occasion way up-country we collected a large internal load of stores to take to another troop location. As so often, the locals helped load the aircraft; men, women and children. Some 10 minutes after take-off, with stores packed to the roof of the cabin, and much to the amazement of my aircrewman, a Dyak child about 12 years old appeared over the top of the stores. He had been helping and, unnoticed by all, had got loaded in behind everything. A small, unplanned diversion soon had him home; a very proud young man who had flown in one of the 'big birds'!

Nanga Gaat – B Flight 848 NACS – August/September 1965

After a relatively short time in Sibu, 'B' Flight deployed forward to Nanga Gaat to take over helicopter support operations in that remote forward area of 3rd Division. The Forward air base at 'the Gaat' had been constructed at the confluence of two fairly large rivers that, once again, played an important role in the mobility of the local people. Life there was both delightful and very different from Sibu, with the base being engineered and locally-constructed jungle huts that were, in part thanks to excellent mosquito-nets around our bunks, amazingly comfortable. Food was fairly basic and, thanks to the initiative of both our cooks and some of the other more adventurous members of 'B' Flight, amazingly varied. Fresh fish were not too hard to come by, thanks to our use of the odd stick of plastic explosive thrown into the river. That practice caused something of a frown from an Army Major General who, during a visit to Borneo from UK, asked our chef what we used for bait. He turned out to be an avid fly-fisherman and, while he clearly enjoyed his meal, considered our methods 'not very sportsmanlike'!

We were at 'the Gaat' to support a company of 3 Royal Malay Regiment (3 RMR) whose tactical area of operations (TAOR) extended far to the south and south east towards the Indonesian border. We were the last Royal Navy helicopters to work from this extremely remote jungle air base, as we were due to be permanently relieved by the RAF some 6 weeks from our arrival.

Our work, similarly to that from Sibu, was primarily to support ground infantry operations with the movement of people and supplies that would, on foot or by river, have taken days or even weeks, whereas for us it was minutes or hours. Getting the fuel to give us that essential payload/range we needed to successfully accomplish our task, involved the RAF dropping drums of AVTUR into remote areas, and often onto sandbars on the bends of one of the larger rivers. When on extended missions, we carried a portable refuelling pump, along with water-test kits to ensure that the fuel we took from the drums was not contaminated.

While flying from 'the Gaat', we occasionally worked with the UK's Joint Service hovercraft Unit (Far East) that was operating along much of the Rajang River. Capt Stuart Syrad RM was in command, which made it particularly rewarding for a fellow Marine.

Fig 48. 848 Squadron 'B' Flight at Nanga Gaat August 1965

All too soon the time came to leave 'the Gaat', but we were intent on not doing so without a suitable show for both RAF and the locals. A formation fly-past with a difference was decided upon. So it was that we took an underslung load of 4 drums of AVGAS to a nearby jungle hill-top, where I re-familiarized my experience as a Commando recruit training officer on the grenade range to wire the drums for a spectacular explosion to coincide with the fly-past a safe distance away. Blowing up 4 cans of AVGAS proved a very different experience from doing the same to unexploded grenades on the range! The explosion was huge and, by the grace of God, did no harm to the aircraft in formation or myself, not nearly far enough down from the hilltop. The 'Crabs' were unimpressed but the natives thought that, once again, we had used some divine power!

18th September saw another, and final, farewell formation fly-past for the people of Sibu, as we flew back to sea to re-embark in *Albion* for the return to Singapore. Little did we know as we joined *Albion* that Prime Minister Ian Smith of Rhodesia was about to declare a 'Unilateral Declaration of Independence' (UDI) from the UK. Our return to Singapore was suddenly extremely brief, as we were soon steaming full-speed across the Indian Ocean. We were to pick up 45 Commando RM from Aden, after which the plans were a little hazy since we neither had the range to cross Mozambique nor was that country likely to let us cross its airspace. The next problem was what to do with a Commando Carrier with two flights of helicopters embarked (the other two being recently deployed to Labuan and Bareo in Sarawak) that had sailed with such obvious haste from Singapore. So it was that I spent two weeks in Kenya doing an elephant count with two aircraft for Tsavo National Park, followed by a month, as the new commander of 'C' Flight 848 NACS, doing the up-country support task in Aden, having taken over temporarily from the RAF. It was late 1965, just before Christmas, that we returned to Singapore and prepared for our turn in the Brunei/Bareo TAOR.

Late 1965 we were briefly supporting another unit change-over in the Kuching area of Sarawak's 1st Division when we suffered the loss of my flight second-in-command, Lt Bruce Brown RN. While approaching a landing site his Wessex Mk 5 helicopter had a 'runaway up' on one engine. That, probably the most feared twin turbine-engine helicopter emergency, led to the abrupt loss of one rotor blade, with all on board being lost. Bruce was wonderful person and an outstanding officer who, to this day I have no doubt, would have gone far in the Naval Service.

Bareo – 'C' Flight, 848 NACS – January/February 1966

Early January 1965 saw 'C' Flight 848 NACS being deployed from HMS *Albion* through Labuan and up-country to take over support operations for 2nd/6th Gurkha Rifles at Bareo in the 4th Division of Sarawak. Bareo was both a unique and delightful forward operating base. 'C' Flight was located at 2nd/6th Gurkhas' battalion headquarters base, which was on the eastern side of the grass-strip airfield that was just large enough to take an RAF Twin Pioneer aircraft, and gave us plenty of operating space. The climate was near-perfect since its height, at some 3000 ft above sea level, ensured a daily temperature at the base in the mid-80°F but without the humidity associated with living on the Equator at sea level. The Gurkha engineers had also made us some amazingly comfortable accommodation. Fortunately, having been born in the Far East, curry is a favourite dish of mine, since we dined fairly frequently on 'Gurkha Bart', a special curry that, other than the chicken or beef base, we were better off not knowing what else may be included in the ingredients!!

In addition to supporting the operations of 2nd/6th Gurkhas, we had two other priority tasks; the support of the Gurkhas' signal station on Gunong Murud, and of SAS and other special forces patrols deep into Sarawak's 3rd Division.

Gunong Murud was especially challenging. The Gurkha signal base was strategically vital to military operations throughout that area, and indeed was into the more isolated areas of Sarawak's 3rd Division to the west and Sabah to the east. The problem was that the signal station was at the peak of Gunong Murud, over 8000ft above sea level, where the flight envelope of the Wessex Mk 5 was significantly constrained by the 'thin air'. While the signal station could be supported by foot patrol it took days for a patrol to get there walking up the long ridge to the top, which meant that it would not have been a realistically sustainable location without helicopter support. While its sheer height was a challenge, its geography was an even bigger one as the mountain dropped some 2000+ feet almost vertically on three sides of the ridge that led to the summit. Huge updraughts and downdraughts made approach to the landing site on Gunong Murud particularly 'hairy' and a suitable task only for experienced pilots. As if those challenges were not enough, the mountain-top was in cloud some 80+% of the time, which meant that either myself or the Flight Second-in-Command, Lt Iain Mackenzie RN, had to remain at the Bareo base each day in case it cleared for us to resupply its garrison. On one occasion the weather had been particularly troublesome and the mountain had remained in cloud for nearly three weeks. The Gurkha Signals garrison was starting to get seriously low on provisions and other essential supplies. In turn I started to get daily signals from the new Air Commander Borneo's headquarters questioning why we had 'failed' to resupply the base. Our answers were clearly unconvincing, so it was that one morning around 10 a.m., and soon after the cloud that enveloped the runway at Bareo most mornings had cleared, an RAF Twin Pioneer landed with COMAIR on board. Gunong Murud had not let us down, so we pointed out the base of the mountain and the cloud with a very hard centre, and explained again that we just had to wait and hope for a clearing that was sufficiently sustained not to be a dangerous 'sucker's gap". COMAIR was due to return to Labuan mid-afternoon but, shortly before he was due to go, Gunong Murud showed herself in her full glory. Our Wessex aircraft was, as always, preloaded waiting for just such an event, so I took COMAIR with us. As usual the Gurkhas 'popped a smoke', to help us set up our approach in the safe updraught zone, and we landed safely. While on the pad, however, Mother Nature did her thing by bringing back the cloud cover and enveloping the summit. Shutting down on the summit and potentially blocking the landing pad was not operationally acceptable. Furthermore, the site was too small to turn the helicopter around, so it was a site where you went in from the updraught side and came out on the downdraught side where the aircraft's forward speed was taking you safely away from the mountainside. We unloaded the stores very hastily and took off, going almost immediately on to instrument flight and, shortly after, hit the downdraught. As expected we were soon descending at over 1000 feet/minute at full power. Fortunately, although that period always seemed like an age, we soon broke through the base of the cloud some 400 yards from the mountainside and returned without further excitement to Bareo. COMAIR, an RAF fixed-wing pilot by background, was very quiet throughout the exit from the mountain and left for Labuan immediately we got to Bareo, where his 'Twin Pin' was already started and waiting for him; his staff never questioned our resupply of Gunong Murud again!

Patrols deep into 2nd/6th Gurkha TAOR included the support of their forward companies in the Ba Kelalan and Punong Kelalan area, where their bases were extremely close to the Indonesian border. This made for very 'interesting' flying, as we were very vulnerable to possible enemy fire on the approach to, and departure from, those sites. Indeed, the 2nd/6th Gurkha bases were on a ridge that looked directly into Indonesia. While 2nd/6th Gurkhas had excellent observation of both the enemy's infantry and artillery across the border that was just a few hundred yards away, the reverse was also true of the Indonesians' lines of sight for us if we got a little high on the approach or departure from the base landing sites that were just behind the ridge line. Sometimes a slightly higher approach was extremely difficult to avoid, due to the need to allow for some serious updraughts and downdraughts from the adjacent ridges. That was certainly a test of our flying skills, as the alternatives were to face the wrath of a serious downdraught or the possible accuracy of direct enemy fire. Fortunately the Gurkhas were extremely adept with their use of smoke and the Indonesians were not as 'quick to the draw' as they could have been, so we had no incidents.

In addition to supporting the operations of 2nd/6th Gurkhas, much of the work we did from Bareo was supporting SAS long-range patrol activities. These sorties frequently took us way south to the most remote parts of both 3rd and 4th Division, close to the Indonesian border. Despite the remoteness, missionary activists had penetrated parts of the area, which led to a very special event one morning. Having dropped off a Special Forces patrol we had some time before the incoming one was due, so we shut down near a very remote jungle village in the Long Balen area. While most of the natives we met in that area wore barely anything that could be described as 'clothing', the adults from this village were clothed; clearly the influence of missionaries. When our crewman produced his camera, however, the reaction was as if we were pointing a gun at our intended subjects, who ran off into the jungle. Uncertain of what we had done, we waited for our incoming patrol but, before long the locals returned, ready to be photographed, mostly almost stark naked with their tattoos in full display. It seemed that, while the western clothing placated the missionaries' zeal for purity, ceremonial occasions such as a photograph required appropriate 'best' attire!!

Looking back, flying in Borneo and Sarawak during the period of Confrontation with Indonesia was both hugely challenging and immensely rewarding. The role of Royal Navy helicopters, both in support of our forward deployed troops and in winning the 'hearts and minds' battle, was huge and something to be historically very proud of.

Para Rescue - Bario 14th and 15th March 1966

By Lieutenant Mike Smith and Sub-Lieutenant David Baston RN 848 Squadron (Pilots Wessex Mk 5)

Mike Smith and I were tasked to search for a Section (nine men) of the Paras who were in difficulties near the Border Ridge in a section of the country which was used for training. We searched for their 'SARBE' (search and receive beacon) for a whole day and, although we found their approximate position, we were unable to locate them visually by nightfall. We returned the following morning and winched our crewman (believed to have been Jan Burr) down through the jungle canopy, who spotted them nearby but, upon being winched back up into the aircraft, told us that he had been nowhere near the ground. The canopy was 100 - 150 ft above ground and in this case was on a very steep slope near the top of the ridge at about 4500ft amsl. Mike Smith then climbed down from the cockpit to the cabin so that the winchman could winch him down, in order for him to be in communication with me in the cockpit.

I had to fly very carefully and push well down into the canopy, keeping just the blades above the tree-tops and the tail rotor in a convenient hole, in order for Mike to reach the ground at the end of the winch-wire, where he found that five of the nine Paras were in serious condition with, variously: a deep parang wound, a crushed pelvis (having slipped astraddle a log) and three other cases of serious fever for various reasons. Mikes initial intention was to organise a 'working party' (to include himself) and to cut down one or two large trees in order to make space for me to fly the aircraft down. However, despite Mike's super, extra-large, made-from-a- lorry-leaf-spring parang, this quickly proved to be impossible. Trees were about four to five feet in diameter, with supporting buttresses growing out to about 8 feet at the ground. Although the buttresses were soft and easy to cut through, within two or three inches into the tree the wood became so hard that it was like trying to chop through iron. Mike told the Paras that he would have to go back up and find help.

Having winched Mike up, we flew to a nearby Gurkha camp and, with the help and advice of the Sergeant Major, an explosives expert, we set off with Mike hanging in the strop on the end of the message-bag rope (150 feet long) attached to the hook of the winch cable which, when lowered, would give an extra 90 feet. About his body Mike was carrying a reel of safety fuse, a reel of Cordtex (high-speed fuse) and six each of primers and detonators. I flew at the pre-agreed initial speed of about 40 kts, with the crewman looking down for signals from Mike. Mike soon realised that the strop was restricting his blood circulation and made repeated signals to go faster. I flew an approach to the small hole in the tree's canopy where Mike had 'landed' previously, with him hanging below the aircraft on the end of the rope, and toss-bombed him into the hole. We then lowered the winch to complete his descent to the ground. Mike states he only just made it! Having arrived back on the ground, Mike and the Paras made three charges of about 12 lbs of plastic explosive, placed them into a 'V' cut into each of three trees, and packed them with mud. They used both Cordtex and safety fuse to ignite the primers. After the ensuing explosions I was then able, just, to fly down through the now-enlarged hole to within reaching distance of the normal 90ft winch. All the nine Paras and Mike were now winched up and we returned, via the Gurkha camp, to the Paras at our Base at Bareo. The helicopter had suffered slight damage caused by 'landing' on the canopy. Four days later, back in *Albion*, Mike watched the film *Laurence of Arabia*, and was not a little shocked by the scene of Laurence's right-hand-man dying from the explosion of a detonator, which he had lost in his clothing robe, caused by the heat of his body! Mike had carried six in his hand and placed them in his pocket for half an hour, before packing them for the transit!

845 Squadron Activities for the Last Two Months in Borneo

From a Report by Lieutenant Commander A D Levy RN Commanding Officer 845 Squadron,

(Pilot Wessex Mk 5)

The final activities of 845 Naval Air Commando Squadron under my Command in Borneo took place from 1st September to 7th October, 1966.

The operational side of this period was highlighted by the final 'mopping up' of the last Indonesian incursion by a band of Sukarelawan (volunteers) led by Lt Sumbi, which started in late July. All but 4 out of a total of 50 'incursionists' were accounted for with Lt Sumbi being captured. The success of this operation could only be attributable to the determination shown by all participating units. It was a perfect example of Joint Service co-operation, towards which 845 Squadron made a sizeable contribution.

The decision to withdraw 845 Squadron as part of the general withdrawal of British forces from Borneo was taken towards the end of August 1966. Detailed planning was therefore put in place to execute the withdrawal of the forward detachments to Labuan in good time for the arrival of *Bulwark* on 7th October, but not so early as to cause embarrassment to British units remaining in the forward areas.

As well as the withdrawal of Squadron equipment and personnel amounting to about 33,000 lbs, our four aircraft also had to cope with an enormous quantity of ammunition, machinery, stores and personnel belonging to the Army units based in forward areas for which there were no fixed-wing airstrips; altogether a very large task indeed.

It was agreed that the Bario and Sepulot detachments should be withdrawn to Labuan on 1st and 2nd October and that, should the aircraft be required for tasking thereafter, they would operate from Labuan. In the event, Sepulot was evacuated in one day on 1st October but, for operational reasons, Bario's withdrawal was postponed to 3rd October and was completed on the 4th.

Not one single item of stores was unaccounted for on completion of the withdrawal, a tribute to the immense care taken by all concerned.

The final withdrawal of Squadron equipment and stores from Labuan to *Bulwark* was executed by four aircraft within the space of 1½ hours on the morning of 7th October 1966.

Over and above the general Squadron withdrawal, it was planned to use the Naval Wessex aircraft to lift over 100,000 lbs of heavy engineering equipment from Long Pasia and Bario to Brunei. Owing to the size and weight of this equipment, only Wessex aircraft could be used to lift the majority of it. The operation was planned to take place between 7th and 9th October inclusive, using 10 aircraft in all, those ashore being supplemented by the aircraft embarked in *Bulwark*. The overall withdrawal of British troops and equipment, of which the engineering plant was only part, was to be known as 'Operation Playboy'.

It was felt by the Squadron that, owing to the notorious unpredictability of the Borneo weather, it would be prudent to start the withdrawal of the engineering plant as soon as possible, on an opportunity basis. Never having failed on any task undertaken in Borneo, it would have been a bitter blow to the Squadron to sail from Labuan with only a proportion of this particular task completed because of inclement weather. About mid-September, therefore, the Sepulot detachment, which throughout the first half of the month was under-employed, began the heavy lift from Long Pasia. The Bario detachment, which had been fully employed throughout the month, began its heavy lift in the last week of September.

The lift from both locations was hampered by very poor weather conditions, which persisted from the last week of September through to the time of *Bulwark's* arrival. However, all pilots, including the four who had joined from Singapore on 19th September, were familiar with the routes and, despite the necessity to dogleg around frequent and very heavy storms, the lift went on.

Fast talking was required at times to prevent the Headquarters planners from stopping the lift. They were worried that, having asked for assistance from *Bulwark*, there would be nothing left for the ship to do on its arrival. They were also worried about the hours being used by the Wessex during September, which not only hit the top of the graph but went straight through the roof. Eventually, in order to placate the statisticians but continue with the lift, it was decided to use training hours, of which about 40 still remained under our belts, to progress the operation. It was difficult to convince some people that the hours being used were booked anyway and that these used for heavy lifts in September would merely be saved on the October bill.

The arrival of a fifth Wessex on 10th September did much to save the situation. Though it didn't actually fly until 27th September for reasons of maintenance and engine changes, it usefully added a further 40 operational and 10 training hours to our monthly allowance.

Both the heavy lift from Long Pasia and that from Bario were completed by 4th October. It was perhaps a disappointment to *Bulwark* that they were unable to participate in the operation but it was problematic whether, if the commencement of the lift had been left until 7th October and the unfavourable weather conditions had persisted, the task could have been completed at all.

In the last foreseeable Report of Proceedings for a Naval Squadron operating in Borneo after nearly 4 years of continuous Fleet Air Arm service there, I was pleased to record our sincere thanks to all the units with whom we operated side-by-side for their cheerful co-operation at all times.

845 Squadron Activities at Bario for the Last Two Months in Borneo

From a Report by Lieutenant Roger Bryant 845 Squadron, (Pilot Wessex Mk 5)

During this period, the last traces of Naval aviation were removed from Sarawak. Our withdrawal date was fixed for 1st/2nd October 1966, but was put back to 3rd/4th, on which dates we moved the detachment to join that from Sepulot at Labuan. On 22nd September, Flight Lieutenant Joy and Lieutenant Alan Rock joined the detachment and, on the 25th, Lieutenant Tony Horton left for the United Kingdom and a QHI course.

There were no material improvements made to our site during the period since, our withdrawal being so close, they were considered unnecessary. All building materials, including air-drop baseboards, were used in the new construction on Red Hill.

The Lister generator was never connected to the Camp's electrics again. Spares did arrive, and the generator was assembled. Although the engine worked well, the generator failed and the following day it was broken down to be air-lifted to Brunei. Power was supplied to the detachment bars and messes by the Hatz generator.

The operations against the Indonesian 'communist' incursionists continued and, on 3rd September, Lieut SUMBI (the Leader), and three henchmen were captured near the Sungi Trusan. His subsequent interrogation produced some very interesting and extremely hot information. This left six still at large. Corporal Ibrahim of the TNKU (ex-Brunei Revolt Army) was caught with one other in the middle of the month and, although patrols continued, little hope was left of picking up the stragglers alive, and it was hoped that they either fell victims to the jungle or that Special Branch would trace them in the future.

During the latter half of the month, we progressed the lift of the

Gurkha Engineers' heavy plant to Brunei. This was of the order of 19 underslung loads and was completed before the end of September.

An interesting training trip was made to Seria with a buffalo, three pigs, a goat and six hens for the festival of 'D'Shera' (the Gurkha Christmas). This was for the benefit of the 2nd/6th Gurkha Rifles and 67 Independent Field Squadron, Gurkha Engineers - a small 'thank you' for all the work they had done for the Flight in Borneo.

Tony Horton had a partial ECU-bearing failure on a shingle bar on the Trusan and flew the aircraft back to Bario empty. The replacement ECU was found to be in a worse condition after installation and also had to be replaced. Both engine changes were achieved within 48 hours. No other major tasks were carried out. We experienced considerable windscreen-wiper trouble, and this became significant during the badweather towards the end of the month, though no tasks were affected. 'X' flew nearly 90 hours in September - a very fine maintenance achievement.

845 Squadron Activities at Sepulot for the Last Two Months in Borneo

From a Report by Lieutenant Roger Edmonds RN 845 Squadron, Detachment Commander, Sepulot (Pilot Wessex Mk 5)

From 1st September 1966 the 845 Sepulot Detachment was involved mainly with withdrawing units from the forward areas to the main bases at Brunei and Labuan until, on 1st October, the detachment was itself withdrawn to Labuan.

Nevertheless, a very limited amount of support was also provided for the 2nd/6th Gurkha Rifles, Border Scouts and Police Field Force, consisting of re-supply and re-deployment of patrols for these units.

The weekly commitment of lifting heavy stores forward for the Australian Sappers engaged on the Kekingau-Sepulot road continued until that unit was ordered to withdraw, and the final lift was to move some heavy stores back to the Sappers' main base.

The withdrawal from the Central residency involved the detachment in three separate operations; the withdrawal of the heavy engineering plant of 67 Gurkha Independent Field Squadron, the withdrawal of 845 Squadron's detachment from Sepulot to Labuan and, finally, the withdrawal of heavy equipment from Sepulot.

It was originally planned that the 80,000 lbs of plant at Long Pasia would be lifted out during Operation 'Playboy'. However, it was decided to withdraw it on an opportunity basis and the task was completed by 4th October.

The back-loading of the 845 Squadron detachment from Sepulot was easily completed on 1st October and the heavy underslung equipment at Sepulot, consisting of a generator and Land Rover, was withdrawn to Labuan by 5th October.

The 2nd/6th Gurkha Regiment Tactical HQ gave a splendid party at the end of the month to mark the departure of the detachment from Sepulot.

In conclusion, the two Wessex were never fully employed at this location and the withdrawal phase provided the most valuable experience of the whole of our period in Sabah. The members of the detachment at Sepulot enjoyed their stay and made many friends with the Gurkhas.

The Tail-End of Confrontation

By Lieutenant Alan Rock Pilot 845 Squadron (Wessex Mk 5)

At the beginning of February 1966 I was transferred from 706 Squadron (Wessex 1 HAS), with my last flight on 2nd Feb doing a night-dunking trip in Falmouth Bay with Geoff Gadson as my student, to 707 Squadron for a very short Wessex Mk 5 conversion. My conversion consisted of Familiarisation (Fam) 1 and 2 on a Wessex Mk 5 on 8th February in 707, having finished ground school, followed the next day by Fam 3, 4 & 5, the last two being solo trips. On 10th Feb I joined 845 Squadron and completed two IF trips, one formation trip and one load-lifting trip! In actual fact, my OFT was all done front-line in the next 2-3 months.

On 13th Aug 845 Squadron embarked in *Bulwark* for the Far East. An advance party of aircrew and maintainers was flown out to Borneo to relieve most of the 848 personnel based in Borneo with 4 aircraft sometime before this date, to allow them to come home with *Albion*.

On 25th Aug we passed *Albion* on her way home, at the top end of the Red Sea. I did some transfers & photography sorties with her.

On 16th Sep we disembarked to Sembawang. The next entry in my log book is a sortie from Labuan to Bario on 16th Sep, so I must have got to Labuan by fixed wing, but I don't remember the trip.

There followed several sorties moving people and stores around in preparation for the final withdrawal from Borneo, until my last flight in Borneo on 4th Oct. I believe that we re-embarked in *Bulwark* on 6th Oct as the ship had departed from Singapore on the 5th with the rest of the Squadron. My next entry, on 12th Oct, is a mutual IF sortie with Roger Edmonds from *Bulwark*. I have a feeling I was a bit 'Brahms & Liszt' in Labuan the night before we embarked and Harry Joy, the Flight Commander, being RAF, did not consider I was fit enough to fly an aircraft back to the ship! I have an indistinct memory of being rudely greeted on board by John Ramsdale, who was Duty Officer that day! He came looking for me and found me feeling sorry for myself in the back of one of the aircraft.

So my total time in Borneo was about 14-21 days. Total flying time only 31.35 hours - not exactly a large contribution to Confrontation. The four aircraft I flew were 'V', 'W', 'X' and 'Z'. These were 848 aircraft and I have 2 colour photographs of me entering a clearing on 25th Sep, and on one you can see a bit of the 'A' for *Albion* on the tail. These aircraft had not featured in my log book before. 'V' & 'Z' did not feature in my log book after 4th Oct until I left the Squadron the following April. They probably ended up as FIR/Hangar Queens.

Pilots who flew with me in Borneo at that time were Harry Joy (a New Zealander on 2 years' exchange with the RAF), who eventually retired back there, Mike Shuttleworth, a Royal Marine, brother to twins Ian & Richard, Roger Bryant and Tony Horton. The last two were ex-848 and had therefore been in Borneo for some time. Aircrewmen who flew with me were CPO Ellis, PO Jackson, POs Powell and Redgrave and PO Ben Hazel, who had served in Borneo with 845 from 1962 to 1964 and subsequently in 848.

Postscript

Return to Nanga Gaat

By Lieutenant David Rowe RM

Many who served in Sarawak during Confrontation probably wished that they could go back to their locations after things had returned to normal. In February 1968 I was lucky enough to do just that. During 1963/4, I was stationed for six months at Nanga Gaat in the Third Division of Sarawak. It was used as a Forward Air Base by 845 Naval Air Commando Squadron to support operations on the Indonesian Border, and it was to Nanga Gaat that I returned.

Having spent nearly three months in *Bulwark* in the Gulf of Muscat, standing-by for Aden, I cajoled my Commanding Officer into allowing me to make my journey on the Squadron's return to Singapore. An Indulgence Flight to Kuching fell through at the last minute but, undaunted, I flew by Malaysian-Singapore Airways to Kuching and arrived there at 1100. Customs and Immigration proved a little difficult at the airport; some people have short memories! Whilst I was at the airport, I walked down to Semengo Camp. It looked very shabby, with the Malaysian Barracks next door. It was now used as a camp for a Government Agricultural Field Force.

I caught a taxi into Kuching and went to the residence of Tun Sri Temenggong Jugah, the paramount chief of the Ibans. He had adopted me as a tribal son before my departure in 1964. He and his family were delighted to see me and we spent most of the day talking about old times and personalities. My limited vocabulary of Sea Dyak was very stretched, not having been used for almost four years. The Temenggong was still as ebullient as ever. He had, however, had to curtail his drinking. That evening I ate a Chinese meal in Kuching with the Temenggong and some local personalities. The face of Kuching had changed a little from Confrontation days; the new buildings included a large shopping complex by the open market.

The next morning I was driven in the official car at 0630 to catch my aircraft to Sibu. I arrived at Sibu at 0800 and had coffee at the airport bar, which was still run, though not as profitably, by Ah Bee. He was very pleased to hear my news and asked to be remembered to everyone. He had obviously sunk some of his profits into a new set of gold teeth. My remark about each tooth being engraved with a unit crest caused much laughter!

The buildings around the airfield, which were used by 845 Squadron, had fallen into disrepair and the bungalows which had been used for Messes were vacant. No Malaysian Forces were stationed in the Third Division at that time.

I went by taxi into the town and called on the Resident, Peter Tinggom, who may be remembered as the District Officer of Kapit. He was in good spirits, excused himself for being busy, and invited me to lunch at the Sarawak Hotel later. With time on my hands, I arranged a seat on the steam launch to Kapit, 110 miles up the Rajang River, and then wandered round Sibu. No visible changes had taken place since my last visit, but there were obviously some planned as a fair amount of construction work was in progress. I called in at the Cinza Bar, which had not changed at all, although the female attractions appeared to be of a new generation! 'Your Old China' was still in charge and insisted on offering me a cigar; previously, all I had been offered was the door! After a couple of coffees I moved to the Sarawak Hotel for lunch.

Lunch was another superb Chinese meal, so good in fact that I almost missed my launch for the up-river trip. However, a true pierhead jump put me safely on board.

The launch trip proved to be quite an experience. The trip lasted 14 hours and I was the only European on board. The accommodation was basic: wooden benches around the sides provided the seats and your bunk was the deck. Lavatory facilities were provided by a hole in the stern deck, with the engine's water-cooling piped in as a flush! There were some rather odd items of cargo and these, together with the livestock and passengers, provided a strong reminder that one was in 'the Exotic East'. I eventually assumed a horizontal position and dozed off. I woke up on reaching Kapit but, as it was still dark, I went back to sleep.

When I eventually awoke again, I found that the launch was alongside the New Wharf. I walked to the flat where some of my 'family' were living, and very soon was having a much-needed shower.

Transport up-river from Kapit was to prove difficult and I had to wait there for two days. The town has had a face-lift and now had a new market, shops and two hotels. One of the hotels was now owned by the victualling contractor, Sin Joo, who had supplied rations to the Gurkhas and the Navy for over four years.

The two days were spent in visiting old friends and taking part in the 'Berjaya' celebrations which were going on. One of these was a cockfight, fought with the wicked, metal spurs which the locals use. Old cockfighting hands from Nanga Gaat will be interested to know that the Iban bloodstock was superior to the Chinese.

On Monday morning I left in a longboat to go upriver for another 50 miles; I planned to go right up to the Sun-gei Merirai and call in at Nanga Gaat on the way back. However, I could not resist calling in for a couple of hours as we were passing. After coffee and something stronger, I set off and arrived at the longhouse at Sungei Merirai. Most of the familiar longhouse had gone and a very-much-improved version was in the last stages of completion. Running water for my shower came, via some very familiar piping, from a nearby stream. I later found out that most of the plumbing from our Forward Air Base was distributed amongst the longhouse. Similarly the PSP which was used to reinforce the helicopter spots had been distributed and was being used as a walkway.

The next day, I went down-river to Nanga Gaat and was met by Penghulus Jimbong and Kumbong and, of course, Sani. Lanting had been divorced and had moved on, which was bound to happen. The two Penghulus had brought plenty of alcohol, which they insisted that we drank immediately, so it was some time before I could look around at what had been my home for six months.

The only buildings left were the large wooden basha, the operations hut and the Border Scouts basha. Everything else had gone, even the 'Anchor Inn', the only two-bar, revolving-door pub in Borneo. The helicopter spots had all gone and were overgrown, together with all the other fixtures that had been so familiar. Even the old Chinaman and his shop had been replaced by a new shop built into the wooden basha. The electric generator had been broken down since November and the water came from the river. In a nutshell, the place had reverted almost to the condition it was in when the Squadron first arrived. The only real improvement was a clinic built across the river. This had been badly needed when we arrived and the withdrawal of the Naval Sick Bay had prompted the government to provide something similar. The memorial to the members of the security forces who lost their lives at Nanga Gaat was being kept in immaculate condition, a tribute to the friendship which the local people, who erected the memorial, have for the British Forces.

Fig 49. Nanga Gaat Memorial

Glossary

2 I/C	Second in Command
AA1	Aircraft Artificer 1st Class
ACT	Aircraft Control Team
AED	Ship's Air Engineering Department
AMCO	Air Maintenance Control Office
AMSL	Height above mean sea level
ASW	Anti Submarine Warfare
AOG	Aircraft on the Ground i.e. Unserviceable aircraft awaiting spares.
AVCAT	Aviation Turbine Fuel (for jet engines; usually only available in aircraft-equipped ships)
AVGAS	Aviation Gasoline (petrol for internal-combustion-engined aircraft)
AVTUR	Aviation Turbine Fuel (for jet-engined aircraft; usually available ashore)
BASO	Brigade Air Staff Officer

Basha	A hut made with local foliage
BF	Before Flight Inspection of Aircraft
CAF	Chief Air Fitter
CCO	Clandestine Communist Organisation
CASEVAC	Casualty Evacuation (usually by helicopter)
Christmas Tree	An unserviceable aircraft which is 'robbed' of parts to make another aircraft serviceable
C-in-C	Commander-in-Chief
Claret	UK Authorisation to operate a small distance into Indonesian territory
CO	Commanding Officer
COMAIR	Air Commander (of an area involving several air units)
COMBRITBOR	Commander British Forces in Borneo
COMFEF	Commander Far East Fleet
CP	Command Post
DZ	Dropping Zone, usually for parachuted stores dropped by fixed-wing aircraft
FAE	Front Line Aircraft Equipment. The authorised number of Squadron aircraft
FIR	First in Reserve Aircraft. Extra aircraft carried above Squadron complement to be 'broken out' if a F.A.E aircraft were to be lost or damaged beyond repair, or if extra Squadron operational aircraft were required and authorised

FOB	Forward Operating Base
FOCINFEF	Flag Officer Commander-in-Chief Far East Fleet
FRB	Forward Refuelling Base
FREDs	Small Dummy Parachutes with explosive charges
Hanger Queen	A long term unserviceable aircraft liable for similar treatment as a 'Christmas Tree' see above
HDS	Helicopter Delivery Service
HF	High Frequency Radio for longer range coverage
LS	Landing Site for one or more aircraft
LST	Landing Ship Tank
LZ	Landing Zone for several aircraft
MEDEVAC	Medical Evacuation (by helicopter or vehicle)
NA	Naval Airman
NACS	Naval Air Commando Squadron
NAS	Naval Air Squadron
OFT	Operational Flying Training
ORI	Operational Readiness Inspection
POAH	Petty Officer Aircraft Handler
PFF	Police Field Force
PSP	Pierced Steel Planking
PWD	Public Works Department
R and R	Period of Rest and Recuperation for personnel

following an extended period of operations.

RMR	Royal Malay Regiment
Robbing	A term used to describe the removal of parts from an aircraft to make another one serviceable
Roulement	Term used by the British Army to signify major combat units that are employed in short tours of duty
SARBE	Search and Rescue Beacon radio fitted to aircrew lifejackets
SP	Senior Pilot (and normally second in command of a NACS)
SAS	Special Air Service (Army)
SBA	Sick Berth Attendant
SBS	Special Boat Service (Royal Marines)
SITREP	Situation Report
SS 11	Surface-to-Surface wire guided missile sometimes fitted to Wessex helicopters for Air-to-Ground firing
TAOR	Tactical Area of Responsibility
Topo	Topographical Surveyors brought in to improve the quality of maps
UDI	Unilateral Declaration of Independence
UHF	Ultra High Frequency radio normally used by RN aircraft for short range transmissions
Ulu	Slang term for 'somewhere in the Jungle' e.g. 'Up the Ulu'

VIP	Very Important Person
X/Y or xth/yth	e.g. 1/7, meaning the First battalion of the Seventh Regiment

Index

Figure Index

Acknowledgements

As Editor, I would like to thank all of the contributors for sending me their stories without which this book would not have happened. I would also like to acknowledge the help given me by the Fleet Air Arm Museum in letting me search through the official Squadron reports which allowed me to find accounts of the squadron activities to fill in some of the gaps in the contributors' submissions. My thanks also go to Joyce Dawson who kindly read through the manuscript and offered excellent detailed advice on many areas of presentation.

Finally, I am very grateful for the help, support and advice from Captain Alan Hensher, my erstwhile Commanding Officer in 845 Squadron at the start of our Borneo activities, both for his help, and advice throughout the 4½ years of the gestation of the book and finally his material support in getting the book published.

Brian Skinner, February 2012